Educati

Education Matters

Global Schooling Gains from the 19th to the 21st Century

ROBERT J. BARRO

AND

JONG-WHA LEE

OXFORD
UNIVERSITY PRESS

OXFORD
UNIVERSITY PRESS

Oxford University Press is a department of the University of Oxford.
It furthers the University's objective of excellence in research, scholarship,
and education by publishing worldwide. Oxford is a registered trade mark of
Oxford University Press in the UK and in certain other countries

Published in the United States of America by
Oxford University Press
198 Madison Avenue, New York, NY 10016,
United States of America

© Oxford University Press 2015

CIP data is on file at the Library of Congress
ISBN-13: 9780199379231

9 8 7 6 5 4 3 2 1

Printed in the United States of America on acid-free paper

CONTENTS

In the past half century, human capital has emerged as one of the most active areas of research in economics. This research depends fundamentally on good data, and our efforts at constructing useful measures of educational attainment for a broad range of countries go back 20 years.

This book presents and discusses a new long-term data set on educational attainment of the populations of up to 146 countries from 1870 to 2040. We then use the new data to analyze linkages across countries and over time between education and important economic and political variables, such as economic growth, fertility, and democracy. Discussions in this book go beyond existing studies by presenting new data, improving the analysis, and describing original findings.

The seminal theoretical and empirical work by Becker, Ben-Poranth, Mincer, and Schultz contributed to the development of new models and evidence that relate human capital, attained by schooling and training, to earnings and incomes at individual and national levels. Research on human capital became more vibrant with the (re)emergence of interest in economic growth in the late 1980s. The new growth theory initiated by Paul Romer motivated theoretical and empirical studies that investigate the role of human capital in economic development, productivity growth, and innovation.

The development of longitudinal panel data sets on educational attainment for a large number of countries was one of our earlier contributions to this field. We started the project in 1993 for conferences at the World Bank and the Bank of Portugal. Our first two joint papers, "International comparisons of educational attainment," in 1993, and "Sources of economic growth" in 1994, were published as products from these conferences. Since then, we have made progress in several ways—updating the estimates of educational attainment, improving the estimation methodologies, and extending the analysis from quantity to quality of education. Throughout this process, we have retained the focus of assessing human capital as an influence on economic and political variables, including economic growth, fertility, and democracy.

This book, a further development of our work on human capital, makes several new contributions:

- We present newly constructed estimates of educational attainment for population by age and gender back to 1870.
- We project educational attainment up to 2040.

- We provide a newly constructed data set on the quality of education based on internationally comparable test scores at five-year intervals.
- The data sets presented here are available at our website (http:/www. barrolee.com/).
- Utilizing two data sets—one comprising a large number of countries from 1960 to 2010, and the other with a more limited number of countries from 1870 to 2010—we analyze the effects of human capital on economic growth, fertility, and democracy.

We have written this book to contribute to ongoing research and policy debates on the assessment of educational achievement, in a nation or worldwide, and on its linkages to economic, political, and social development. We hope it will appeal to both academic researchers and policymakers who work on educational and human development issues in various fields, such as education, economics, sociology, and political science.

ACKNOWLEDGEMENTS

In writing this book, we have benefited from outstanding research support by Hanol Lee, a Ph.D. student at Korea University, who has helped us since 2007 with collecting data and conducting statistical analyses. Many student research assistants, including Seulki Shin and Siying Cao, have also provided valuable research assistance at various stages of this project. Special thanks are due to Eunbi Song for her dedicated assistance in collecting data and preparing the manuscript.

This book has also benefitted from valuable comments and feedback on our earlier papers on human capital and economic growth from participants at workshops and seminars since 1993. We are also grateful to UNESCO Institute for Statistics and national statistical agencies for providing updated data on the distribution of educational attainment of the population by age. We are also indebted to many individuals who have pointed out errors in our earlier estimates. They are not responsible for any errors we may have made.

We thank the Korea Research Foundation for a research grant (KRF-2006–342-B00010) that has supported this project. In 2006, KRF initiated a program to support distinguished Korean scholars to engage in long-term research. Lee was honored to be one of the first recipients of the grant in the field of humanities and social science.

We have had a great experience working with the people at Oxford University Press, including Scott Parris, Cathryn Vaulman, and Stephanie Raga. We appreciate their support in making this book available to the world in a timely manner and with a wonderful presentation.

Robert J. Barro
Jong-Wha Lee

ABBREVIATIONS AND ACRONYMS

ALLS	Adult Literacy and Life Skills Survey
BRICS	Brazil, China, India, Russia, and the South African Republic
CGDP	Current-price Real Gross Domestic Product
CONFEMEN	Conference of Ministers of Education of French-Speaking Countries
DHS	Demographic and Health Surveys
FYR	Former Yugoslav Republic
GDP	Gross Domestic Product
GLS	Generalized Least Squares
IAEP	International Assessment of Educational Progress
IALS	International Adult Literacy Survey
IEA	International Association for the Evaluation of Educational Achievement
IFS	International Financial Statistics
IIASA	International Institute for Applied Systems Analysis
IMF	International Monetary Fund
ISCED	International Standard Classification of Education
LLECE	Latin American Laboratory for Assessment of the Quality of Education
MLA	Monitoring Learning Achievement
MYS	Mean Years of Schooling
MYSE	Mean Years of Schooling Equivalent
NAEP	National Assessments of Educational Progress
NCES	National Center for Education Statistics
OECD	The Organisation for Economic Co-operation and Development
OLS	Ordinary Least Squares
OSG	OECD Standardization Group
PASEC	Programme on the Analysis of Education Systems
PIAAC	Programme for the International Assessment of Adult Competencies
PIRLS	Progress in International Reading Literacy Study
PISA	Program for International Student Assessment
PPP	Purchasing Power Parity

PWT	Peen World Table
SACMEQ	Southern and Eastern Africa Consortium for Monitoring Educational Quality
SAR	Special Administrative Region
TFP	Total Factor Productivity
TIMSS	Third International Mathematics and Science Study
UN	United Nations
UNESCO	United Nations Educational, Scientific and Cultural Organization
UNICEF	United Nations Children's Fund
USA	United States of America
WDI	World Development Indicators
WLS	Weighted Least Squares
WWII	World War II

Education Matters

Introduction

"Fourthly, of the acquired and useful abilities of all the inhabitants or members of the society. The acquisition of such talents, by the maintenance of the acquirer during his education, study, or apprenticeship, always costs a real expense, which is a capital fixed and realized, as it were, in his person. Those talents, as they make a part of his fortune, so do they likewise that of the society to which he belongs."

—ADAM SMITH, *An Inquiry into the Nature And Causes of the Wealth of Nations, 1776.*

1.1 OVERVIEW

Education is an important means to personal development. It is also a foundation for the economic, political, and social development of a nation. In many countries, education is recognized as a fundamental human rights and a priority for sustainable development. As recently as the year 2000, the majority of the world's governments adopted the Millennium Development Goals (MDGs), committing to accomplish universal primary education and eradicate gender disparity in all levels of education by no later than 2015.

A vast literature—from many disciplines, including economics, education, politics, and sociology—has analyzed the evolution of educational expansion in the world and assessed the role of education in economic, political, and social development. Undoubtedly, these analyses depend on high-quality data that measure educational attainment across nations over the long term.

This book presents long-term data on educational attainment measures for a broad number of countries and systematically analyzes the role of educational attainment in economic, political, and social development.

Human capital, multifaceted and complex, is difficult to precisely and quantitatively measure in individuals (Barro and Lee, 2001). Educational attainment is widely used as a proxy for the component of human capital stock that is obtained at schools. There have been a number of attempts to measure educational attainment by population across countries.

In our earlier studies, we constructed a complete data set of educational attainment of the population, aged 15 and over, in 146 countries at five-year intervals from 1950 to 2010. The estimates are disaggregated by gender and five-year age intervals.[1]

This book aims to make new contributions by updating and extending the existing data set. Most importantly, it presents newly constructed estimates of historical educational attainment for the total populations and the female populations from 1870 to 1945 for 89 countries. In addition, it constructs projections for educational attainment, available by gender at five-year age intervals, for the next 30 years, up to 2040, for 146 countries.

Human capital, particularly attained through education, has been emphasized as a critical determinant of economic development.[2] In addition, the level of educational attainment has a strong impact on social and political outcomes, such as infant mortality, fertility, the education of children, democracy, and the rule of law.[3] However, it has been argued that human capital's role in economic growth is not quantitatively substantial.[4] Some recent papers have also found that education does not play a significant role in enhancing democracy.[5] We make use of our new data on educational attainment measures for a broad number of countries and explore the effects of human capital on economic, social, and political development.

We begin, in the following section, with a brief overview of education's expansion over the past two centuries. We look at the key features that have influenced the emergence of the modern educational system and the worldwide expansion of education.

In chapter 2, we present estimates of enrollment ratios at all education levels—primary, secondary, and tertiary—for both the total and the female populations since 1820 for a sample of 89 countries and compare the evolution of school enrollments among nations and across regions. We then move to constructing estimates of educational attainment from 1870 to 2010.

The final data set in the chapter includes an updated version of our previous estimates of educational attainment for 146 countries at five-year intervals, from 1950 to 2010, available by gender and five-year age intervals. In addition, it presents newly constructed estimates of historical educational attainment for the total and the female populations, from 1870 to 1945, for 89 countries. Using the new data set, we assess the trends in educational attainment globally and by major regions from 1870 to 2010. We also look at the evolution of gender inequality in educational attainment.

Chapter 3 provides our projections for educational progress in the next 30 years. We first discuss the methodology for estimating school enrollments and the population structure that is needed to generate projections for educational attainment. The increase over time in the average years of schooling for the population aged 15 and over is mainly determined by an increase in the average years of schooling for those aged 15–24, as well as a change in population structure. We examine the extent to which the continuous inflow of a better-educated young population into developing countries could help reduce the gap with advanced countries, in average years of schooling for the total and the female populations over the next 30 years.

Using the new data set, chapter 4 analyzes the cross-country linkages between education and important economic, political, and social variables, such as economic growth, fertility, and democracy. We adopt "development accounting" and "growth accounting" techniques to analyze the extent that differences in educational capital can explain differences in the level and growth rate of output per worker across countries. The main empirical analysis is based on a general framework of cross-country regressions, which considers the experience of an individual country in a global context. The empirical results show how education relates to economic growth, as well as fertility and democracy.

Chapter 5 investigates these relationships over a longer period of time. We have constructed a long-term macroeconomic panel data set consisting of internationally comparable data on per worker GDP growth, fertility, educational attainment, and indicators of democracy over the past 140 years since 1870.

Chapter 6 turns to the discussion of educational quality in addition to educational quantity. The estimates of educational attainment do not take into account differences in the quality of schooling across countries, nor do they directly measure human skills obtained in schools. We discuss various indicators of school outcomes, including internationally comparable test scores for students at the primary and secondary levels and direct measures of adult skills. We then explain how various indicators are related to the educational attainment measure. We construct a complete data set of educational quality, as measured by an aggregate test score combining mathematics and science scores for primary and secondary schooling in 134 countries at five-year intervals from 1965 to 2010. We then attempt to construct an aggregate human capital stock measure that combines both average years of schooling and average quality of schooling.

Chapter 7 concludes the book by summarizing main findings and arguments of the previous chapters, and discussing emerging challenges related to education and human development.

1.2 THE ORIGIN AND GLOBAL EXPANSION OF EDUCATION

We begin with a summary of key features of the worldwide expansion of educational attainment.[6]

Primary Education

Traditionally, education served children from the more privileged classes, training them as elites who would govern and administer the country or empire (Cummings, 2003). The shift away from this narrow base of education occurred gradually, starting in the second half of the 18th century. One influence came from the intellectual work of prominent scholars such as Bacon, Locke, Montaigne, and Rousseau. Rousseau's *Emile* (1762), for example, emphasized the social importance of education free from the restraints of tradition and authority (as cited in Kandel, 1930). Primary education expanded rapidly during the late 18th and early 19th centuries with the spread of compulsory mass schooling in the industrialized regions of the world.

In Western Europe, the first major national education systems featured an expanding framework of secular public schools, based on compulsory schooling laws and strong state administrations (Benavot, Resnick, and Corrales, 2006). Prior to these laws, families and religious institutions played the central role in the education of children. The first legally binding rules that required children to attend school were enacted in Prussia and Denmark about 200 years ago (Soysal and Strange, 1989). In the United Kingdom, Queen Victoria introduced compulsory primary education in the Education Act of 1870. The state envisaged educational reforms as a means to deprive churches of their power (Morrison and Murtin, 2009, Annex).

New nation-states enacted legal provisions for compulsory public primary schooling in order to solidify their authority and promote national unity (Benavot, Resnick, and Corrales, 2006). Public education was a direct link between the state and the masses. The public also increasingly viewed the socialization and training offered in public schools as important, as well as an improvement over education acquired at home or through religious institutions (Benavot, Resnick, and Corrales, 2006).

Since the founding of the early colonies in the North America, democratic and egalitarian views, supported by strong Protestant principles, pervaded the development of mass schooling (Benavot, Resnick, and Corrales, 2006). Because individual states, rather than the federal government, exercised the power to control education, the results were not uniform. Northeastern states in the United States developed public school systems, administered by state and county boards of education, in the early 19th century. By the end of the century, primary education had become almost universal in Northeastern states.

In the Soviet Union, the national education system was an outcome of the political transformation and Communist ideology that took effect after the Bolshevik Revolution of 1917. The centralized public education system developed with the full support of the state for the collective development of the nation. The Soviet model influenced the development of education systems in other Communist countries, including Cuba, the People's Republic of China, and Vietnam (Benavot, Resnick, and Corrales, 2006).

The modern education systems in China and in Japan were outcomes of major political transformations, as well as the integration of domestic cultural values with Western ideas. In pre-Communist China, early modern education provided lessons on Western subjects, while continuing to place importance on the Chinese culture (Marlow-Ferguson and Lopez, 2002). The reforms in education that occurred during the late 19th and early 20th centuries encouraged compulsory mass education and the imitation of Western models. In 1905, the Qing dynasty dismantled the system of civil service examinations and introduced a Western system of primary, secondary, and tertiary levels of education. After the founding of the People's Republic of China in 1949, the education system was largely influenced by the Soviet model. In Japan, the Elementary School of Ordinance was promulgated in 1885 following the Meiji Restoration. This ordinance made primary education compulsory.

Subsequent education reform resulted in the establishment of a centralized system that reduced cross-regional differences.

India's primary education system underwent two significant expansions. The first occurred between 1901 and 1917 under British rule as part of attempts to educate the masses through compulsory education. The second expansion was caused by new principles of primary education, mainly focusing on crafts and the availability, after India's independence, of universal, compulsory, and free education (UNESCO, 1958).

Most developing countries, as well as former colonies of Africa, Asia, and Latin America, experienced a sharp expansion in public primary education after 1945. Meyer, Ramirez, and Soysal (1992) argued that the rapid expansion of primary education was the result of the intensification of the nation-state model, reflecting the desire of newly independent states to be linked to the Western model of nation-states, a feature of which was mass education. Sociologists and economists have found that the important determinants of educational expansion in the late 19th and early 20th centuries included state capacities, ideologies, demographic changes, and per-capita GDP (Benavot, Resnick, and Corrales, 2006).

Some researchers have argued that international governmental organizations contributed to the promotion of universal primary schooling in developing regions, especially after World War II. Many international organizations (e.g., the UNESCO, the World Bank, and the OECD) contributed to the diffusion of Western-style education models and to the worldwide emergence of universal education (Benavot, Resnick, and Corrales, 2006). On December 10, 1948, the United Nations adopted the Universal Declaration of Human Rights, in which Article 26 enshrined the right to free and compulsory elementary education. Moreover, the publication of the educational yearbook and compendia (e.g., UNESCO, 1958) contributed to the worldwide expansion of important ideas concerning educational and institutional developments.

The worldwide expansion of universal primary education after World War II included attempts to raise the quality of schooling. For example, in Europe, there was a movement to improve educational quality by introducing new systems of training and recruitment of teachers and by offering classes to students who needed special care. The qualitative improvement of education was supported, as the International Covenant on Economic, Social and Cultural Rights states, by "the progressive introduction of free education" (UNESCO, 1993).

Secondary and Tertiary Education

In the latter half of the 19th century, primary education's great expansion continued in an increasing number of countries. However, enrollment in secondary and tertiary schools remained low. Universal access to secondary education began to expand in industrialized countries during the first half of the 20th century. However, the pace of these changes varied greatly among countries.

In Western Europe, many nation-states maintained as late as the 1930s the traditional system of universal primary education, along with secondary education offered mainly to more privileged classes (UNESCO, 1961). Secondary education, in the forms of the gymnasium, lycée, and grammar school, provided upper-class children access to an advanced level of liberal education and college preparatory programs (Benavot, Resnick, and Corrales, 2006). Later, European states embarked on educational reforms to open secondary education to all children with talent and capacity, regardless of their social status. In France, secondary education provided in communal or private schools, or in lycée established by the state, was intended to concentrate on the training of intellectual elites. Since the beginning of World War I, there had been a crescendo of criticism urging an increase in opportunities to make secondary and tertiary education available for anyone with talent, wherever they were found (Kandel, 1930). In the United Kingdom, the Education Act of 1902 established a national education system while preparing for compulsory secondary education (Benavot, Resnick, and Corrales, 2006).

Many countries made efforts to increase the education facilities available for post-primary education, while simultaneously broadening the enrollees to include children from all social classes. The rapid increase in primary school enrollment, and subsequently in graduates, in the late 19th and early 20th centuries, created a demand for secondary education. A rise in income also enabled parents to support their children's post-primary education without relying on additional income earned from a child's labor.

The principle of universal access to lower secondary education gained momentum in most European countries after World War II. Many European governments inaugurated radical reforms in secondary schooling, including the extension of compulsory education, which led to the massive expansion of secondary school enrollment. These educational reforms in Europe over the 20th century were influenced by the preceding rapid expansion of secondary education in the United States.

In the United States, secondary education became more prevalent as it was tied to ideals of liberty and democracy. The first secondary schools in the North American colonies, established during the 17th and early 18th centuries, were similar to Latin grammar schools in Europe (Benavot, Resnick, and Corrales, 2006). After American independence, the collapse of the European elite system was fostered by the widely accepted idea of a free and publicly controlled system of secondary schooling. As early as 1816, the Constitution of Indiana stated that "it shall be the duty of the general assembly as soon as circumstances will permit, to provide by law for a general system of education, ascending in regular graduation from township schools to a state university, wherein tuition shall be gratis and equally open to all" (Kandel, 1930, p.423). The English Classical School for boys, founded in Boston in 1821, was the first public high school in the world (Kandel, 1930). The United States saw unprecedented growth of secondary education in the early 20th century.

In Japan, the secondary education system comprised mainly middle schools and vocational schools. This educational system's transformation coincided with the development of industry. As stated by the Order of 1872, middle schools functioned as institutional channels that prepared students for higher education, while vocational schools were responsible for educating technicians. In the early 20th century, there was a great expansion in secondary education, featuring the establishment of girls' high schools, the extension of compulsory education, free public schools, and industrial and economic development (UNESCO, 1961).

The first modern institutions for secondary education in China were established by Christian missionaries at the end of the 19th century. Almost simultaneously, the chief officials serving the court of the Qing dynasty founded China's own educational institutions as part of their Westernization movement. Western languages and science became the core subjects of study. In 1922, the Educational System Reform Act introduced the track of the US system, which followed a duration of 6 years for primary, 6 years for secondary, and 4/5 years for tertirary education (UNESCO, 1961). After 1949, China's educational system was largely influenced by the Soviet system (Deng and Treiman, 1997). In the early 1950s, a unified system of middle schools was established. China abolished all private middle schools and implemented standardized curricula and textbooks for secondary education (Marlow-Ferguson and Lopez, 2002). During the Cultural Revolution of 1966–1968, almost all secondary institutions were closed (Unger, 1982).

In India, before 1900, secondary schools utilized English as the medium of instruction and provided university preparatory programs for students, highlighting the importance of literary subjects. With the qualitative improvement of education, the free secondary education movement, and the use of Indian languages as a replacement for English as the medium of instruction, secondary education began to expand. The expansion accelerated "owing to an upsurge in political and social consciousness" in the early 20th century (UNESCO, 1961).

In the postcolonial states of Africa, Asia, and Latin America, the elitist system of secondary education remained for a while after World War II as a legacy of the colonial period. Secondary schools served mainly as institutional channels for university entrance and the attainment of elite status (Benavot, Resnick, and Corrales, 2006). The governments did not have the resources to improve secondary education, so they gave priority to the provision of universal primary education.

During the first half of the 20th century, there was also continuing progress in tertiary school enrollments, following the growth of secondary school enrollments in the most advanced countries. This progress accelerated during the latter half of the century. The modern tertiary education system was largely influenced by European universities, which provided a picture of higher education that focused on "science, technology, the arts and the humanities" (UNESCO, 1966). The development of tertiary education during the early 20th century was caused by several factors, including the increase in demand for higher education following the expansion of secondary education, the demand for professionals in new industries, the reinforcement of national unity, the growth of female participation in higher schooling, and the general expansion of education in developing countries (UNESCO, 1966).

European universities experienced three major reforms before World War II: "the expansion of specialist and technical universities" initiated in Hungary in the 18th century; "State universities with the autonomy and academic freedom"; and "free and equal access to higher education based upon examination" (Garrouste, 2010). These reforms mostly resulted from the new models of education created in Germany, England, and France. The German model focused on autonomy, the English model on the independence of institutions, and the French model on state control and utilitarian views. After World War II, the opening of higher education to the public and the abolition of restrictions on private universities contributed to the expansion of tertiary education in Europe.

In colonial America, early tertiary schools served the wealthy sons of planters and merchants, as well as children who would later enter the ministry. In 1636, the first college, known as Harvard College, was founded in the Massachusetts Bay town of Cambridge. At the beginning, learning at Harvard was dominated by the sacred principals of the Puritans. However, the approach developed later into a broader model of tertiary education. The spread of commerce and new settlements increased demand for higher education, leading to the expansion of tertiary education. Moreover, the ideals of democratization and "the unreachable quest for perfection in the nature of mankind" contributed to the expansion of tertiary schooling (Marlow-Ferguson and Lopez, 2002).

The first national university in China, the Capital University (later Peking University), was set up in 1898 (UNESCO, 1966). After the founding of the People's Republic of China, the education system was influenced by the Soviet model. American-style liberal arts colleges were abolished, and Soviet-style comprehensive universities (*zonghexing daxue*) were established. Nationally unified teaching plans, curricula, and textbooks were introduced for every academic specialty (Marlow-Ferguson and Lopez, 2002). At that time, college admission criteria focused heavily on a student's family background. Students from working-class families were deemed to have the best "origin." During the Cultural Revolution (1966–1976), the system of university entrance examinations was halted, and many tertiary-level institutions remained closed until 1977 (Deng and Treiman, 1997), when the national unified college entrance exams were restored and selection based on political virtue was abolished.

After World War II, the expansion of higher education became a worldwide phenomenon. Tertiary education expanded steadily in developing regions. According to the cross-national analysis of tertiary enrollment ratios in Schofer and Meyer (2005), the expansion of higher education since 1950 was influenced by new global trends of democratization, the expansion of human rights, and the development of science and technology.

Female Education

There has been steady progress toward gender equality in access to education. As the principle of equality of opportunity and democratization of education slowly gained momentum, girls gained increasing access first to primary, then later to secondary and tertiary education.

In the early history of educational development, the under-representation of girls at all levels of schooling highlighted gender inequalities in the access to educational attainment. Women's achievement of the right of access to universal education, including changes in education laws to allow mixed-sex schools, represented an important historical movement that promoted women's economic, social, and political status to a level equal with men. The rise of girls' enrollment in primary schools was a significant step toward accomplishing universal education.

In Europe, influences on the development of girls' education came from intellectual works, such as Fenelon's *De L'education des Filles* (1681) and Rousseau's *Emile* (1762), which emphasized the social importance of educating women (as cited in Kandel, 1930).

With the worldwide expansion of free and universal primary education to newly developed countries by the early 20th century, girls in these countries gained the right to receive primary education.

Most European countries introduced compulsory education for all children in the late 19th and early 20th centuries, with the implication that girls had access to primary education since the 19th century.

In the American colonies, seven years after the Boston educational system was established in 1635, the law allowed access to primary education for all children. This provision was a significant development in the history of education, as it was the first law related to universal education to be established in an English-speaking country. In 1789, a committee led by Samuel Adams introduced a new school program for girls in public schools. Several schools in New England towns began to teach girls in the late 18th century.

In Western Europe and the United States, secondary education for girls began, in an organized form, in the 19th century (Kandel, 1930). It advanced, in many cases, alongside the establishment of teacher certification and normal schools (Benavot, Resnick, and Corrales, 2006).

In Europe, secondary schools were first built for the daughters of the upper classes and expanded in the 19th century to include daughters of the middle classes. In Germany, there were 56 public secondary schools for girls in 1840 (Kandel, 1930). In addition, girls were first permitted to take courses and exams to enter universities in 1893. The French government established organizations and imposed the regulations necessary for girls' higher education in 1819. However, it was not until 1867 that a movement began for the state to provide secondary education to girls, supplementing private schools. In the United Kingdom, women were first admitted to pursue degrees at the University of London in 1880 (Kandel, 1930).

In the United States, the availability of education for both genders became more prevalent as a reflection of the ideals of liberty and democracy. The first girls' high school was opened in 1826. The movement toward equal opportunity led to coeducation, as girls were allowed to receive schooling in Boston Latin School, originally available only to boys. In 1852, the High School for Girls, the country's first public girls' high school, was established. The first women's college, Mount Holyoke Seminary, was established in 1837, accelerating the development of female higher education.

In traditional China, women were excluded from receiving education comparable to that available to men. Women's education instead focused on teaching family traditions and social ethics, with an emphasis on how to behave as a virtuous wife and good mother (Lee, 1995). Female education began to take root in China mostly through schools established by Christian missionaries. The first girls' school was founded shortly after the Opium War (1840–1842), under the reign of Dao Guang. Although the Qing government, in 1907, announced its approval of women's education in private colleges and primary schools, it was not until the late 1920s that women were officially enrolled in Peking University (Lee, 1995).

In recent decades, the principle of equal access for women to educational opportunities gained momentum in the developing regions of Africa, East Asia, South Asia, and the Middle East. At present, the rights of boys and girls to free and compulsory education is recognized in educational legislation in almost all of the countries in the world.

International Comparisons
of School Enrollment
and Educational Attainment,
1870–2010

"An investment in knowledge pays the best interest."
—BENJAMIN FRANKLIN

We quantitatively assess educational expansion worldwide and compare educational attainment across countries since the 19th century. These analyses require high-quality data that measure educational attainment across nations over the long term.

There are a number of different measures of educational attainment to be used when comparing countries. School enrollment ratios measure the educational investment of new entrants. These ratios are widely available across countries, at least for the period after World War II, and have been used in numerous studies.[1] They are available for three levels of education: primary, secondary, and higher.

The underlying data on school enrollment are subject to problems of data collection. Most of the information collected by UNESCO comes from annual surveys of the educational institutions in each country. The typical practice involves the person responsible for administering each institution to answer questions about that institution. Chapman and Boothroyd (1988) note that "in several countries, headmasters have been observed to inflate reported enrollment based on their experience that higher enrollment figures lead to more resources (supplies, textbooks, budget) being allocated to the school." Another potential source of bias in the enrollment figures lies in the fact that the data refer to the number of registered students at the beginning of each school year. The actual number of children attending school during the year can be substantially lower if dropout rates are high.[2]

Enrollment ratios do not gauge the aggregate stock of education possessed by the adult population; this stock matters for its contemporaneous influence on production and on social and political life. School attainment reflects past inflows into schooling, as reflected in the enrollment of the school-aged population. These flows accumulate to create future stocks of educational attainment. Because the educational process takes many years, there is a long lag between flows and stocks.

Many researchers have attempted to construct direct measures of the stock of educational attainment. The adult literacy rate is widely available and has been frequently used to measure the stock of human capital of adults. Literacy concepts tend, however, not to be comparable across countries, because the measure is not based on a common and consistent criterion. In addition, literacy captures only the first stage in the process of human capital formation. It ignores other aspects of human capital, such as numeracy, logical and analytical reasoning, and various types of technical knowledge.

The most widely used measure of the stock of educational attainment is the number of years spent in school. Earlier studies, notably those by Psacharopoulos and Arriagada (1986, 1992), used census and survey data to compile information about the educational attainment of the labor force and the adult population. The main shortcoming of these data is that the coverage is too small: many countries have only a single observation. In addition, the time period covered differs among countries.

In our earlier studies (Barro and Lee, 1993, 1996, 2001, 2013), we constructed a data set of educational attainment for a broad group of countries. The most recent data set provides estimates of educational attainment for the population, aged 15 and up, for 146 countries at five-year intervals from 1950 to 2010. The estimates are disaggregated by gender and by five-year age intervals. The data are available at seven levels of education: no formal education, incomplete primary, complete primary, lower secondary, upper secondary, incomplete tertiary, and complete tertiary. We used the data to construct the average number of years of schooling for the adult population, at all levels combined, and at the primary, secondary, and tertiary levels.

The estimation procedure used the available census/survey observations on attainment as benchmark stocks. These data show the distribution of educational attainment in the population over age 15, classified by gender and five-year age group, for individual countries. Unfortunately, the census/survey information does not cover all five-year periods for most countries.

In our earlier studies (Barro and Lee, 1993, 1996, 2001, 2013), we constructed estimates for missing observations by combining enrollment rate data with the available census/survey information. This method produced reasonably accurate estimates of educational attainment over time and across countries at five-year intervals.

This chapter goes beyond the existing studies by constructing cross-country data for school enrollments and educational attainment over the long term. Our data set now includes measures of school enrollment since 1820 and educational attainment since 1870.[3]

We present the data set for enrollments at all education levels—primary, secondary, and tertiary—since 1820 for a sample of 89 countries. We then summarize the data and methodology used to construct the estimates of educational attainment. The final data set on educational attainment combines two data sets. The first contains estimates of educational attainment for both the total and female population for 146 countries, at five-year intervals, from 1950 to 2010. This data set improves on our previous work by incorporating newly available census/survey observations and adopting improved estimation methodologies. The second data set is the newly constructed data on educational attainment for the total and female populations for the age groups 15–24, 25–64, and 15–64 from 1870 to 1945 for 89 countries. Combining these two data sets, we highlight the main trends of educational attainment for the world and major regions from 1870 to 2010.

2.1 SCHOOL ENROLLMENT TRENDS FROM 1820 TO 2010

School enrollment provides valuable information about educational investment and expansion of a society. An increase in school enrollments does not necessarily correlate with improved education, especially in terms of quality, but it is a useful indicator of the educational investment made in a society's youth. Enrollment numbers also provide essential information for constructing estimates of a population's educational attainment over time.

We analyze the evolution of school enrollment, using comprehensive data on historical enrollment ratios disaggregated by gender and education level: primary, secondary, and tertiary. The estimates are constructed at five-year intervals from 1820 to 1945 for a sample of 89 countries. The historical estimates for this time span are combined with information from UNESCO publications since 1950 to get a full time series on enrollment ratios up to 2010.

We use "adjusted enrollment ratios," which are appropriate for cross-national comparisons of educational expansion at primary and secondary schools. These adjusted ratios modify the gross enrollment ratios to account for repetition of grades in primary and secondary schools. The gross enrollment ratio, whether unadjusted or adjusted, is a standard flow measure of educational investment of new entrants in a society and is widely used for cross-country comparisons. However, the adjusted ratio is superior to the unadjusted one as a reflection of the inflow of the youth population.[4] Due to data limitations, we use unadjusted gross enrollment ratios for tertiary education.

The original historical data on school enrollments are compiled from various sources. These data on primary, secondary, and tertiary enrollments for the total and female populations are used to construct complete time-series estimates of enrollment ratios.

UNESCO has collected and published comprehensive and reliable enrollment data, especially in its annual statistical yearbooks, for all of the countries in the world, but its information is limited to the post-World War II period. Before that, the League of Nations and other international agencies made similar efforts. Available compendia (Banks and Wilson, 2013; Mitchell, 2003a, 2003b, 2003c; UNESCO, 1958, 1961, 1966; Benavot and Riddle, 1988; Lindert, 2004) provide historical enrollment statistics for many independent states and colonies. Additional historical statistics, especially those on female enrollment, are available from the US Bureau of Education's *Report of the Commissioner of Education* (various years), Barnard

(1854), and Monroe (1911). We have also compiled data from other sources, including national statistical publications.[5]

We have compiled all available enrollment ratios for primary, secondary, and tertiary levels at five-year intervals from 1820 to 1945 using these various sources. Where necessary, the underlying data were applied to the nearest five-year date. We focus on a group of 89 countries and colonies, for which we are able to construct complete estimates for enrollment ratios in primary, secondary, and tertiary schools for the total and female populations. The number of countries for which actual enrollment data for total population is available is high, especially for the period after 1870 (see Table 2.1). The total number of actual observations available fills 72%, 58%, and 56% of the possible cells for primary, secondary, and tertiary levels, respectively, for the 89 countries from 1870 to 1945. Data are less available for the period before 1870, but they often exist after 1900 for many non-Western independent countries as well as former colonies. The number of actual figures that are available for the female population is more limited, filling in about 17%, 13%, and 12% of the cells for primary, secondary, and tertiary enrollment, respectively, for the female population between 1870 and 1945. The limited availability of data for the female population also reflects the later establishment of female education in developing countries and former colonies. Many countries that had not reported figures,

Table 2.1 THE NUMBER OF AVAILABLE ENROLLMENT CENSUS/SURVEY
OBSERVATIONS BY YEAR, 1820–1945

Year	Total Population			Female Population		
	Primary	Secondary	Tertiary	Primary	Secondary	Tertiary
1820/25	9	8	22	0	0	0
1830/35	19	8	33	1	0	0
1840/45	22	15	46	4	1	0
1850/55	38	21	48	5	0	0
1860/65	50	27	56	4	0	0
1870/75	68	39	63	6	0	0
1880/85	94	65	76	33	6	6
1890/95	109	90	88	47	6	8
1900/05	126	94	96	57	6	8
1910/15	132	108	98	43	11	8
1920/25	147	126	118	17	10	6
1930/35	165	143	126	16	64	53
1940/45	167	149	128	15	74	77
Total *1820–1945*	*1,146*	*894*	*998*	*248*	*178*	*166*
1870–1945	*1,008*	*814*	*793*	*234*	*177*	*166*

NOTES: The figure refers to the number of available actual enrollment figures for the two indicated years in the sample of 89 countries in which we have constructed complete data for enrollment at primary, secondary, and tertiary levels for total and female population.

especially for secondary and tertiary schools, during the earlier period had not yet established a formal education system for girls. The missing observations for those countries could be zero, or very low.

Gross enrollment ratios are calculated by dividing gross enrollments by the relevant school-age population of the individual countries. The historical demographic data on age distribution for national populations are available from Mitchell and the United Nations' *Demographic Yearbook* (1955) and the League of Nations' *Statistical Yearbook* (various years). Additional data were obtained from national sources. We compute the shares of the population—5–9, 10–14, 15–19, and 20–24 years old—in the total population from the sample of all available country-years observations at ten-year intervals, from 1820 to 1940. We fill in missing observations of the population structure through interpolation and extrapolation of the available data.[6] Using the estimated shares of the school-age population, 5–9, 10–14, 15–19, and 20–24 years old, we estimate the shares of country-specific school-age populations corresponding to each level of education. This calculation takes into account the variation in the duration of schooling at each level for each national educational system.

The next step uses school repetition rates at the primary and secondary levels to construct adjusted gross enrollment ratios. Because data on repetition ratios are available from the 1950s, our estimates for the adjusted enrollment ratios are calculated by assuming the same values for repetition ratios in the period 1850–1945.

Because the historical enrollment data are not complete for most countries at five-year intervals from 1820 to 1945, we have to construct estimates for a significant number of missing cells, especially in the cases of developing countries or former colonies. We use interpolation and extrapolation techniques to fill in missing observations for adjusted enrollment ratios. First, we use a linear interpolation estimate when feasible, in situations for which the missing observation is located between two actual enrollment figures. When interpolation is not feasible, we use backward estimates based on a logistic trend.[7]

Table 2.2 summarizes the complete data, showing the trends in adjusted enrollment ratios of school-age population groups for the total and female populations for the world and by group from 1850 to 2010 for 89 countries.[8] The table considers two broad groups: 23 "advanced countries" and 66 "developing countries."[9] The developing group is further broken down into five regions: Asia/Pacific (13 countries), Eastern Europe (5), Latin America/Caribbean (23), the Middle East/North Africa (8), and Sub-Saharan Africa (17). Regional averages are weighted by each country's school-age population at each education level.

Table 2.2, Part A shows that the proportion of the school-age population that attends school increased significantly at all levels since 1850. For the world as a whole, primary enrollment ratios increased from 9.8% in 1850 to 47.4% in 1940. Secondary and tertiary education also expanded during this period, although slowly; the secondary enrollment ratio rose from 0.3% to 8.3%, while tertiary education rose from less than 0.1% to 1.3%.

Enrollments expanded significantly after World War II. In 1950, the world's enrollment ratio was 56% for primary education and 12% for secondary education.[10]

Table 2.2 TRENDS OF ADJUSTED ENROLLMENT RATIOS (%) OF THE SCHOOL-AGE
POPULATION GROUPS FOR TOTAL AND FEMALE POPULATION BY GROUP AND
REGION, SELECTED YEARS BETWEEN 1850 AND 2010

	A. Total Population							
	1850	1880	1910	1940	1950	1970	1990	2010
World (89)								
Primary	9.8	22.0	34.0	47.4	55.6	73.3	88.5	98.5
Secondary	0.3	1.2	2.8	8.3	11.8	33.6	47.7	74.2
Tertiary	0.05	0.2	0.4	1.3	2.2	10.9	16.1	32.5
Advanced (23)								
Primary	37.7	69.6	85.8	90.1	94.6	94.1	97.6	99.5
Secondary	0.9	3.3	7.1	20.9	28.2	64.8	79.5	93.4
Tertiary	0.2	0.5	1.2	2.9	4.7	24.6	45.3	72.6
Developing (66)								
Primary	2.0	6.2	14.9	34.4	42.8	68.8	87.1	98.3
Secondary	0.1	0.4	1.0	3.7	5.8	22.8	41.2	71.3
Tertiary	0.01	0.03	0.1	0.6	1.3	5.6	9.3	26.1
Asia/the Pacific (13)								
Primary	0.2	2.2	7.0	23.7	37.7	66.8	89.3	99.7
Secondary	0.1	0.3	0.8	2.2	4.9	22.2	40.8	72.4
Tertiary	0.00	0.01	0.04	0.2	0.6	4.6	6.5	22.9
Eastern Europe (5)								
Primary	14.8	26.5	50.4	95.6	99.9	98.7	89.2	98.2
Secondary	0.3	0.9	2.3	12.3	15.5	56.8	87.7	87.5
Tertiary	0.03	0.1	0.3	2.8	6.3	20.6	42.7	72.7
Latin America/the Caribbean (23)								
Primary	7.4	17.0	28.3	51.7	55.3	75.2	90.0	99.5
Secondary	0.1	0.3	0.6	2.3	4.2	19.5	36.3	82.8
Tertiary	0.02	0.1	0.2	0.5	0.9	6.6	17.9	38.3
Middle East/North Africa (8)								
Primary	0.5	1.8	6.3	25.0	30.4	61.0	91.2	99.5
Secondary	0.02	0.1	0.3	2.4	6.0	20.4	48.6	68.4
Tertiary	0.02	0.02	0.03	0.2	0.8	4.7	12.3	32.1
Sub-Saharan Africa (17)								
Primary	1.5	5.1	6.2	17.4	28.0	45.3	60.9	89.6
Secondary	0.00	0.01	0.1	0.7	2.2	7.4	22.2	42.8
Tertiary	0.00	0.00	0.02	0.2	0.3	1.3	3.8	8.7
	B. Female Population							
	1850	1880	1910	1940	1950	1970	1990	2010
World (89)								
Primary	8.1	18.4	30.5	40.4	50.9	71.0	84.2	98.1
Secondary	0.1	0.6	2.2	7.5	11.2	30.7	44.3	75.1
Tertiary	0.00	0.02	0.2	1.0	1.4	7.5	15.2	33.5
Advanced (23)								
Primary	31.1	60.0	84.8	91.0	94.0	94.6	97.8	99.5
Secondary	0.5	1.9	6.9	22.1	26.2	63.5	79.8	94.0
Tertiary	0.00	0.03	0.3	2.1	2.4	18.6	46.2	77.6

Table 2.2 (CONTINUED)

	B. Female Population							
	1850	1880	1910	1940	1950	1970	1990	2010
Developing (66)								
Primary	1.6	4.3	10.1	24.7	36.6	65.8	82.2	97.9
Secondary	0.00	0.02	0.3	2.1	5.7	19.2	37.0	72.1
Tertiary	0.00	0.01	0.1	0.6	0.9	3.1	7.9	26.4
Asia/the Pacific (13)								
Primary	0.1	0.4	2.2	11.7	30.3	63.6	83.2	99.8
Secondary	0.00	0.01	0.2	1.1	4.8	16.2	35.1	72.7
Tertiary	0.00	0.00	0.01	0.1	0.2	1.7	4.9	22.0
Eastern Europe (5)								
Primary	13.4	25.6	41.4	88.7	95.7	97.8	89.1	98.0
Secondary	0.01	0.1	0.6	6.9	17.0	80.5	91.8	96.7
Tertiary	0.01	0.08	0.5	3.0	6.1	20.5	47.8	85.0
Latin America/the Caribbean (23)								
Primary	3.1	10.5	27.7	47.8	54.1	77.2	87.1	99.3
Secondary	0.00	0.03	0.2	2.1	3.8	16.5	41.1	85.9
Tertiary	0.00	0.00	0.03	0.2	0.5	4.5	16.4	41.7
Middle East/North Africa (8)								
Primary	0.1	0.3	1.7	12.6	19.2	46.7	84.6	98.5
Secondary	0.00	0.02	0.2	1.3	2.8	13.4	42.4	70.4
Tertiary	0.00	0.00	0.03	0.2	0.4	2.6	8.6	32.2
Sub-Saharan Africa (17)								
Primary	0.1	0.6	2.6	17.7	26.2	42.6	59.9	87.4
Secondary	0.00	0.01	0.1	0.7	1.5	5.4	16.7	42.1
Tertiary	0.00	0.01	0.04	0.1	0.2	0.5	2.6	8.2

NOTES: Regional averages are weighted by each country's school-age population. See Appendix Table for the list of countries included in each region/group.

Thereafter, the average primary enrollment ratio increased further, to 73% in 1970 and almost 99% in 2010. Secondary and tertiary enrollments also exploded after World War II. The average secondary enrollment ratio jumped from 12% in 1950 to 34% in 1970 and 74% in 2010. Similarly, tertiary education showed strong growth in the postwar period. By 1970, the percentage of the college-age population enrolled in tertiary schools across the world reached 11%, and it increased to about 33% by 2010.

For the 23 advanced countries, primary education expanded rapidly with the spread of compulsory primary schooling during the late 18th and early 19th centuries. The average primary enrollment ratio significantly increased, from 38% in 1850 to 90% in 1940. Secondary enrollment ratios also showed strong growth, rising from 0.9% to 21% over the same period. In contrast, the average tertiary enrollment ratio remained below 3%, until 1940. The growth of secondary and tertiary enrollment ratios accelerated after World War II. Secondary enrollment ratios jumped to

65% in 1970, and tertiary enrollment ratios increased to 25%. In 2010, secondary and tertiary enrollment ratios reached 94% and 73%, respectively.

For the group of 66 developing countries, enrollments also showed significant growth, at all levels, since 1850. The average primary enrollment ratio increased from a mere 2% in 1850 to 34% in 1940, 69% in 1970, and 98% in 2010. Secondary enrollment ratios, starting from almost 0% in 1850, increased to 4% in 1940 and then jumped to 23% by 1970. The increase in primary and secondary enrollment ratios in the post–World War II period reflects educational expansion worldwide, including in large countries such as Brazil, China, and India. Tertiary education was still underdeveloped in 1940; the average tertiary enrollment ratio remained at less than 0.6%. However, it expanded rapidly over the past half century, rising to 5.6% in 1970 and 26% in 2010.

Among the developing regions, the expansion of school enrollments over the late 19th and early 20th centuries was most prominent in the Eastern European region, which includes Albania, Bulgaria, Hungary, Poland, and Russia (Table 2.2 and Figure 2.1). This evolution reflects strong, state-led educational development in the context of the relatively advanced economic and social systems of these countries. By 1940, the average enrollment ratios reached 96% at the primary level, 12% at the secondary level, and 2.8% at the tertiary level.

For most developing countries and former colonies in Asia, Africa, and Latin America, the expansion of education occurred later than in the Eastern European countries. Table 2.2, Part A shows that Latin America had relatively high levels of school enrollments at all three levels during the late 19th and early 20th centuries, before World War II. In 1940, for example, the average primary enrollment ratio was 52% in Latin America, compared to 25% in the Middle East/North Africa, 24% in Asia/Pacific, and 17% in Sub-Saharan Africa. For secondary and tertiary education levels, enrollment ratios remained low in the developing countries of Asia, Africa, and Latin America until World War II. Since then, there has been significant growth in primary, secondary, and tertiary enrollment ratios in all of the developing regions.

Figure 2.1 displays the changes of the average enrollment ratios among the school-age population groups for each education level, classified by group and region. Although the educational progress of the developing region as a whole was relatively strong over the past century and a half, the average enrollment ratios in this region lagged far behind the advanced regions, at all education levels, throughout the period. The strong educational progress made by developing countries over the past 50 years has significantly narrowed the gap in primary enrollment ratios with the advanced regions, almost bringing the developing world to the same level as the advanced countries. Yet, there are still substantial gaps in secondary and tertiary enrollment ratios. The gap between the developing and advanced countries in secondary enrollment ratios remains high in 2010 at 22 percentage points on average (93% for advanced countries compared to 71% for developing countries). The gap in tertiary enrollment ratios remains much higher in 2010, at 47 percentage points (73% for advanced countries compared to 26% for developing countries). The levels of secondary and tertiary enrollment ratios

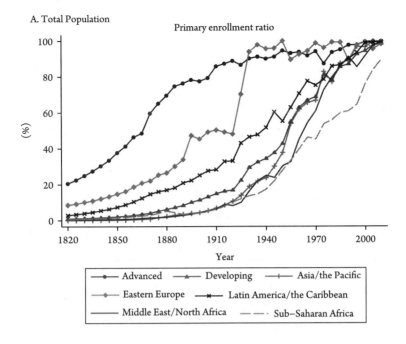

A. Total Population

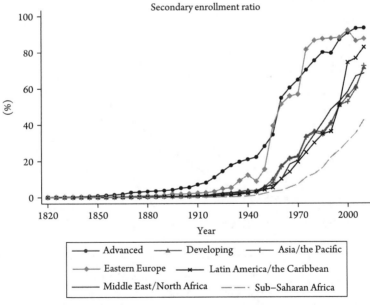

Figure 2.1 Trends of Average Enrollment Ratios by Group and Region, 1820–2010

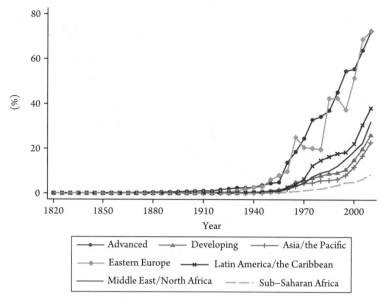

Tertiary enrollment ratio

B. Female Population

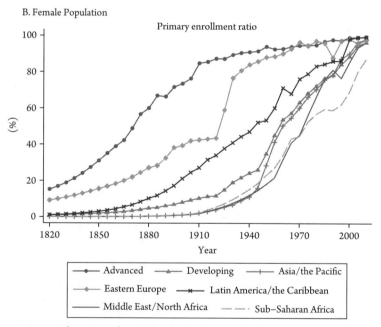

Primary enrollment ratio

Figure 2.1 (continued)

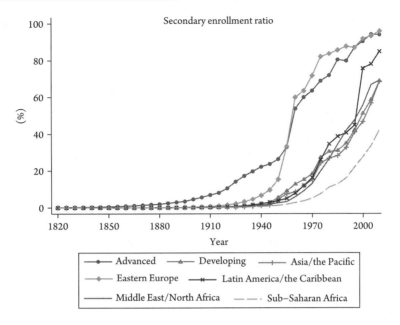

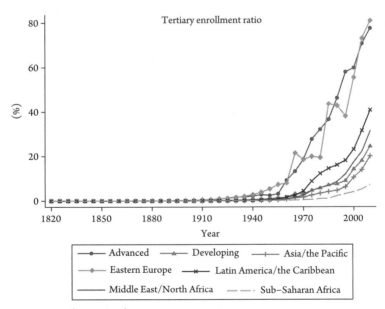

Figure 2.1 (continued)

in 2010 in the developing regions are comparable to those of the advanced countries in 1970 (see Figure 2.1).

Figure 2.1 shows regional variations in the growth of secondary and tertiary enrollment ratios among five developing regions in the post–World War II period. Eastern European countries maintained the highest levels of enrollment ratios throughout these years. Developing countries in Asia/Pacific, the Middle East/ North Africa, and Latin America showed strong gains since the war. By contrast, secondary and tertiary enrollment ratios in the Sub-Saharan African countries grew at slower rates over the same period. Their secondary and tertiary enrollment ratios are still very low compared with other developing countries.

Table 2.2, Part B summarizes the estimates of school enrollment ratios for the female population since 1850 for 89 countries. They show significant progress in all regions, including a group of advanced countries and five developing regions. For the world as a whole, female primary enrollment ratios increased from 8% in 1850 to 40% in 1940, 71% in 1970, and 98% in 2010. Secondary and tertiary education also expanded over time: the secondary enrollment ratio rose from 0.1% in 1850 to 7.5% in 1940 and then jumped to 31% in 1970 and 75% in 2010, while the ratio for tertiary education remained below 1.0% until 1940 and rose to 7.5% in 1970 and 34% in 2010. In the advanced countries, average female primary enrollment ratio increased significantly, from 31% in 1850 to 91% in 1940, whereas it increased from 1.6% to 25% in the developing countries. Average female secondary enrollment ratio reached 22% in 1940 for the group of advanced countries; however, it was only 2.1% for the group of developing countries. In the developing countries, the secondary enrollment ratios for the female population grew rapidly after World War II, along with those for the total population. In contrast, female enrollment ratios at the tertiary level remained low worldwide until 1950 and began to rise since then.

Figure 2.2 compares the enrollment ratios for females with those for males at each education level for the regional groups from 1820 to 2010. The figures show the "gender ratio," defined as the proportion of females to males in enrollment ratios at each education level.[11] In the advanced regions, the gender disparity in primary education was small even in the 19th century. For secondary and tertiary education,

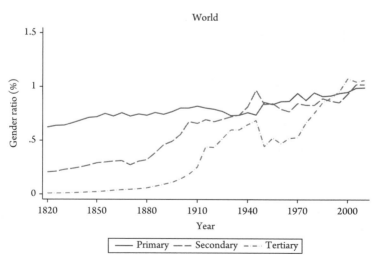

Figure 2.2 Trends of Gender Ratios in Enrollment Ratios, Worldwide and by Group, 1820–2010

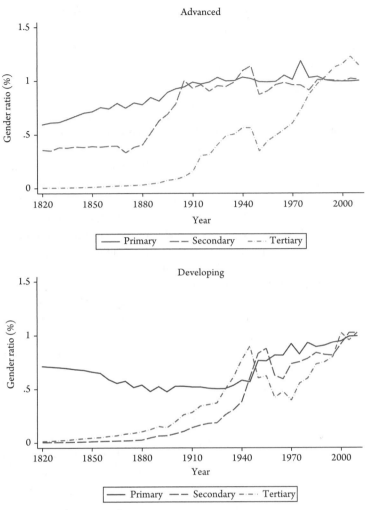

Figure 2.2 (continued)

there has been a substantial rise in gender equality over the past century. The ratios rose steadily from 0.2 in 1850 to 1.02 in 2010 for secondary education, and from 0.01 to 1.06 for tertiary education.

In advanced and developing regions, gender inequality has declined steadily at all levels of education from 1820 to 2000. Note that the gender gap in secondary and tertiary education has rapidly decreased over recent decades in developing regions, resulting in almost equal enrollment ratios for both genders.

2.2 DETERMINANTS OF SCHOOL ENROLLMENTS

We investigate the determinants of school enrollment ratios by adopting a regression approach. The relationship between educational investment—as measured by enrollment ratios by level of education—and economic factors that were identified in the existing literature is estimated.

The literature suggests that the major determinants of enrollment ratios are income per-capita, income distribution, parental education, fertility, and public education expenditures.[12]

Parental income determines whether a household can afford to send children to school. Poor households are unable to pay for tuition fees and school supplies, and are often unable to forego the income from their children's employment. They also need their children's assistance with chores.

The educational level of parents also influences their desire to see their children placed in school, as well as the child's academic performance once they are attending. More educated parents may have a stronger desire to provide for the education of their children. A more educated adult population, including competent teachers available to instruct classes, is also more capable of cultivating and training students. Empirical studies have supported the significant influence of the parent's income and education level on their investment in their children's education (for example, Haveman and Wolfe, 1995; Hanushek and Luque, 2003).

A more equal distribution of income implies that more families can afford to let their children attend school and invest in their children's education. In the case of developing countries, some poor families may lack the resources and access to credit necessary to finance education. Flug et al. (1998) found that income inequality has a significant negative effect on secondary enrollment ratios.

According to the literature (for example, Becker and Lewis, 1973; Becker and Barro, 1988), families face a trade-off between having more children and having fewer, but better educated, children. This implies that the demand for children falls as the cost of nurturing and educating children becomes more expensive; human capital expenditures per child are inversely related to fertility. Kalemli-Ozcan (2003) argued that the quantity-quality trade-off is realized, when households who consider the uncertainty on child survival increase educational investment with response to decline in the mortality.

Heyneman and Loxley (1983) found that, although a student's academic achievement is influenced by both school resources and family background, school resources are more important in poor countries.[13] According to several other empirical studies, social spending on education has a significant positive impact on educational performance (Anand and Martin, 1993; Psacharopoulos and Patrinos, 2004). By contrast, a number of empirical studies showed that education spending has a limited effect on educational outcomes (Flug et al., 1998; Mingat and Tan, 1998).

Specifically, we test and estimate these relationships with the following equation:

$$
\begin{aligned}
\text{Enrollment ratio}_j = \ & \alpha + \beta_{1j}\ln\left(\text{GDP per capita}\right) + \beta_{2j}\ln\left(\text{GDP per capita}\right)^2 \\
& + \beta_{3j}\text{Gini} + \beta_{4j}\ \text{Ave. Yrs Sch}_{40\text{-}64} + \beta_{5j}\text{Fertility} \\
& + \beta_{6j}\text{Public education expenditure}_j \\
& + \sum_{i=1}^{5}\delta_{i,j}{}^{*}\text{Regional dummies}_i + \mu_j
\end{aligned}
\tag{2.1}
$$

The dependent variables are the enrollment ratios at level j (primary, secondary, or tertiary). We run regressions for both the total population and female population.

GDP per-capita data are from the Penn World Table (PWT version 8.0),[14] and income inequality data, as measured by the gini coefficient, are from the Standardized World Income Inequality Database, constructed by Solt (2013).[15] For parental education, the average years of schooling among 40–64 year-olds from our educational attainment dataset are used. Data on total fertility rates are from the United Nation's consolidated online database. We construct current public education expenditures by educational level (as a percent of GDP) from the data available in the UNESCO *Statistical Yearbooks* (various years).

Country or region-specific effects, such as cultural and religious factors, can also influence school enrollment. Some studies have argued that East Asian culture has a significant positive impact on educational expectations and performance (Stevenson et al., 2008; Leung, 2006). The regressions include regional dummies to control for factors common to a given region. The regressions also include dummy variables for year, to represent unexplained, but common, global factors that have influenced enrollment ratios in the period between 1960 and 2010.

The Tobit models, which take into consideration the censuring of dependent values between 0 and 100, are applied to an unbalanced panel, consisting of data from 95 countries over the five ten-year periods from 1960 to 2010. We adopt random GLS estimation techniques. The panel Tobit model cannot adopt fixed-effects estimation techniques.

One concern in the empirical specification is reverse causation from school enrollment to any contemporaneous explanatory variable. For example, the relationship between contemporaneous enrollment and GDP may indicate that high enrollment causes high income. To reduce this potential bias, we use ten-year lagged values of both GDP per capita and fertility rate as independent variables. Current public education expenditure is an average ratio calculated over the previous five years.

Figure 2.3 examines whether the panel data confirms these theoretical predictions. Figure 2.3a indicates a strong positive relationship between income and enrollment ratios, which is strong at both the primary and secondary levels. Figure 2.3b shows that enrollment ratios are negatively related with income inequality, although the relationship is weak. Figure 2.3c demonstrates that enrollment ratios increase with parental education, while they decrease with fertility, as indicated in Figure 2.3d. Finally, Figure 2.3e shows that enrollment ratios are positively related to current public education expenditures.

Table 2.3 presents our regression results for the specification. Columns (1)–(3) show the results of the regressions for the enrollment ratios of the total population. As expected, we find a significant positive relationship between per-capita income and enrollment ratios, which is nonlinear for both primary and secondary enrollment ratios, as shown by the significant coefficients for the squared per-capita income term. That is, when holding all else constant, primary and secondary enrollment ratios increase alongside average per-capita income, although at a decreasing rate. However, the coefficient of the squared per-capita income is statistically significant only at the 10% level for secondary enrollment ratios. The relationship between tertiary enrollment ratios and per-capita income is also statistically significant and

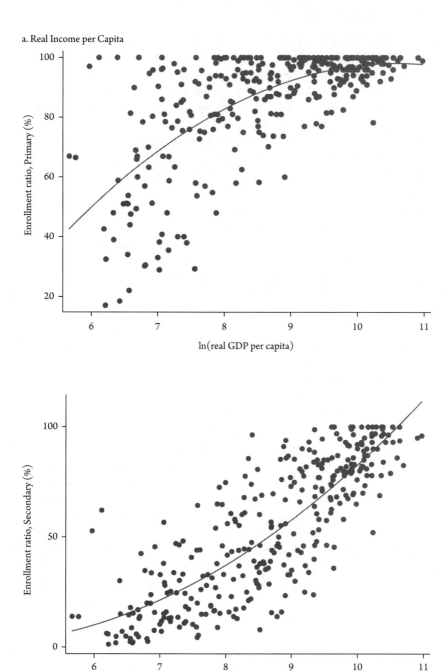

a. Real Income per Capita

Figure 2.3 Relationships of Enrollment Ratios with Income, Income Inequality, Parents' Education, Fertility Rate, and Public Education Expenditure, 1960–2010

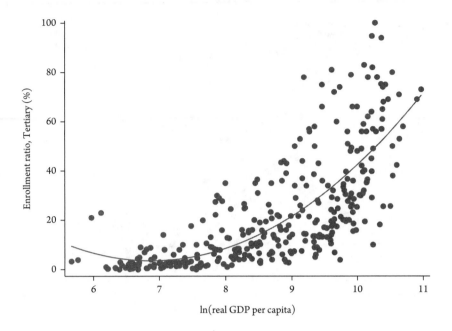

b. Income Inequality

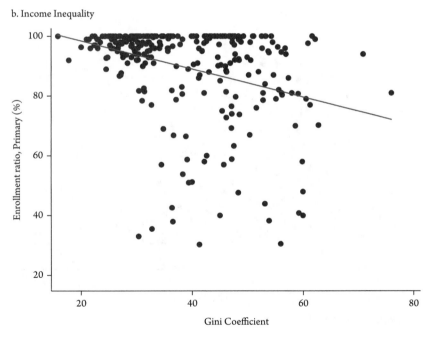

Figure 2.3 (continued)

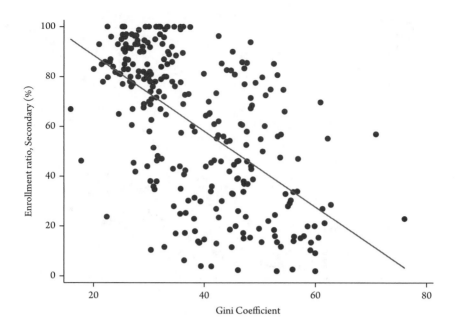

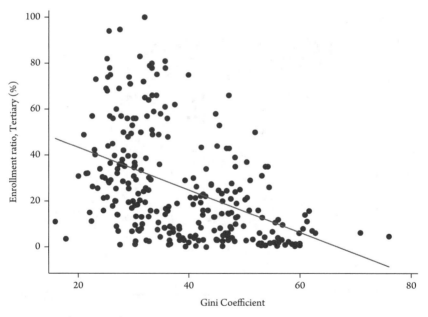

Figure 2.3 (continued)

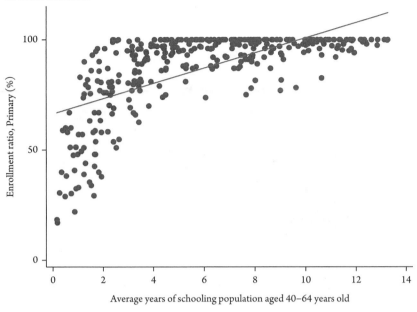

Average years of schooling population aged 40–64 years old

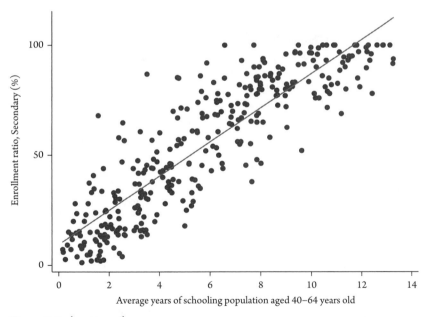

Average years of schooling population aged 40–64 years old

Figure 2.3 (continued)

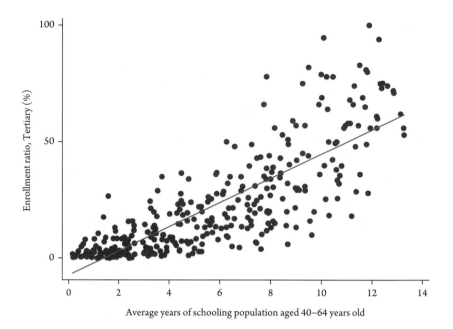

Average years of schooling population aged 40–64 years old

d. Total Fertility Rate

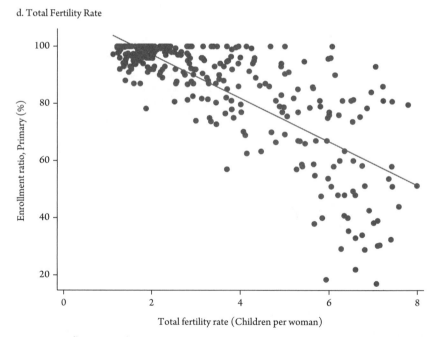

Total fertility rate (Children per woman)

Figure 2.3 (continued)

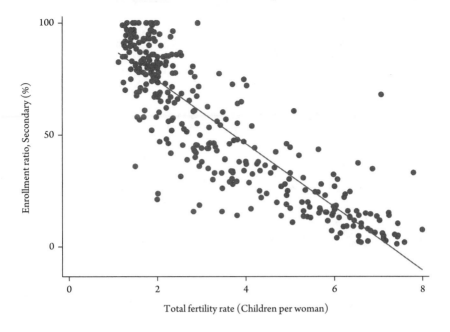

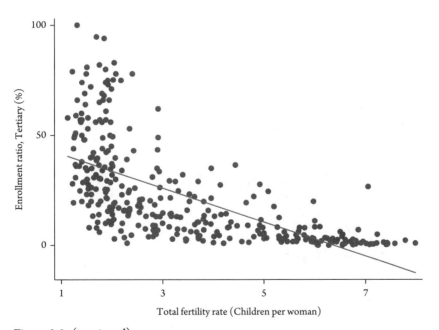

Figure 2.3 (continued)

e. Public Education Expenditure

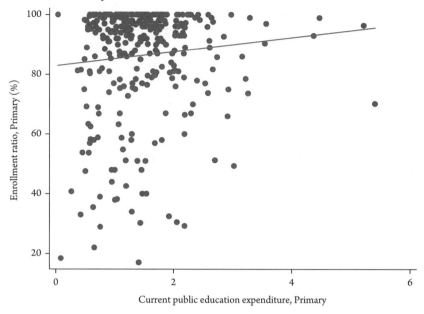

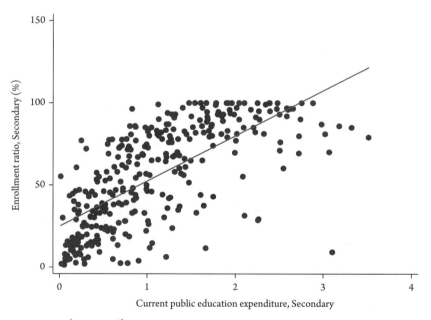

Figure 2.3 (continued)

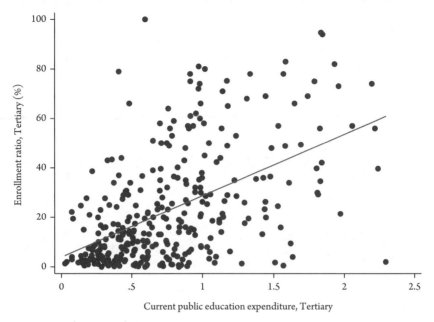

Figure 2.3 (continued)

nonlinear. The coefficients of both the per-capita income and its squared terms are, respectively, positive and negative. Hence, as per-capita income increases, tertiary enrollment ratios also increase at a growing rate.

The estimates for the parents' education are also positive and strongly significant across all levels, especially at the secondary and tertiary levels. This indicates that, on average, while controlling for other factors, a population with a higher level of education is more likely to invest in children's education, and is thus more likely to see its level of education increase over time.

Investments in primary and secondary education decrease significantly with the total fertility rate, which means that, holding all else constant, larger families are less likely to invest in primary or secondary education for their children (on a per-child basis). Intriguingly, however, our estimates indicate that a strong positive and significant relationship exists between tertiary enrollment and the fertility rate, under different specifications. This implies that, all else being equal, countries with larger families are more likely to have a higher investment in tertiary education.

Meanwhile, the coefficient for income inequality is negative for primary and secondary enrollment ratios. This suggests that, holding all other variables equal, countries with lower income inequality would tend to have a higher investment in primary and secondary education.

Our estimates also show that enrollment ratios are positively related to current public education expenditure at all levels. However, this relationship is strongly significant for the secondary enrollment ratio only under both specifications.

Columns (4)–(6) of Table 2.3 show the results of the regressions for the enrollment ratios for the female population. The results are quite similar to those in columns (1)–(3).

Table 2.3 DETERMINANTS OF ENROLLMENT RATIOS

	Total Population			Female Population		
	Primary	Secondary	Tertiary	Primary	Secondary	Tertiary
ln(Real GDP per Capita)$_{t-10}$	65.190***	20.53**	-49.85***	81.16***	19.58**	-53.73***
	(9.202)	(8.662)	(8.819)	(10.22)	(9.064)	(10.33)
ln(Real GDP per Capita)$_{t-10}$ Squared	-3.962***	-1.023*	3.384***	-4.793***	-0.922	3.613***
	(0.560)	(0.536)	(0.536)	(0.623)	(0.561)	(0.629)
Average Years of Schooling, 40–46 years old$_t$	1.019*	3.074***	1.683***	1.647**	3.048***	1.643***
	(0.551)	(0.471)	(0.472)	(0.587)	(0.494)	(0.535)
Education Expenditure, by Level$_t$	2.981***	3.304***	5.771***	4.171***	3.634***	6.976***
	(0.827)	(1.061)	(1.416)	(0.906)	(1.121)	(1.624)
Total Fertility Rate$_{t-10}$	-2.169***	-4.238***	1.954***	-2.134**	-5.609***	2.433***
	(0.791)	(0.725)	(0.682)	(0.876)	(0.754)	(0.773)
Income Equality Index$_t$	-18.88**	-14.63*	10.36	-11.06	-13.90*	10.87
	(8.392)	(7.892)	(7.392)	(9.586)	(8.383)	(8.788)
Advanced	15.35***	8.356**	13.20***	11.99**	2.542	14.37***
	(4.912)	(3.799)	(4.086)	(5.364)	(4.069)	(4.686)
Asia/the Pacific	11.93***	6.987***	12.20***	8.018**	2.097	13.77***
	(3.472)	(2.707)	(2.970)	(3.809)	(2.892)	(3.407)
Europe/Central Asia	3.057	2.584	20.55***	-1.608	-1.412	25.91***
	(5.587)	(4.408)	(4.716)	(6.003)	(4.658)	(5.386)

	(1)	(2)	(3)	(4)	(5)	(6)
Latin America/the Caribbean	11.00***	3.792	12.35***	8.492**	3.723	13.75***
	(3.484)	(2.701)	(2.946)	(3.784)	(2.872)	(3.372)
Middle East/North Africa	7.390*	10.91***	7.997**	1.929	4.944	7.692*
	(4.296)	(3.255)	(3.648)	(4.700)	(3.570)	(4.225)
No. of countries	95	95	95	91	91	91
No. of observations	329	329	329	314	314	314

NOTES: Dependent variables are adjusted enrollment ratios for primary and secondary education and gross enrollment ratios for tertiary education, for total and female population. The panel specification uses data from 95 countries over the six years, 1960, 1970, 1980, 1990, 2000, and 2010. Period dummies are included. Standard errors are in parentheses.

Asterisks denote significance levels: * 10%; ** 5%; *** 1%. Absolute value of z/t statistics in parentheses.

In summary, cross-country regressions confirm the important roles of parents' income and education, the number of children, income inequality, and public expenditure for educational investment.

2.3 ESTIMATING EDUCATIONAL ATTAINMENT, 1950–2010

We summarize here the data and methodology for constructing estimates of educational attainment for the population over age 15 at five-year intervals from 1950 to 2010. The estimates are disaggregated by gender and by five-year age group.

Census Data

The newly constructed estimates make use of information from available survey/census data, disaggregated by age group.

The benchmark figures on school attainment are collected from census/survey information, as compiled by the United Nations Educational, Scientific and Cultural Organization (UNESCO), Eurostat, national statistics agencies, and other sources.[16] Table 2.4 presents the distribution of countries by the number of census/survey observations available since 1945. For the total population aged 15 and over, 191 countries have at least one observation, and 132 countries have three or more

Table 2.4 BREAKDOWN OF NUMBER OF COUNTRIES BY NUMBER OF CENSUS/SURVEY OBSERVATIONS

Number of Observations (1945–2010)	Number of Countries					
	All		Advanced		Developing	
	MF	F	MF	F	MF	F
1	36	33	1	1	35	32
2	23	26	0	0	23	26
3	28	30	1	1	27	29
4	30	28	1	1	29	27
5	20	22	4	4	16	18
6	26	24	6	6	20	18
7	17	15	6	6	11	9
8	4	3	1	1	3	2
9	5	5	3	3	2	2
10	1	1	1	1	0	0
11	0	0	0	0	0	0
12	1	1	0	0	1	1
Total	191	188	24	24	167	164

NOTE: The data refer to census/survey observations for educational attainment for the total (MF) and female (F) populations in each group.

Table 2.5 THE NUMBER OF AVAILABLE OBSERVATIONS BY CENSUS/SURVEY YEAR

Census/Survey Year (to nearest 5-year value)	Number of Countries					
	All		Advanced		Developing	
	MF	F	MF	F	MF	F
1945	5	4	1	1	4	3
1950	26	26	8	8	18	18
1955	16	14	1	1	15	13
1960	73	69	15	15	58	54
1965	30	30	4	4	26	26
1970	92	87	18	18	74	69
1975	45	44	7	7	38	37
1980	93	91	18	18	75	73
1985	27	24	5	5	22	19
1990	86	81	14	13	72	68
1995	28	28	4	5	24	23
2000	93	93	17	17	76	76
2005	56	56	17	17	39	39
2010	91	91	23	23	68	68
Total	761	738	152	152	609	586

NOTE: The data refer to census/survey observations for educational attainment for the total (MF) and female (F) populations in each group.

observations. Table 2.5 shows the distribution of countries by census/survey year since 1945 (when the underlying figures are applied to the nearest five-year value). For the total population over age 15, for example, 73 observations are available for 1960, 92 for 1970, 93 for 1980, 86 for 1990, 93 for 2000, and 91 for 2010. We have compiled a total of 761 census/survey observations.[17] These data include the countries/territories for which we could not construct complete estimates of educational attainment due to other missing information. We have constructed complete estimates for 146 countries by utilizing the census/survey observations as benchmark figures on educational attainment.[18]

The census/survey figures report the distribution of educational attainment in the population over age 15 by gender and five-year age group. The classification scheme by schooling level follows the UNESCO's "International Standard Classification of Education" (ISCED), which attempts to facilitate comparisons of education statistics and indicators across countries by using uniform and internationally agreed on definitions.[19] Based on the UNESCO classifications, we have obtained data that correspond to six levels of education:

No Schooling: those who have no formal schooling at all and those who completed less than one year of primary schooling.
Incomplete Primary Level: those who have received at least one year of primary education but did not complete the final year of primary school.

Complete Primary Level: those who completed the final year (or in some cases, completed the penultimate year) of primary school (ISCED category "1") but did not advance to secondary school.

Lower Secondary Level: those who entered the lower stage of secondary school (ISCED category "2") but did not advance to the higher stage of secondary school.

Upper Secondary Level: those who entered the higher stage of secondary school (ISCED category "3"), whether or not they completed the full course, but did not proceed to post-secondary, tertiary-level studies.

Higher Level: those who undertook post-secondary, tertiary-level education (ISCED categories "5," "6," and "7"), whether or not they completed the full course.

There are also census/surveys that present the disaggregation of higher education as complete and incomplete components. The incomplete higher level includes those junior-college and university attendees without degrees, while the complete higher level includes university graduates with degrees and postgraduates (Kaneko, 1986). The classification of national educational systems according to the international standard is not always perfect. For example, many countries have "post-secondary and non-tertiary schools" (ISCED category "4"). These programs are not significantly more advanced than those in ISCED 3. Programs in ISCED 4 typically have durations of six months to two years. In most cases, they are classified into the "upper secondary" category. However, comparing the education standards of post-secondary educational institutions across nations is often a complex endeavor.

Based on the available census and survey data, we estimate missing observations from 1950 to 2010 for each country. We calculate the estimation in two steps: first, we estimate the missing observations at a broad, four-level classification—no formal education (h_u), primary (h_p), secondary (h_s), and tertiary education (h_h)—and then we estimate the breakdown of primary, secondary, and tertiary education into subcategories. Primary includes incomplete primary (h_{pi}) and complete primary (h_{pc}), while secondary (h_s) includes lower secondary (h_{si}) and upper secondary (h_{sc}). Tertiary education (h_h) also includes incomplete (h_{hi}) and complete tertiary (h_{hc}).

Estimating Missing Observations at the Four Broad Levels[20]

From 1950 to 2010, we calculate, at five-year intervals, the educational attainment of the population by five-year age groups in four broad categories. The available census data do not always report data according to these four broad categories. When a census provides numbers only for a combination of several categories—such as no formal education, incomplete primary, and complete primary—we use decomposition methods to separate them into categories.[21]

We fill in most of the missing observations at the four broad levels using forward and backward extrapolation of the census/survey observations on attainment. The estimation procedure extrapolates census/survey observations on attainment by age group in order to fill in missing observations with an appropriate time lag.

Denoted by $h_{j,t}^a$ the proportion of persons in age group a, for whom j is the highest level of schooling attained; j = u for no school, p for primary, s for secondary, and h for higher, at time t. There are 13 five-year age groups, ranging from $a = 1$ (15–19 years old) to $a = 13$ (75 years and over).

The forward extrapolation method assumes that the distribution of educational attainment of the age group a at time t is the same as that of the age group that was five years younger at time t-5:

$$h_{j,t}^a = h_{j,t-5}^{a-1} \tag{2.2}$$

where age group a denotes $a = 3$: 25–29 age group, . . ., $a = 11$: 65–69 age group. This setting applies to persons who have completed their schooling by time t-5. As explained below, we adjust this formula by considering different mortality rates, by education level, for the older population, aged 65 and over. For younger groups, under the age of 25, we adopt a different method, which considers that part of the population is still in school during the transition period from t to $t + 5$.

The backward extrapolation is expressed as:

$$h_{j,t}^a = h_{j,t+5}^{a+1} \tag{2.2a}$$

where age group a denotes $a = 2$: 20–24 age group, . . ., $a = 10$: 60–64 age group.

Thus, a person's educational attainment remains unchanged between ages 25 and 64. One assumption here is that, in the same five-year age group, the survival rate remains the same regardless of a person's educational attainment. When we look at the information from available censuses, stratified by educational attainment and the population structure by age group in previous or subsequent five-year periods, we find this assumption holds for the population aged 64 and under but not for older age groups. In a typical country, the mortality rate is higher for older people who are less educated. The assumption of uniform mortality can then cause a downward bias in the estimation of the total educational stock.

If we consider the differences in survival rates by education levels, the forward extrapolation method is expressed by:

$$h_{j,t}^a = h_{j,t-5}^{a-1} \cdot (1 - \rho_j^a) \tag{2.3}$$

where ρ_j^a is the age-specific mortality rate over the five-year period for the population in age group a (a = 12, 13), for whom j is the highest level of schooling. For the population aged 65 and older, we allow for different mortality rates based on education levels. Note that the survival rate is a relative variable that measures the survival rate of each educational attainment group as a fraction of the overall survival rate of the relevant age group. The overall survival rates for each five-year age cohort are reflected in the change in population structure over time, derived from population census data for individual countries.

By utilizing information from available censuses, by age group, in the previous and/or next five-year periods, we have estimated the survival rates $(1-\rho_j^a)$ for the older populations in the age group—65–69, 70–74, and 75 and up—by education levels. Due to the limited availability of observations, we estimate survival rates for two broad groups of education levels: first, a less-educated population (the uneducated and people who have reached the primary level) and a more-educated population (who have reached at least secondary schooling), and second, for broad groups of advanced countries and developing countries. The estimation results show that more-educated people have lower mortality (higher survival) rates.[22]

Table 2.6 summarizes the backward and forward estimation procedure by age group. We perform either backward or forward extrapolation when at least one benchmark figure is available from either an earlier or later period. If more than one benchmark figure is available, we use the figure from the closest period as the benchmark figure. In the backward extrapolation for the population aged 75 and older, we allow the procedure to run up to three consecutive times. The backward extrapolation, from the estimate of the population aged 75 and older, is likely subject to substantial measurement error because of its broad age range. This restriction prevents the backward extrapolated estimate for the oldest population, aged 75 and older, from being continuously used for the backward extrapolation, thereby influencing the estimates for the population under 65 years.

Because of the limitations on the number of repetitions, the backward estimation cannot fill in all missing observations in the earlier periods, particularly for the older population groups in countries that do not have actual census/survey information. We construct the estimates to fill in these missing cells using two methods.

Table 2.6 Rules for Estimating Missing Observations through Forward and Backward Extrapolation

Age Group (a)	Backward Extrapolation	Forward Extrapolation
15–19	$h_{j,t}^{15-19} = h_{j,t+5}^{15-19} - \Delta enroll_{j,t}^{15-19}$	$h_{j,t}^{15-19} = h_{j,t-5}^{15-19} + \Delta enroll_{j,t}^{15-19}$
20–24	$h_{j,t}^{20-24} = h_{j,t+5}^{25-29}$	$h_{j,t}^{20-24} = h_{j,t-5}^{20-24} + \Delta enroll_{j,t}^{20-24}$
25–29, ..., 60–64	$h_{j,t}^{a} = h_{j,t+5}^{a+1}$	$h_{j,t}^{a} = h_{j,t-5}^{a-1}$
65–69, 70–74	$h_{j,t}^{a} = h_{j,t+5}^{a+1} \cdot (1-\rho_j^a)^{-1}$	$h_{j,t}^{a} = h_{j,t-5}^{a-1}$
75 and over	$h_{j,t}^{75+} = h_{j,t+5}^{75+} \cdot (1-\rho_j^a)^{-1}$	$h_{j,t}^{75+} = h_{j,t-5}^{70-74} \cdot (1-\rho_j^a)$

NOTE: $h_{j,t}^a$ is the proportion of people in age group a, for whom j is the highest level of schooling attained at time t, $\Delta enroll_{j,t}^a$ is the change in enrollment ratios over time (after taking account of time lag and graduates' advance into the next education cycle) for age group a in level j at time t, and $(1-\rho_j^a)$ is the survival ratio for age group a in education level j over the five years at time t.

First, we construct "flow estimates" based on enrollment ratios (explained in the next section). Alternatively, we construct estimates based on the typical age-group profile from the distribution of educational attainment, derived using available data from countries in the same region, advanced or developing. The ex post simulation, using the actual census/survey estimates between 1950 and 1970, indicates that the "enrollment-based flow estimates" are well matched with the actual census/survey figures in the period 1950–1970 (see Figure 2.4). Hence, in most cases, we use the "enrollment-based flow estimates." For the countries in which flow estimates for specific age groups are not compatible with the forward-extrapolated census/survey figures in the other five-year age groups, we use the alternative estimates based on the average regional profile.

We have evaluated the accuracy of the forward- and backward-extrapolation method by carrying out ex post simulations, as described in Barro and Lee (1993), and found that the method provides reliable estimates for missing observations. An important issue is how forward- and backward-flow estimates can be combined when both are available for a missing cell. We have carried out a simulation exercise in which we conduct a regression for the "observed" actual census values of the various levels of educational attainment using the estimates generated from forward- and backward-flow estimates (based on both five- or ten-year lead and lagged values

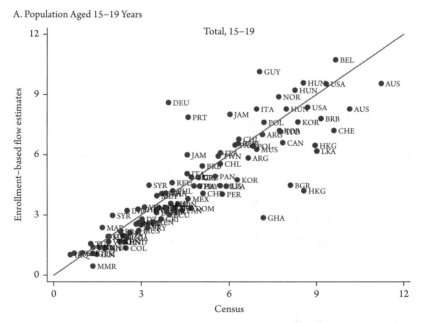

A. Population Aged 15–19 Years

Figure 2.4 Comparison of Years of Schooling between Enrollment-Based Flow Estimates and Census Data for Total Population Aged 15–19 and 20–24 Years, 1950–1970

NOTES: The "flow estimates" are constructed using enrollment ratios for age-specific population groups and compared to the actual/survey figures over the period 1950–1970.

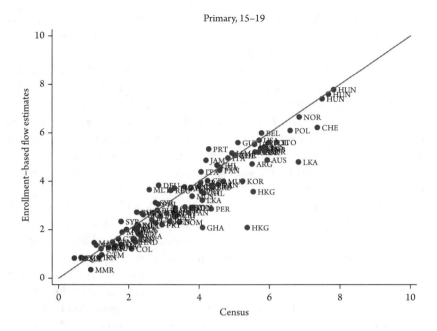

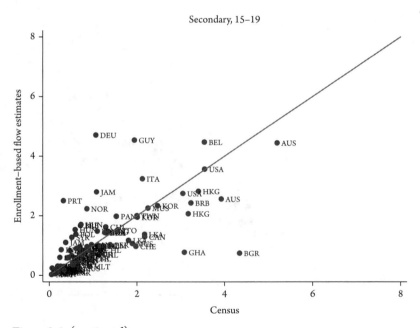

Figure 2.4 (continued)

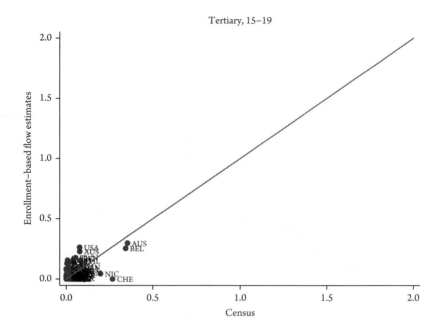

Tertiary, 15–19

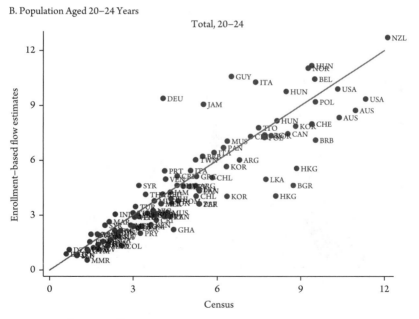

B. Population Aged 20–24 Years

Total, 20–24

Figure 2.4 (continued)

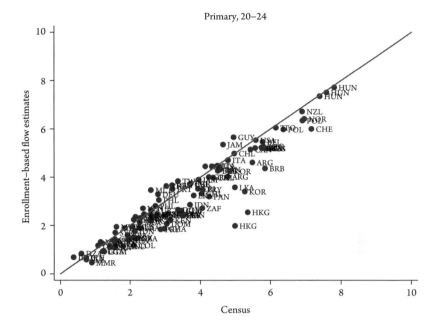

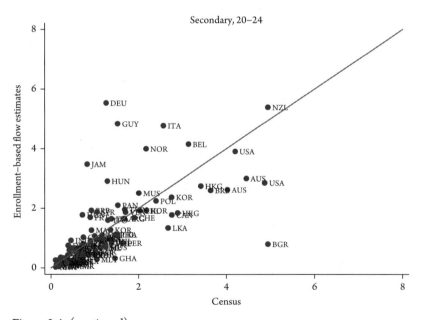

Figure 2.4 (continued)

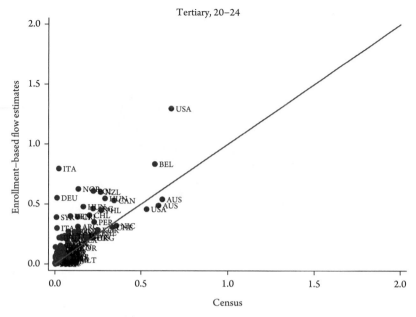

Figure 2.4 (continued)

from actual censuses). We use the regression results to construct a weighted-average of the forward- and backward-flow estimates.[23]

Direct forward extrapolation is not applicable for the two youngest age groups, between the ages of 15 and 24 ($a = 1$: 15–19 age group and $a = 2$: 20–24 age group), because parts of the population is in school during dates t and $t + 5$. We use attainment and enrollment data to estimate the missing attainment data for these age groups. We assume that the change in (age-specific) enrollment leads to a proportional change in attainment over time with a time lag. Hence, for these age groups, we use estimates for the same age group from the previous period as a benchmark, and we adjust this benchmark figure according to the change in enrollment over time.[24]

For the backward extrapolation, we use this method for the 15–19 age group, but not for the 20–24 age group, because direct backward extrapolation of the estimate for the 25–29 age group from a later period can, without adjustment, be applied to the 20–24 age group (see Table 2.6).

We carry out ex post simulations to assess the accuracy of the estimates for the 15–19 and 20–24 age groups by comparing them with the actual survey figures. We find that they are well matched (see Figure 2.5), except for a few observations for Germany and Singapore, which show big discrepancies in the backward extrapolations for the 20–24 age group at the secondary (for Germany) or tertiary level (for Singapore). However, measurement errors increase if the forward and backward procedures are repeated too many times. We decide that the forward extrapolations for the 15–19 and 20–24 age groups, and the backward extrapolations for the 15–19 age groups, can be repeated up to eight times; that is, with 40 years lead or lag. We

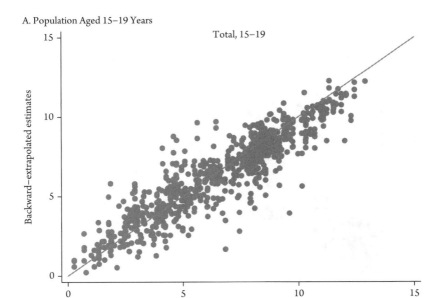

A. Population Aged 15–19 Years

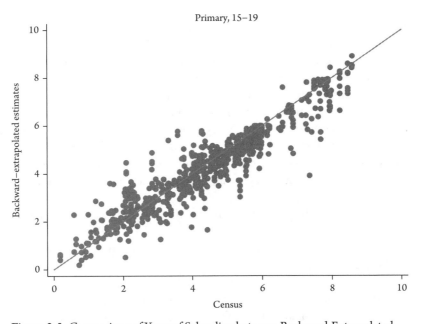

Figure 2.5 Comparison of Years of Schooling between Backward-Extrapolated Estimates and Census Data for Total Population Aged 15–19 and 20–24
NOTES: The backward-extrapolated estimates use the census figure from the same age group from the next period as benchmark and adjust this benchmark figure by the change in enrollment over time. The extrapolated estimates from the repetition up to eight consecutive five-year periods are compared to the actual/survey figures for the 15–19 and 20–24 age groups.

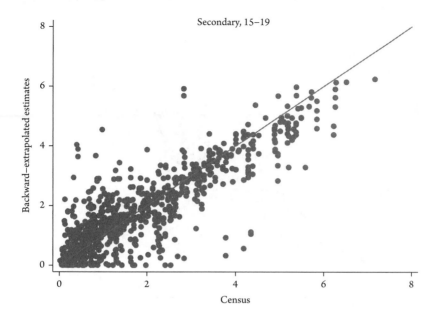

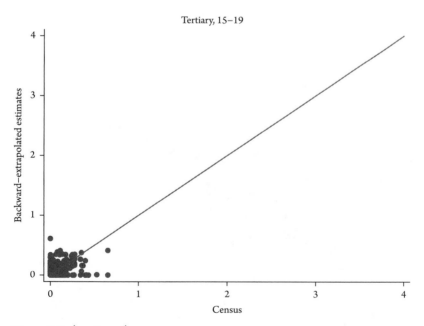

Figure 2.5 (continued)

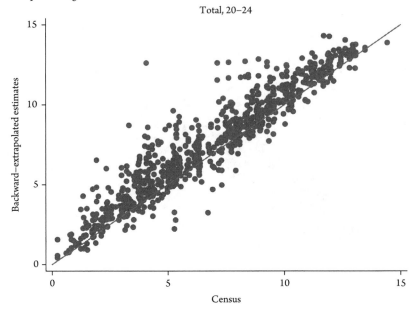

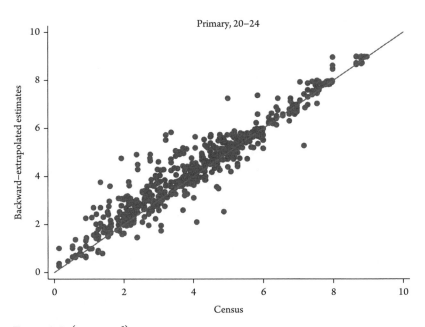

Figure 2.5 (continued)

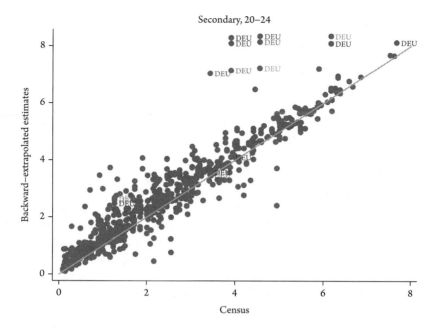

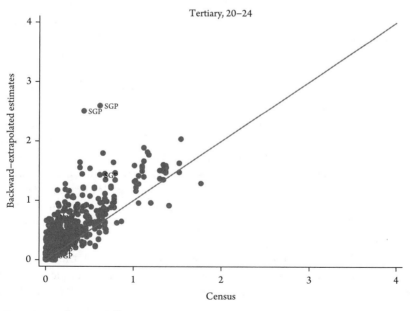

Figure 2.5 (continued)

use the "enrollment-based flow estimates" to fill in the missing observations that still remain after eight repetitions.

Estimating Subcategories of Educational Attainment

After completing the attainment data at four broad levels of schooling, we break down the three levels of schooling into incomplete and complete education using estimates of completion ratios.

We describe here our procedure for estimating the observations that are missing from the subcategories in the primary-schooling category.[25] We fill in the missing cells using information from the available census/survey data. The census/survey data show that 297 observations from 108 countries are available for use in the breakdown of first-level attainment into incomplete and complete categories. The completion rate at the primary level is the number of people who completed primary schooling but did not enter secondary schooling, compared to the number of people who entered primary school. We fill in the remaining missing cells using forward and backward extrapolation of the census/survey observations of completion ratios, with an appropriate time lag. This procedure applies to the age group $a = 3$ (25–29) and above.[26] In the backward extrapolation for the older population, aged 75 and above, we allow the procedure to run up to three consecutive times (that is, 15 years), taking into consideration that the backward extrapolation from the estimate of the population aged 75 and above is likely subject to large measurement errors. For the missing observations in the earlier periods that are not filled in by the backward extrapolation, we use country-specific profiles of completion ratios from the available census figures.

For the countries that do not have actual census observations for the completion ratio, we use the average estimates for a group of advanced or developing countries with the same age group and the same period.

If both forward and backward estimates are available, we combine them using the results of the regression of the "observed" actual census values of the various levels of the completion ratio against the estimates generated from the forward- and backward-flow estimates (based on five-year and ten-year lead and lagged values from actual censuses).[27] We assume that the completion ratios for the 15–19 and 20–24 age groups are determined by an age-specific profile of completion ratios in each country (see Table 2.7).

We apply similar methods to estimate missing observations in the subcategories for secondary and tertiary schooling. There are 348 census observations from 124 countries for the breakdown of secondary-level attainment into lower and upper categories and 169 census observations from 65 countries for the breakdown of higher-level attainment into incomplete and complete categories. In case of secondary-level attainment, for convenience, we use incomplete for lower and complete for upper category. If data for complete country-specific completion ratios are available from both earlier and later periods, we combine backward and forward estimates using averages of the primary/secondary completion weights for groups of advanced and developing countries.[28]

Table 2.7 RULES FOR EXTRAPOLATING COMPLETION RATIOS

Age group (a)	Backward Extrapolation	Forward Extrapolation
Primary and Secondary		
15–19	$c_{j,t}^{15-19} = c_{j,t+5}^{25-29} \cdot \left(c_{j,t+5}^{15-19} / c_{j,t+5}^{20-24} \right)$	$c_{j,t}^{15-19} = c_{j,t-5}^{20-24} \cdot \left(c_{j,t-5}^{15-19} / c_{j,t-5}^{25-29} \right)$
20–24	$c_{j,t}^{20-24} = c_{j,t+5}^{25-29}$	$c_{j,t}^{20-24} = c_{j,t-5}^{20-24} \cdot \left(c_{j,t-5}^{20-24} / c_{j,t-5}^{25-29} \right)$
25–29,…, 70–74	$c_{j,t}^{a} = c_{j,t+5}^{a+1}$	$c_{j,t}^{a} = c_{j,t-5}^{a-1}$
75 and over	$c_{j,t}^{75+} = c_{j,t+5}^{75+} \cdot \left(c_{j,t+5}^{75+} / c_{j,t+5}^{70-74} \right)$	$c_{j,t}^{75+} = sh_{t-5}^{70-74} \cdot c_{j,t-5}^{70-74} + sh_{t-5}^{75+} \cdot c_{j,t-5}^{75+}$
Tertiary		
15–19, 20–24	$c_{j,t}^{a} = c_{j,t+5}^{a}$	$c_{j,t}^{a} = c_{j,t-5}^{a}$
25–29	$c_{j,t}^{25-29} = c_{j,t+5}^{30-34}$	$c_{j,t}^{25-29} = c_{j,t-5}^{25-29} \cdot \left(c_{j,t-5}^{25-29} / c_{j,t-5}^{30-34} \right)$
30–34, 35–39,…, 70–74	$c_{j,t}^{a} = c_{j,t+5}^{a+1}$	$c_{j,t}^{a} = c_{j,t-5}^{a-1}$
75 and over	$c_{j,t}^{75+} = c_{j,t+5}^{75+} \cdot \left(c_{j,t+5}^{75+} / c_{j,t+5}^{70-74} \right)$	$c_{j,t}^{75+} = sh_{t-5}^{70-74} \cdot c_{j,t-5}^{70-74} + sh_{t-5}^{75+} \cdot c_{j,t-5}^{75+}$

NOTE: $c_{j,t}^{a}$ is the completion ratio or the proportion of people in age group a, for whom j is the highest level of schooling attained at time t who have completed j. $sh_t^a = pop_t^a / pop_t^{70-79}$ or the share of the population in age group a (70–74, 75–79) in the population aged 70–79 years at time t.

Average Years of Schooling

The number of years of schooling for the population aged 15 and above, s_t, is constructed as:

$$s_t = \sum_{a=1}^{A} l_t^a s_t^a \tag{2.4}$$

where l_t^a is the population share of group a in the population aged 15 and older, and s_t^a is the number of years of schooling of age group a (a = 1: 15–19 age group, a = 2: 20–24 age group, …, a = 13: 75 and above).

The number of years of schooling of age group a in time t is:

$$s_t^a = \sum_j h_{j,t}^a Dur_{j,t}^a \tag{2.5}$$

where h_j^a is the fraction of group a that has attained the educational level $j = p, s$ (incomplete, complete), h (incomplete, complete), and Dur indicates the corresponding duration in years.

The duration refers to the typical length of primary education and the two levels of secondary education for each country. It is constructed by taking account of changes in the structure of duration over time in a country. Since 1950, data on duration are available from issues of UNESCO, *Statistical Yearbook*. We suppose that, at the primary or secondary level, changes in the duration of schooling applied to students who had just entered primary or secondary school (students between ages 5–9 or 10–14) at the time of the change. For higher education, we use four-year duration for all countries and years, and we assign two years to persons who entered tertiary school but did not complete it.

We use the same sources and methodology to construct a panel data set on the educational attainment of females by age group. The data on the distribution of educational attainment among the population, combined with the information for each country on the duration of school at each level, generate the number of years of schooling achieved by an average person at various levels of schooling and at all levels of schooling combined.

2.4 ESTIMATING HISTORICAL EDUCATIONAL ATTAINMENT, 1870–1945

The history described in section 1.2 shows that that the world has observed a great expansion of education over the past two centuries. The estimated enrollment data demonstrate that, in advanced regions of the world, primary education had expanded rapidly in the 19th century, followed in the 20th century by the emergence and growth of secondary and tertiary education. For most developing countries, modern primary education began to expand in the latter half of the 19th century or the early 20th century, while secondary and tertiary education progressed steadily after World War II.

An interesting issue is how educational capital stocks evolved over the long-term period that started with the beginning of the educational expansion in the 19th century. To investigate this pattern, we construct estimates of historical educational attainment for the total and female populations from 1870 to 1945.[29] By utilizing the estimates of historical enrollment ratios from the 1820–1945 period, as well as the available census data and estimates of educational attainment by age for the 1950–2010 period, we can construct a complete data set of estimates of educational attainment for the total and female populations at the five-year intervals from 1870 to 1945 for 89 countries. The estimates are constructed at five-year age intervals, but we also present the data for three broader age groups, 15–24, 25–64, and 15–64. The sample size of 89 countries is mostly restricted by the availability of female enrollment ratios.

Our new estimates for the total population improve on the estimates in previous studies, such as Morrisson and Murtin (2009) and Baier et al. (2006). Morrisson and Murtin (2009) present a historical database on educational attainment in 74 countries for the period 1870–1960. They compiled historical enrollment data, which they used to generate the educational stock measures. Baier et al. (2006)

used a similar method, based on enrollment ratios, but constructed historical data for only 34 countries.

Our estimates make use of higher-quality enrollment data that are compiled from a larger number of original census sources and more accurately measured. More importantly, our estimation method uses as benchmarks actual census data on educational attainment by age group in the later period. Thus, this new data set makes a contribution by improving the accuracy of estimates of educational attainment in the period 1870–1945. The comparison of our estimates with other estimates is discussed further in section 2.5.

This chapter makes another contribution by constructing a data set on historical educational attainment by gender. No previous study has attempted to construct a historical data set for female and male educational attainment.

Estimation Method

We fill in observations for educational attainment of the total population aged 15–64 by five-year age group from 1870 to 1940 at four broad categories: no formal education (h_u), primary (h_p), secondary (h_s), and tertiary education (h_h). We construct ten five-year age groups, ranging from $a = 1$ (15–19 years old) to $a = 10$ (60–64 years old).

First, we use the backward extrapolation of the estimates (including actual census/survey observations) on attainment by age group over the period 1950–2010. Let $h_{j,t}^a$ denote the proportion of people in age group a for whom j is the highest level of schooling attained: $j = 0$ for no school, 1 for primary, 2 for secondary, and 3 for higher education at time t. The backward extrapolation is then expressed as:

$$h_{j,t}^a = h_{j,t+5}^{a+1} \qquad (2.6)$$

where age group a denotes $a = 2$: 20–24 age group, ... $a = 10$: 60–64 age group.

This procedure assumes that, in the same five-year age group between ages 25 and 64, the survival rate is the same regardless of a person's educational attainment. Following this "backward-extrapolation method," the estimate for the 20–24 age group in 1910 is filled in by the distribution of educational attainment for the 60–64 age group in 1950. We do not extrapolate the educational attainment for the over-65 age group in 1950. Hence, we cannot use the backward extrapolation method to construct estimates before 1910 (these would exceed the maximum limit of eight backward extrapolations).

For the population between the ages of 15 and 24 ($a = 1$: 15–19 age group and $a = 2$: 20–24), we adopt the same procedure used for the estimation of attainment for the period 1950–2010. We construct the estimates by using estimates of the same age group in t-5 and the change in (age-specific) enrollment ratios for the corresponding age groups over time. Based on the ex post simulation we have used in the estimation for the 1950–2010 data set, the backward extrapolations for the 15–19 and 20–24 age groups are repeated up to eight times using the actual census/survey observations in the same age groups in the 1950–2010 data set.

Second, we fill in the missing observations in five-year age groups from 1870 to 1945 by using information from the previous school enrollment rates and the structure of population by age groups. Because there are no available census/survey observations on educational attainment prior to 1945, we cannot use census/survey data as benchmarks for the forward extrapolation.

This estimation procedure (which we call "enrollment-based flow estimation") assumes that the enrollments for various levels of school for the school-age population between 5 and 24 years old lead, with appropriate time lags, to the estimates of the current flows of attainment for the population in the 15–19 and 20–24 age groups. We use the adjusted primary enrollment ratios at times t-5 and t-10, with the information on country-specific duration and starting school age, to estimate the share of those who completed primary education among the population aged 15–19. Similarly, the adjusted secondary enrollment ratios at times t and t-5, with country-specific secondary duration data, are used to estimate the share of those with a secondary education among the population aged 15–19. The share of those with a tertiary education among the population aged 15–19 is calculated by the adjusted tertiary enrollment ratio at time t, multiplied by the fraction of years that correspond to the duration of tertiary school according to the national education system. Similar procedures are used for the 20–24 group, while considering appropriate durations and time lags.

We then fill in missing observations for the older age groups using the forward-extrapolation of the "enrollment-based flow" estimates. We assume that the distribution of educational attainment for the 25–29 age group at time t is the same as that of the 20–24 age group at time t-5 and apply the same procedure for the next age groups:

$$h_{j,t}^{a} = h_{j,t-5}^{a-1} \tag{2.7}$$

where age group a denotes, $a = 3$: 25–29 age group, ... $a = 10$: 60–64 age group.

Note that when both backward- and forward-extrapolation estimates are available, we decide to fill the missing attainment data using the backward-extrapolation estimate. This is because the backward-extrapolation estimates are derived from the original census and survey figures.

We break down the three levels of schooling into incomplete and complete education using estimates of completion ratios. We do not have information pertaining to school dropout rates or completion ratios for individual countries before 1950. We have constructed the completion ratios by using backward extrapolation from the actual data available from 1950 onwards following the same procedure we applied for the estimation in 1950–2010 (see Table 2.7). To fill in the remaining missing observations, we have constructed completion ratios for the 15–19 and 20–24 age groups by using information on the age-specific profile of completion ratios in the nearest year. Then, these estimates are forward-extrapolated to fill in missing observations for the groups over age 25 (see the formula in Table 2.7). The data on the distribution of educational attainment among the population—combined with information for each country on the population structure at each age group and the school duration at each level—generate the number of years of schooling achieved by the average person at various levels of schooling and at all levels of schooling combined, following the formula in equations (2.4) and (2.5).

As explained in section 2.1, we compute the shares of the populations for all sample countries at five-year intervals from 1820 to 1950 by interpolating and extrapolating from the available actual figures. Historical demographic data on the age distributions of national populations are available from Mitchell (2003a, 2003b, 2003c) and the United Nations' *Demographic Yearbook* (1955), League of Nations' *Statistical Yearbook* (various years), and national sources.

We have collected information on the changes in the structure of duration for the period 1930–1955 from UNESCO's *World Survey of Education* (1958, 1961, 1966). We have also compiled information about the duration for the period around 1910 from *A Cyclopedia of Education* (Monroe, 1911) and the European Commission's Eurybase[30] for a limited number of countries. The complete duration data are then constructed by taking account of changes in the duration system over time for each country. Between 1930 and 1950, a total of 33 countries had changed the duration of their primary or secondary education. We assume no change in duration for the earlier years for the countries for which we cannot find information.

2.5 TRENDS IN EDUCATIONAL ATTAINMENT

The full data set consists of estimates of attainment for 146 countries from 1950 to 2010 and 89 countries from 1870 to 1945. The data set for the period 1950–2010 is available for 24 advanced countries and 122 developing countries. The developing group is further divided into five regions: Asia/Pacific (26 countries), Eastern Europe/Central Asia (20), Latin America/Caribbean (25), the Middle East/North Africa (18), and Sub-Saharan Africa (33). Our data set for the earlier period includes a much smaller number of developing countries; a total of 66 countries, including Asia/Pacific (13), Eastern Europe/Central Asia (5), Latin America/Caribbean (23), the Middle East/North Africa (8), and Sub-Saharan Africa (17). Although our data is more limited for the earlier period, the 89 countries in the data set for 1870–1945 include most major countries, consisting of 88% of the world's population in 1945.[31]

We summarize here the educational attainment data for the world and for each region from 1870 to 2010 for the 89 countries that have complete information. Table 2.8 shows data on attainment at the seven levels of schooling for the overall population aged 15–64. The table also reports the average years of schooling achieved by an average person in each region. Regional averages are computed by weighting each country's observation according to its share in the total population aged 15–64 for its region.[32]

In 1870, the world population had a very limited amount of schooling: the average attained schooling was only 0.5 years. The proportion of the uneducated among the total population aged 15–64 reached 90%. Secondary and tertiary education was still undeveloped. Only 0.7% of the total population had some secondary schooling, and only 0.1% had some tertiary schooling. In 1870, education occurred

Table 2.8 TRENDS OF EDUCATIONAL ATTAINMENT OF THE TOTAL POPULATION AGED 15–64 BY GROUP AND REGION

Region (no. of countries) and Year	Population Aged 15–64 (Million)	No Schooling	Highest Level Attained (% of population aged 15–64)						Average Years of Schooling
			Primary		Secondary		Tertiary		
			Total	Completed	Total	Completed	Total	Completed	
World (89)									
1870	701	89.5	9.7	3.6	0.7	0.2	0.08	0.0	0.50
1900	881	78.1	18.8	7.4	2.8	0.7	0.3	0.2	1.11
1930	1130	61.4	29.4	12.4	7.9	2.8	1.2	0.6	2.19
1950	1300	46.6	37.4	17.4	13.7	5.5	2.3	1.2	3.28
1970	1793	32.6	39.3	20.9	23.9	10.1	4.2	2.3	4.67
1990	2736	22.4	30.2	18.4	37.5	19.0	9.8	5.2	6.52
2010	3688	10.8	21.0	14.7	52.7	27.5	15.5	8.5	8.56
Advanced (23)									
1870	175	64.5	32.9	12.2	2.4	0.5	0.2	0.1	1.67
1900	240	36.2	53.9	21.6	8.8	2.0	1.1	0.5	3.32
1930	321	15.3	61.4	30.6	19.8	7.2	3.5	1.6	5.36
1950	380	9.1	58.2	34.5	26.9	13.4	5.8	3.1	6.58
1970	465	6.0	42.4	28.6	40.7	22.6	10.9	6.0	8.16
1990	574	4.4	23.3	17.5	47.2	29.2	25.0	13.5	10.11
2010	650	1.2	9.9	8.5	53.1	38.2	35.8	19.9	11.94
Developing (66)									
1870	525	97.9	1.9	0.8	0.2	0.1	0.0	0.0	0.10
1900	641	93.8	5.6	2.0	0.6	0.2	0.06	0.0	0.28
1930	809	79.8	16.7	5.2	3.2	1.1	0.4	0.2	0.93
1950	920	62.1	28.8	10.4	8.2	2.2	0.9	0.4	1.92

1970	1328	41.9	38.2	18.3	17.9	5.7	1.9	1.0	3.45
1990	2163	27.2	32.1	18.7	35.0	16.3	5.8	3.0	5.57
2010	3038	12.9	23.4	16.0	52.7	25.2	11.1	6.1	7.84
Asia/the Pacific (13)									
1870	398	99.7	0.2	0.1	0.1	0.0	0.0	0.0	0.02
1900	457	98.0	1.6	0.4	0.4	0.1	0.0	0.0	0.09
1930	568	87.6	10.7	3.0	1.5	0.5	0.2	0.1	0.53
1950	656	69.1	23.7	8.4	6.6	1.6	0.5	0.3	1.52
1970	938	45.4	37.5	18.6	15.9	3.9	1.3	0.7	3.13
1990	1550	29.3	30.8	18.8	36.3	15.9	3.7	2.0	5.23
2010	2139	12.8	22.2	15.6	56.6	25.0	8.4	4.7	7.61
Eastern Europe (5)									
1870	69	88.6	10.8	4.7	0.5	0.2	0.06	0.0	0.56
1900	105	78.2	20.2	8.5	1.4	0.5	0.2	0.1	1.02
1930	121	48.9	39.3	13.7	10.9	3.8	0.9	0.6	2.41
1950	95	13.2	59.5	23.0	24.1	7.1	3.2	1.5	4.52
1970	121	4.0	44.2	23.4	45.5	21.6	6.4	3.0	6.71
1990	139	1.9	18.8	13.3	51.9	36.0	27.4	11.8	10.01
2010	143	0.5	3.6	3.1	45.8	35.0	50.3	22.7	11.88
Latin America/the Caribbean (23)									
1870	22	92.7	7.2	1.8	0.1	0.0	0.0	0.0	0.27
1900	34	80.3	18.7	5.1	0.8	0.3	0.2	0.1	0.78
1930	58	57.2	37.3	11.9	4.8	1.8	0.8	0.5	2.08
1950	91	44.4	47.8	16.0	6.8	3.0	1.1	0.7	2.77
1970	147	28.2	53.4	20.9	15.8	6.0	2.6	1.6	4.03
1990	254	15.2	48.7	24.0	27.8	12.8	8.4	4.9	6.22
2010	380	5.4	32.1	22.1	48.9	27.6	13.6	8.5	8.73

continued

Table 2.8 (CONTINUED)

Region (no. of countries) and Year	Population Aged 15–64 (Million)	No Schooling	Highest Level Attained (% of population aged 15–64)						Average Years of Schooling
			Primary		Secondary		Tertiary		
			Total	Completed	Total	Completed	Total	Completed	
Middle East/North Africa (8)									
1870	17	99.4	0.5	0.1	0.1	0.0	0.0	0.0	0.03
1900	23	97.9	1.9	0.3	0.2	0.1	0.0	0.0	0.09
1930	30	93.6	4.5	1.1	1.7	0.6	0.3	0.1	0.38
1950	40	90.4	6.9	2.4	2.1	0.8	0.6	0.4	0.58
1970	59	76.7	13.6	6.1	7.9	3.9	1.7	0.9	1.68
1990	108	42.9	25.2	13.2	26.9	15.2	5.0	3.0	4.74
2010	189	21.4	23.1	15.6	41.3	23.6	14.2	8.7	7.60
Sub-Saharan Africa (17)									
1870	18	98.5	1.5	0.7	0.0	0.0	0.0	0.0	0.08
1900	22	96.1	3.8	2.0	0.1	0.0	0.0	0.0	0.21
1930	30	86.0	10.8	4.4	2.8	0.6	0.4	0.2	0.81
1950	38	75.9	17.3	7.0	6.1	1.4	0.8	0.2	1.47
1970	62	62.5	25.9	8.8	10.6	2.5	1.0	0.3	2.25
1990	111	42.4	35.3	16.7	20.2	6.3	2.1	0.7	4.10
2010	187	30.6	33.9	18.0	32.3	16.7	3.2	1.5	5.74

NOTES: Regional averages are weighted by each country's school-age population. See Appendix Table for the list of countries included in each region/group.

mostly in the advanced regions of the world. The average years of schooling for the total population in advanced countries was 1.7 years. For developing countries as a whole, the average was only 0.1 years.

Table 2.8 shows that education expanded greatly over 140 years after 1870, especially in the 20th century. For the world as a whole, the number of average years of schooling increased from about 1.1 years in 1900 to 3.3 years in 1950 and 8.6 years in 2010. This dramatic increase in educational attainment reflects increases in school enrollment and completion ratios. Primary education began to spread in the early 20th century, followed by the expansion of secondary and tertiary education in the latter half of the 20th century. The proportion of the total population that received a primary education (as the highest level of attainment) increased from about 19% in 1900 to 39% in 1970 and thereafter declined steadily to about 21% in 2010, as more primary-school graduates continued on to secondary-level education. The proportion of those with a secondary education (as the highest level) in the total population increased rapidly, from 14% in 1950 to 53% in 2010. The proportion of the population with a tertiary-level education also rose significantly, from 2.3% in 1950 to 16% in 2010.

This significant progress in educational attainment took place in advanced and developing regions. In 2010, the overall population aged 15–64 in advanced countries was estimated to have an average of 11.9 years of schooling, a significant increase from 3.3 years in 1900 and 6.6 years in 1950. For developing countries as a whole, the average years of schooling reached 7.8 years in 2010, increasing from 0.3 years in 1900 and 1.9 years in 1950.

The increase in the average years of schooling reflects increases in educational attainment at all levels of education. In the post–World War II period, higher secondary and tertiary attainment accounts for most of the rises in number of years of schooling in the advanced countries. The larger part of the increases in developing countries reflects higher primary and secondary educational attainment, particularly following World War II (see Figure 2.6). Specifically, the proportion of the uneducated in the total population aged 15–64 in developing countries declined significantly, from 94% in 1900 to 62% in 1950 and 13% in 2010. The share of those with a secondary education (as the highest level) in the total population increased dramatically from 0.5% in 1900 to 8% in 1950 and 53% in 2010.

Notwithstanding these significant improvements, the gap between developing and advanced countries still remains. The current level and distribution of educational attainment for the overall population aged 15–64 in developing countries is comparable to that of advanced countries in 1970 (see Figure 2.6).

The gap between developing and advanced countries in the average years of schooling among the overall population aged 15–64 remains high (4.1 years) in 2010. It narrowed by only 0.6 years over the past six decades (Figure 2.6). In fact, in the late 19th century, the gap in educational attainment between two groups was 1.6 years, but it continuously increased, to 4.7 years in the 1970s, as education expanded faster in advanced countries than in developing countries. Although the absolute difference in average years of schooling is still significant between advanced and developing countries, there has been a rapid decline in the proportional differences between the two groups. In 1900, the average years

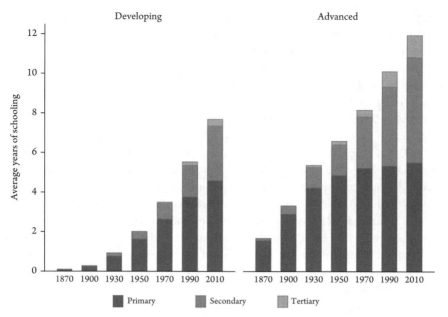

Figure 2.6 Educational Attainment of the Total Population Aged 15–64, 1870–2010

of schooling in the developing countries was only 8% of that in the advanced countries, but has increased rapidly over time to 29% in 1950, 55% in 1990, and 66% in 2010.

The average years of education among the population aged 15–24 in developing countries rose from 3 years in 1950 to about 9 years in 2010 (see Figure 2.7). The improvements in the completion and enrollment ratios at all levels among the younger cohorts in every generation contributed with a lag to the increase in the average years of schooling. The gap in the average years of schooling between younger cohorts from the developing and developed countries has narrowed, but it is not enough to compensate for the large gap that exists between the older cohorts. For example, while the gap between the average years of schooling among 15–24 year-olds from developing and advanced countries has, between 1950 and 2010, narrowed by about two years (4.1 years in 1950 versus 2.3 years in 2010), the gap among those between the ages of 25–64 has declined at a slower rate, narrowing only by 0.3 years over the same period (5.0 years in 1950 versus 4.7 years in 2010) (Figure 2.7). Another factor that has contributed to the slow reduction in the education gap is the decline in the number of youth, as a share of the total population, in recent decades.[33]

Table 2.8 shows regional variations in the growth of educational attainment among the five developing regions over the past 140 years. Among the developing regions, the expansion of educational attainment was most prominent in Eastern Europe; the average years of schooling increased from 1.0 year in 1900 to 4.5 in 1950 and 11.9 in 2010. Developing countries in Asia/Pacific, the Middle East/North Africa, and Latin America also showed strong growth, especially following World War II. In Asia/Pacific, for instance, the average years of schooling was 0.1 in 1900 but increased steadily to 1.5 in 1950 and 7.6 in 2010. By contrast, educational

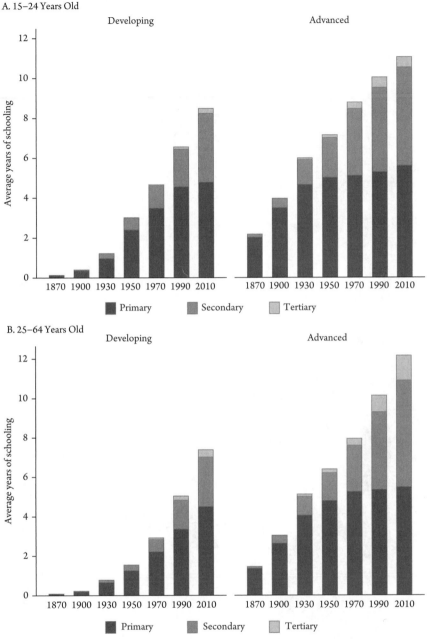

Figure 2.7 Educational Attainment by Age Group, 15–24 and 25–64 Years, 1870–2010

attainment in the Sub-Saharan African countries grew at slower rates during the post–World War II period, rising from 1.5 years in 1950 to 5.7 in 2010. Their enrollment ratios in secondary and tertiary education are still very low compared with other developing countries, as discussed in section 2.1.

Figure 2.8 shows snapshots of educational attainment for the world's working-age population as global maps. The three maps in panel A present the proportions

A. Proportion of Population Who Have Received at Least Some Primary Education

1900

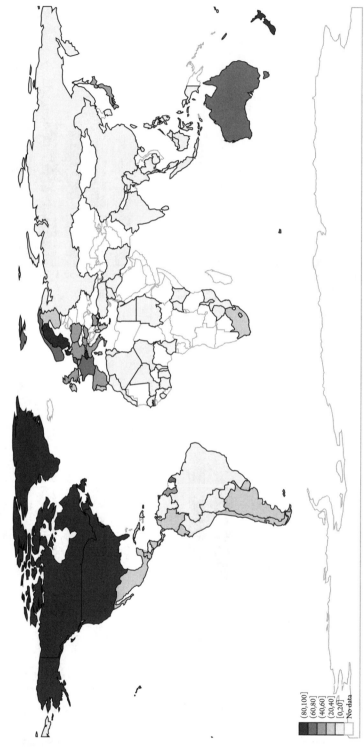

[80,100]
(60,80]
(40,60]
(20,40]
[0,20]
No data

Figure 2.8 Change in Educational Distribution Worldwide, in Selected Years, 1900, 1950, and 2000

1950

[80,100]
[60,80]
[40,60]
[20,40]
[0,20]
No data

Figure 2.8 (continued)

2000

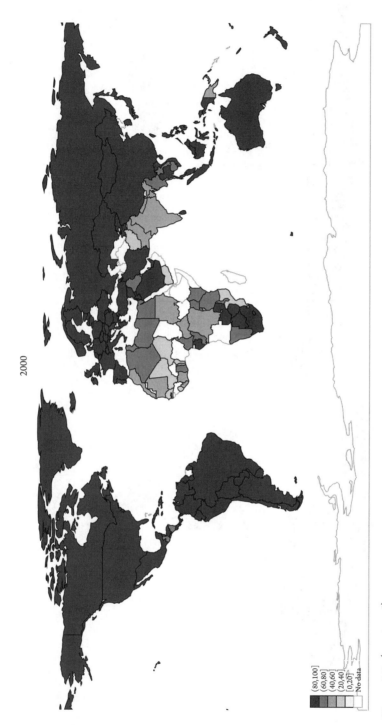

[80,100]
(60,80]
(40,60]
(20,40]
[0,20]
No data

Figure 2.8 (continued)

B. Proportion of Population Who Have Received at Least Some Secondary Education

1900

(80,100]
(60,80]
(40,60]
(20,40]
[0,20]
No-data

Figure 2.8 (continued)

1950

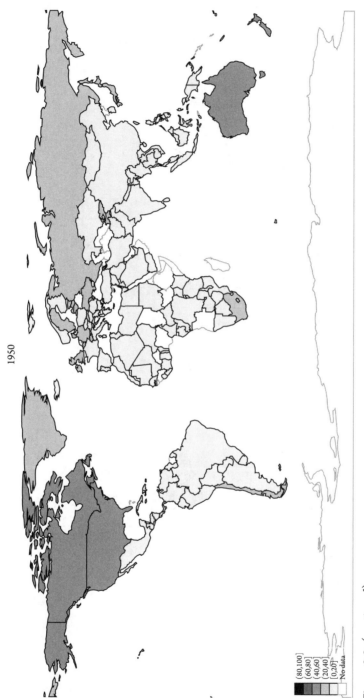

[80,100]
(60,80]
(40,60]
(20,40]
[0,20]
No-data

Figure 2.8 (continued)

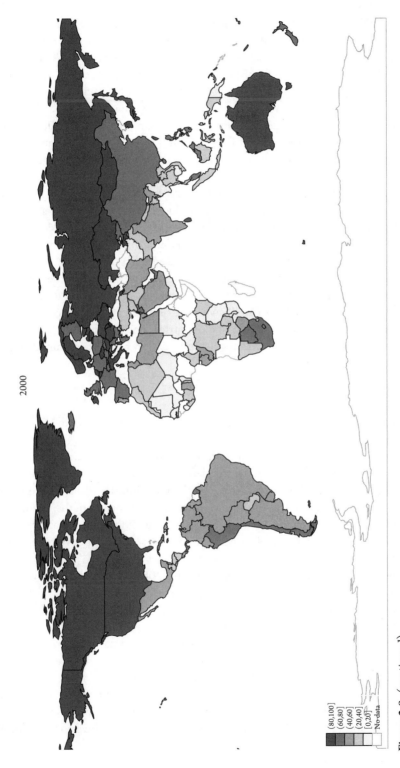

2000

(80,100]
(60,80]
(40,60]
(20,40]
[0,20]
No data

Figure 2.8 (continued)

of the total population that had attained at least a primary level of education for the years 1900, 1950, and 2000. The map for 1900 shows all developing countries in light colors, indicating that the majority of the adult population in the developing world did not attain a primary level of education. In contrast, significant portions of the population in most of the advanced countries, shown in dark colors, had attained a primary education by 1900. In the map for 1950, more developing countries are displayed in darker colors, implying that there were significant improvements in educational attainment at the primary level. In 2000, almost all countries in our sample, except for some sub-Saharan African countries, are shown in very dark colors, indicating that primary education has become almost universal.

Panel B presents three maps that show the proportions of the total population that had received education at the secondary or higher levels over the selected years. In 1900, the majority of adults in most of the world did not attain a secondary education. The map for 1950 shows that secondary education was still not prevalent, except in advanced countries and former Soviet Republics. In contrast, the map for 2000 shows the significant improvements in education attainment at the secondary and tertiary levels throughout the world. In advanced countries and former Communist countries, the portion of adults who had attained at least a secondary level increased to almost 100%. In developing countries, except for some sub-Saharan countries, the majority of the working-age population had also obtained at least some secondary education.

2.6 GENDER DISPARITY IN EDUCATIONAL ATTAINMENT

We have also constructed data on educational attainment for the female population aged 15–64. Table 2.9 shows that the trend of educational attainment of the female population is broadly similar to that of the total population. There was a very limited amount of female schooling in the 19th century. The proportion of the uneducated among the female population aged 15–64 was 81% in 1900. The average extent of female schooling was 3.1 years in advanced countries, while, in developing countries, the average was only 0.2 years.

Female education expanded greatly over the 20th century. For the world as a whole, the average amount of schooling increased from 1.0 years in 1900 to 3.0 years in 1950 and 8.2 years in 2010. This significant progress in educational attainment took place in advanced and developing regions. For the female population aged 15–64 in the advanced countries, the average years of schooling increased from 3.1 in 1900 to 6.4 in 1950 and 11.9 in 2010. In the developing countries, average amount of schooling increased from 0.2 years in 1900 to 1.5 years in 1950 and 7.4 years in 2010. There were significant regional variations in the growth of female educational attainment. In Eastern Europe, the average years of schooling reached 12.0 in 2010, while it was 5.3 in the Sub-Saharan African countries.

Table 2.9 TRENDS OF EDUCATIONAL ATTAINMENT OF THE FEMALE POPULATION, AGED 15–64, BY GROUP AND REGION

Region (no. of countries) and Year	Population Aged 15–64 (Million)	No Schooling	Highest Level Attained (% of population aged 15–64)						Average Years of Schooling
			Primary		Secondary		Tertiary		
			Total	Completed	Total	Completed	Total	Completed	
World (89)									
1870	342	91.1	8.5	3.7	0.4	0.1	0.0	0.0	0.43
1900	434	81.0	16.5	7.1	2.4	0.7	0.2	0.07	0.99
1930	559	65.6	25.9	11.6	7.5	2.6	1.0	0.4	2.00
1950	648	51.4	34.2	15.7	12.7	4.9	1.7	0.8	2.97
1970	890	37.5	37.8	18.8	21.5	9.5	3.3	1.5	4.23
1990	1348	25.1	31.7	17.9	34.5	18.9	8.7	4.2	6.15
2010	1823	14.6	21.2	14.4	49.0	25.7	15.3	8.2	8.17
Advanced (23)									
1870	89	70.0	28.5	12.6	1.4	0.3	0.0	0.0	1.43
1900	121	42.5	48.5	21.3	8.5	2.2	0.6	0.2	3.06
1930	163	17.3	59.6	30.3	20.3	7.0	2.8	1.1	5.25
1950	195	10.1	58.3	34.1	27.0	12.3	4.6	2.1	6.40
1970	236	6.9	42.8	28.4	41.7	23.2	8.7	4.1	7.95
1990	287	5.0	22.9	16.9	49.7	31.1	22.4	11.3	9.96
2010	324	1.5	10.2	8.6	51.2	36.9	37.2	20.3	11.94
Developing (66)									
1870	254	98.5	1.5	0.6	0.0	0.0	0.0	0.0	0.07
1900	313	95.9	4.1	1.6	0.1	0.0	0.0	0.0	0.19
1930	397	85.5	12.0	3.9	2.3	0.8	0.2	0.1	0.67

continued

69

Table 2.9 (CONTINUED)

Region (no. of countries) and Year	Population Aged 15–64 (Million)	No Schooling	Highest Level Attained (% of population aged 15–64)						Average Years of Schooling
			Primary		Secondary		Tertiary		
			Total	Completed	Total	Completed	Total	Completed	
1950	453	69.2	23.8	7.7	6.6	1.8	0.5	0.2	1.50
1970	654	48.5	36.0	15.3	14.2	4.6	1.3	0.6	2.90
1990	1061	30.5	34.1	18.1	30.4	15.6	5.0	2.3	5.12
2010	1499	17.5	23.5	15.7	48.5	23.2	10.6	5.5	7.36
Asia/the Pacific (13)									
1870	190	99.9	0.1	0.0	0.0	0.0	0.0	0.0	0.01
1900	219	99.5	0.4	0.1	0.1	0.0	0.0	0.0	0.02
1930	274	94.4	5.0	1.5	0.5	0.2	0.06	0.0	0.23
1950	315	78.9	16.8	4.8	4.1	1.1	0.2	0.1	0.98
1970	455	53.3	35.1	14.8	10.9	2.9	0.7	0.4	2.47
1990	751	32.6	33.9	18.1	30.6	15.4	2.8	1.4	4.73
2010	1045	18.3	23.0	15.4	51.4	22.4	7.2	4.0	6.98
Eastern Europe (5)									
1870	35	90.7	9.3	3.6	0.0	0.0	0.0	0.0	0.46
1900	54	82.6	17.3	7.4	0.2	0.1	0.06	0.0	0.84
1930	64	55.5	34.4	12.1	9.4	3.4	0.8	0.4	2.14
1950	54	16.1	58.6	21.6	23.0	4.9	2.3	0.7	4.16
1970	65	5.6	45.6	22.8	43.2	17.1	5.6	2.1	6.28
1990	71	1.8	19.7	13.7	51.4	32.8	27.2	9.7	9.80
2010	74	0.4	3.4	3.0	41.4	31.7	54.9	21.0	11.97

Latin America/the Caribbean (23)

1870	11	96.9	3.1	0.9	0.0	0.0	0.0	0.0	0.12
1900	17	86.4	13.0	3.9	0.6	0.2	0.0	0.0	0.55
1930	29	59.5	36.0	11.6	4.2	1.6	0.3	0.1	1.89
1950	45	48.3	44.9	15.8	6.4	3.0	0.5	0.2	2.56
1970	74	31.4	51.2	20.6	15.6	6.3	1.7	1.0	3.82
1990	129	15.3	48.9	24.4	27.9	13.6	7.9	4.5	6.19
2010	193	5.6	31.1	21.3	48.8	28.2	14.5	8.9	8.80

Middle East/North Africa (8)

1870	8	99.9	0.1	0.0	0.0	0.0	0.0	0.0	0.01
1900	11	99.2	0.7	0.1	0.1	0.0	0.0	0.0	0.04
1930	15	96.2	3.1	0.7	0.7	0.2	0.1	0.0	0.20
1950	19	94.9	3.8	1.3	1.2	0.4	0.2	0.1	0.29
1970	30	86.2	8.5	4.1	4.5	2.2	0.7	0.4	0.96
1990	54	55.1	20.8	12.2	21.0	11.8	3.1	1.9	3.67
2010	94	27.5	20.9	15.4	39.0	23.1	12.7	8.0	7.09

Sub-Saharan Africa (17)

1870	9	99.9	0.1	0.0	0.0	0.0	0.0	0.0	0.01
1900	11	99.3	0.6	0.2	0.1	0.0	0.0	0.0	0.04
1930	15	91.2	5.8	2.3	2.8	0.5	0.3	0.1	0.57
1950	20	82.0	11.8	4.8	5.7	1.3	0.6	0.1	1.18
1970	31	71.5	19.1	5.8	8.8	1.9	0.7	0.1	1.74
1990	56	50.1	32.5	15.0	15.9	4.9	1.5	0.4	3.42
2010	93	35.7	31.9	17.4	29.7	15.5	2.8	1.2	5.30

NOTES: Regional averages are weighted by each country's school-age population. See Appendix Table for the list of countries included in each region/group.

Table 2.10 EDUCATIONAL ATTAINMENT BY GENDER, 1870–2010

Region (no. of countries) and Year	Average Years of Schooling (population aged 15–64)		Gender Ratio (F/M, %)
	Females (F)	Males (M)	
World (89)			
1870	0.43	0.56	75.8
1900	0.99	1.22	81.0
1930	2.00	2.37	84.6
1950	2.97	3.59	82.8
1970	4.23	5.10	83.0
1990	6.15	6.89	89.3
2010	8.17	8.94	91.5
Advanced (23)			
1870	1.43	1.92	74.3
1900	3.06	3.59	85.2
1930	5.25	5.48	95.8
1950	6.40	6.78	94.4
1970	7.95	8.38	94.8
1990	9.96	10.26	97.1
2010	11.94	11.94	100.0
Developing (66)			
1870	0.07	0.13	58.2
1900	0.19	0.37	52.0
1930	0.67	1.17	57.1
1950	1.50	2.33	64.3
1970	2.90	3.99	72.6
1990	5.12	6.01	85.2
2010	7.36	8.30	88.7
Asia/the Pacific (13)			
1870	0.01	0.03	24.8
1900	0.02	0.15	13.7
1930	0.23	0.80	28.1
1950	0.98	2.03	48.2
1970	2.47	3.75	65.9
1990	4.73	5.71	82.7
2010	6.98	8.22	84.9
Eastern Europe (5)			
1870	0.46	0.66	68.8
1900	0.84	1.21	69.0
1930	2.14	2.70	79.5
1950	4.16	5.00	83.1
1970	6.28	7.19	87.4
1990	9.80	10.22	95.9
2010	11.97	11.79	101.6
Latin America/the Caribbean (23)			
1870	0.12	0.41	29.2
1900	0.55	1.02	53.5

1930	1.89	2.28	83.0
1950	2.56	2.99	85.5
1970	3.82	4.24	90.1
1990	6.19	6.26	98.9
2010	8.80	8.66	101.6
Middle East/North Africa (8)			
1870	0.01	0.05	19.6
1900	0.04	0.14	26.8
1930	0.20	0.54	37.5
1950	0.29	0.86	33.8
1970	0.96	2.40	40.0
1990	3.67	5.80	63.2
2010	7.09	8.11	87.5
Sub-Saharan Africa (17)			
1870	0.01	0.14	7.3
1900	0.04	0.37	9.7
1930	0.57	1.04	55.1
1950	1.18	1.76	66.9
1970	1.74	2.77	62.8
1990	3.42	4.78	71.6
2010	5.30	6.18	85.7

NOTES: Averages of schooling years are the averages weighted by school-age population for each country that belongs to the regional group.

Table 2.10 uses these results, comparing the regional figures for females with those for males, by region, from 1870 to 2010. The table shows the "gender ratio," defined as the ratio of female-to-male attainment (expressed as a percentage).

Table 2.10 shows that gender equality has improved in all regions over the past 140 years. For the world population, aged 15–64, the ratio of female-to-male average years of schooling rose from 81% in 1900 to 83% in 1950 and 92% in 2010. The ratio increased dramatically, from 52% in 1900 to 64% in 1950 and 89% in 2010, for the population in developing countries aged 15–64. Over the past century, the ratios rose notably in Sub-Saharan Africa (10% in 1900 to 86% in 2010), Asia/Pacific (14% to 85%), and the Middle East/North Africa (27% to 88%). In contrast, the ratios in the advanced, Eastern European, and Latin American regions remained at high levels throughout the period, currently reaching over 100%.

During the late 19th century, gender equality did not improve much. To the contrary, in developing regions there was a slight increase in gender inequality. This result derives from low enrollments for both genders at the earlier period of the century, combined with an increase, initially, mainly for the male population (Figure 2.2). Figure 2.9 shows the trends in gender ratios in average years of schooling at each level of education and at overall levels, both worldwide and by group, for the youth population, aged 15–24.

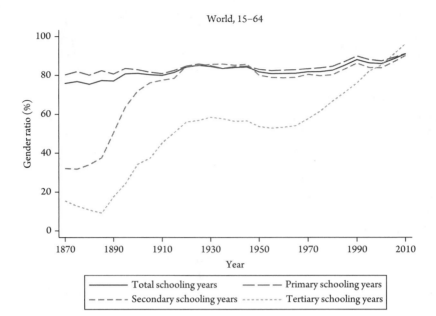

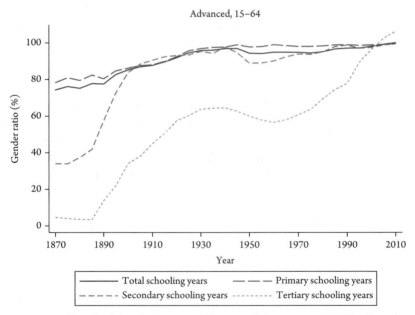

Figure 2.9 Trends of Gender Ratios in Educational Attainment, Worldwide and by Group, for Population Aged 15–64

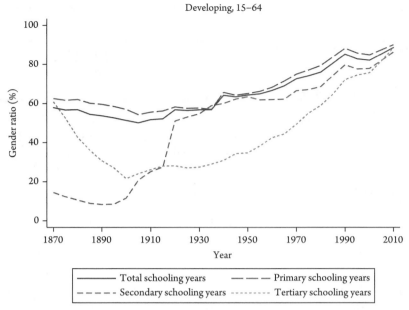

Figure 2.9 (continued)

2.7. COMPARISON WITH OTHER DATA SETS

We now compare our estimates of educational attainment for the overall population aged 15–64 with other estimates. First, we want to check our new estimates with the estimates by Cohen and Soto (2007), who constructed a data set for the average years of schooling for 95 countries at ten-year intervals for 1960–2010. Their data and methodology are similar to ours for the period 1950–2010. They used forward-flow and backward-flow methods to fill in missing observations by extrapolating from the census/survey observations on educational attainment by five-year age groups. However, there are significant differences in terms of census/survey data sources and estimation methods. Most of our estimates are based on actual UNESCO censuses on attainment by age and are consistent across nations over time, whereas Cohen and Soto relied on forward or backward extrapolation based on a more limited number of census/survey observations, sourced from OECD and UNESCO in the recent periods.[34]

Table 2.11 shows the means and standard deviations of average schooling years in levels and ten-year differences for the sample of overlapping observations from our new data set and Cohen and Soto's (2007) data set during the period 1960–2010. The two estimates are highly correlated in levels, with a correlation coefficient of 0.95, but less so in the ten-year differences, with a correlation coefficient of 0.37. The estimates for advanced countries are less correlated than those for developing countries in both levels and ten-year differences.

Lutz et al. (2007) constructed a data set of the distribution of educational attainment by five-year age groups for 120 countries at five-year intervals from 1970 to

Table 2.11 COMPARISON OF AVERAGE YEARS OF SCHOOLING BETWEEN DIFFERENT ESTIMATES

A. This data set and Cohen-Soto	Obs.	Correlation	*This data set*		*Cohen-Soto*	
			1960	2010	1960	2010
World						
Levels	540	0.95	3.58 (2.52)	8.04 (2.79)	4.03 (2.85)	7.40 (3.05)
10-year differences	450	0.37	0.99 (0.59)		0.82 (0.42)	
Advanced countries						
Levels	132	0.89	7.04 (2.19)	11.58 (1.54)	8.14 (2.10)	11.66 (1.77)
10-year differences	110	0.03	0.87 (0.70)		0.71 (0.26)	
Developing countries						
Levels	408	0.95	2.06 (1.70)	7.19 (2.50)	2.23 (1.91)	6.37 (2.53)
10-year differences	340	0.46	1.03 0.55		0.85 0.45	

B. This data set and Morrisson-Murtin	Obs.	Correlation	*This data set*			*Morrisson-Murtin*		
			1870	1910	1950	1870	1910	1950
World								
Levels	630	0.93	0.78 (1.16)	2.07 (1.72)	3.83 (2.60)	1.64 (1.76)	2.93 (2.50)	4.27 (2.88)
10-year differences	560	0.50		0.36 (0.31)			0.31 (0.28)	
Advanced countries								
Levels	198	0.87	1.67 (1.39)	3.91 (1.69)	6.58 (2.16)	3.51 (1.96)	5.86 (2.23)	7.69 (2.20)
10-year differences	176	0.07		0.57 (0.33)			0.49 (0.32)	
Developing countries								
Levels	432	0.92	0.13 (0.33)	0.55 (0.88)	1.53 (1.59)	0.27 (0.47)	0.53 (0.97)	1.50 (1.62)
10-year differences	384	0.70		0.18 (0.25)			0.16 (0.22)	

Table 2.11 (CONTINUED)

NOTES: Figures in this table represent overlapping observations only. This data set consists of a total of 1,898 observations on average years of schooling for the total population over 15 years old for 146 countries at five-year intervals from 1950 to 2010, and 1,424 observations for 89 countries at five-year intervals from 1870 to 1945; Cohen-Soto (2007) has 570 observations for 95 countries at ten-year intervals from 1960 to 2010; Morrison-Murtin (2009): 666 observations for 74 countries at ten-year intervals (1870–1950). Numbers in parentheses are standard deviations.

SOURCE: Authors' calculations based on Cohen-Soto (2007), Morrison-Murtin (2009) data sets, and own data.

2000. They used the information from censuses/surveys that were available in 2000 as benchmarks and adopted a backward extrapolation method to construct missing observations for the period 1970 to 1995. Since their estimation is based on very limited census information and other sources of surveys, their measurement errors would be large. In addition, they used fixed country-specific values in estimating educational attainment for the younger population groups between the ages of 15 and 24 that attend school. This methodology differs from ours because we make use of information on school enrollment. We discuss the baseline data and methodology of Lutz et al. (2007) in detail in the next chapter, when we compare their projections for educational attainment in 2040 with our projections.

We can also compare our historical estimates for the overall population aged 15–64 with the estimates made by Morrisson and Murtin (2009). They present a historical database of educational attainment in 74 countries for 1870–1960 and combine them with Cohen and Soto's data set from 1970 to 2010. Morrisson and Murtin adopted a methodology similar to our "enrollment-based flow" estimation. They have compiled historical enrollment data, which they used to generate their educational stock measures.

We have compiled a larger number of actual enrollment ratios than Morrisson and Murtin (2009). More importantly, we have also utilized the backward extrapolation of the estimates based on actual census/survey observations on attainment by age group.

Table 2.11 shows that the estimates for advanced countries in our new data set are, on average, lower than those in Morrisson and Murtin (2009) for the overall period, 1960–2010. The two estimates diverge for earlier periods. For developing countries, our new estimates are, on average, close to Morrisson and Murtin's estimates in earlier years, but higher for estimates in 2010.

Table 2.11 shows means and standard deviations of the average schooling years, by levels and by ten-year differences, for the sample of observations that overlap between the new data set and that of Morrisson and Murtin (2009) for the period 1960–2010. The two series are highly correlated in levels, with a correlation coefficient of 0.93, but less so in ten-year differences, with a correlation coefficient of 0.50. The estimates for advanced countries are less correlated than those for developing countries in both levels and ten-year differences. The estimates for advanced

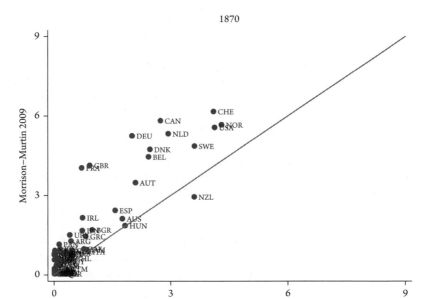

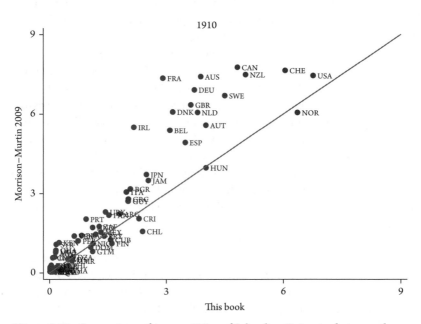

Figure 2.10 Comparison of Average Years of Schooling Estimates between the New Data Set and Morrisson and Murtin (2009), for Selected Years, 1870, 1900, and 1950

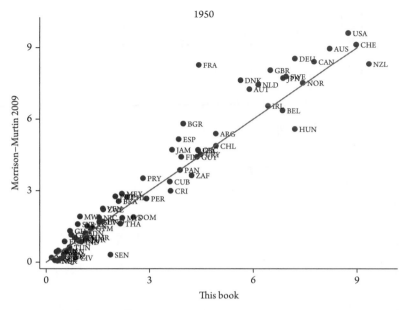

Figure 2.10 (continued)

countries in the Morrisson and Murtin data set are on average higher than ours for the overall period, 1870–1950. Figure 2.10 plots the two estimates in the common sample of observations in 1870, 1900, and 1950. They are closely correlated, but some differences can be seen, especially in some advanced countries. Morrisson and Murtin acknowledge that their estimates for some advanced countries, including France and Canada, are outliers.

Appendix Table. AVAILABILITY OF EDUCATIONAL ATTAINMENT CENSUS/SURVEY DATA BY COUNTRY

Region/ Country		No. of Censuses	Original Census Year												
			1950	1955	1960	1965	1970	1975	1980	1985	1990	1995	2000	2005	2010
Middle East and North Africa															
Algeria	V	5		1954		1966*	1971						2000	2006	
Bahrain		5				1965#	1971				1991		2001		2010
Cyprus		6	1946#		1960						1992		2001	2005	2010
Egypt	V	2						1976		1986					
Iran	V	5		1956		1966						1996		2006	2010
Iraq	V	2		1957		1965									
Israel		5			1961		1972		1982					2006	2010
Jordan		3			1961				1979						2010
Kuwait		7					1970	1975	1980	1985		1995		2006	2008
Libya		3				1964#		1973		1984					
Malta	V	5	1948			1967						1995		2005	2011
Morocco	V	1					1971								
Qatar		3								1986				2004	2011
Saudi Arabia		1												2004	
Syrian Arab Republic	V	4			1960		1970						2002		2009
Tunisia	V	6				1966		1975	1980	1984		1994			2010
United Arab Emirates		2						1975						2005	
Yemen		1						1975#							

Sub-Saharan Africa

Country	V	N												
Benin	V	3						1979#		1992*		2000		
Botswana		4			1964#	1971		1981#		1991				
Burundi		1								1990				
Cameroon	V	1					1976							
Central Africa		2					1975		1988					
Congo		1							1984					
Cote d'Ivoire	V	2							1988			1998 +		
D.R. Congo		1	1955											
Gabon		1									1993			
Gambia		3					1973				1993	2000		
Ghana	V	3		1960#		1970								2010
Kenya	V	4		1962		1969		1979						2010
Lesotho		4			1966		1976						2006	2008
Liberia		3		1962#			1974#							2008
Malawi	V	4			1966		1976		1987			1998		
Mali	V	2					1976							2010
Mauritania		1							1988					
Mauritius	V	7	1952	1962		1972			1983	1990		2000		2011
Mozambique	V	2						1980			1997			
Namibia		3		1960						1991		2001		
Niger	V	1					1977							
Reunion	V	2	195#4		1967#									
Rwanda		1						1978						
Senegal	V	3					1976						2006	2011
Sierra Leone	V	1			1963#									
South Africa	V	7		1960		1970		1980*	1985		1996	2001		2011

continued

Appendix Table (CONTINUED)

Region/ Country		No. of Censuses	Original Census Year												
			1950	1955	1960	1965	1970	1975	1980	1985	1990	1995	2000	2005	2010
Sudan	V	2		1956						1983					
Swaziland		4				1966		1976		1986				2007	
Togo		3					1970		1981						2009
Uganda	V	5			1959#		1969				1991		2002		2010
United Republic of Tanzania		2											2000		2010
Zambia		4					1969		1980#		1990	1993#			
Zimbabwe	V	2									1992		2002		
Latin America and the Caribbean															
Argentina	V	7	1947#		1960#		1970		1980#		1991		2001	2003	
Barbados	V	3					1970		1980				2000		
Belize		5			1960		1970		1980		1991				2010
Bolivia	V	4						1976			1992		2001		2009
Brazil	V	6	1950				1970	1976	1980					2004	2010
Chile	V	7	1952		1960#		1970		1982		1992		2002		2010
Colombia	V	5	1951					1973#				1993		2006	
Costa Rica	V	7	1950			1963	1968	1973					2000	2007	2011
Cuba	V	3		1953			1970		1981				2002		
Dominican Republic	V	4			1960#		1970						2001		2011
Ecuador	V	7	1950		1962			1974	1982		1990		2001		2010
El Salvador	V	6	1950		1961#		1971*				1992			2006	2010
Guatemala	V	7	1950			1964#		1973	1981				2002 +	2006	2012

82

Guyana	V	3				1970		1980				2002		
Haiti	V	4	1950			1971		1982	1986*					2011
Honduras	V	4		1961			1974	1982		1991		2001		
Jamaica	V	5		1960				1980	1983	1990		2000		2010
Mexico	V	7		1960#		1970*#				1990			2006	
Nicaragua	V	3	1950			1971*		1980					2005	2010
Panama	V	7	1950	1960		1970*		1980		1990		2000	2006	2010
Paraguay	V	8	1950	1962#		1972#		1982		1992		2002		2010
Peru	V	6		1961		1972		1981			1993		2007	2009
Trinidad and Tobago	V	4				1970		1980		1990				
Uruguay	V	6			1963	1975			1985		1996		2006	2010
Venezuela	V	6	1950			1971		1981		1990				2009
East Asia and the Pacific														
Brunei Darussalam	V	3		1960		1971		1981						
Cambodia	V	2										1998		2009
China	V	4				1971		1982		1990*		2000		2010
Hong Kong, China	V	9			1966	1971	1976	1981	1986	1991		2001	2006	2010
Macau, China	V	5				1970				1991#		2001 +	2006	2011
Fiji	V	5			1965	1976			1986		1996		2007	
Indonesia	V	6		1961		1971		1980		1990		2000#		2009
Lao, People's Democratic Republic	V	1									1995			
Malaysia	V	5		1957#				1980*		1991		2000		2010

continued

Appendix Table (CONTINUED)

Region/Country		No. of Censuses	Original Census Year												
			1950	1955	1960	1965	1970	1975	1980	1985	1990	1995	2000	2005	2010
Mongolia		3									1989		2000		2010
Myanmar	V	4		1953#				1973		1983	1991				
Papua New Guinea		3					1971		1980				2000#		
Philippines	V	9	1948	1956	1960#		1970	1975#	1980#		1990#		2000		2008
Republic of Korea	V	12		1955#	1960	1965	1970	1975	1980	1985	1990	1995	2000	2005	2010
Singapore		6					1970		1980		1990		2000#	2006	2011
Taiwan	V	5				1965#		1975	1980*				2001	2005	
Thailand	V	6			1960		1970		1980				2000	2006	2010
Tonga		4								1986#		1996		2006	2011
Viet Nam		3							1979		1989				2009
South Asia															
Afghanistan		1							1979						
Bangladesh		4			1961#			1974	1981				2001		
India	V	5			1961		1971#		1981		1991		2001		
Maldives		3								1985			2000	2006	
Nepal		5			1961		1971		1981*		1991		2001		
Pakistan		6			1961#				1981		1990		1998	2006	2009
Sri Lanka	V	5				1963	1969		1981				2001+		2009
Europe and Central Asia															
Albania	V	2											2001		2011
Armenia		1											2001		

84

Country	V	N	1950s	1959–61	1963–66	1970–71	1975–78	1980–81	1983–86	1988–94	1999–2002	2004–07	2009–12
Bulgaria	V	5	1956		1965					1992	2001		2011
Croatia		3								1991	2001		2011
Czech Republic		7		1961		1970		1980		1991	2001	2006	2011
Estonia		3								1989	2000		2011
Hungary	V	7		1960	1963	1970		1980		1990	2001		2011
Kazakhstan		3								1989	1999	2007	2009
Kyrgyzstan		2									1999		
Latvia		2								1989	2000		
Lithuania		4								1989	2001	2007	2011
Republic of Moldova		3								1989		2004	2010
Poland	V	6	1953#	1960		1970	1978			1988	2002		2010
Romania		6			1966		1977*			1992	2002		2010
Russian Federation	V	6		1959		1970				1989+ 1994*+	2002+		2010
Serbia		6	1953*			1971		1981		1991	2002		2011
Slovakia		6		1961		1970		1980		1991	2001		2012
Slovenia		5		1961+		1971+		1981+		1994+	2002+		
Tajikistan		2								1989			2010
Ukraine		2				1970					2001		
Advanced Countries													
Australia	V	6			1966	1971		1981		1991	2001	2006	2011
Austria	V	6		1961#		1971		1981		1991		2005	2010
Belgium	V	5		1961#		1970					2001	2006	2010
Canada	V	10	1951	1961		1970	1975		1986	1991 1994	2001	2006	2010
Denmark	V	5							1983	1991 1994	2001		2011

continued

85

Appendix Table (CONTINUED)

Region/Country		No. of Censuses	Original Census Year												
			1950	1955	1960	1965	1970	1975	1980	1985	1990	1995	2000	2005	2010
Finland	V	9	1950		1960		1970#		1980	1985	1990		2000	2006	2009
France	V	6		1954#	1962				1982		1990			2004	2010
Germany	V	7					1970#	1978	1980	1985				2006	2010
Greece	V	7	1951		1961				1981		1991		2001	2005	2010
Iceland		1			1960										
Ireland	V	7				1966	1971		1981		1991		2002	2006	2011
Italy	V	7	1951		1961		1971		1981				2001+	2005	2010
Japan	V	5			1960		1970		1980		1990				2010
Luxembourg	V	3									1991		2001		2010
Netherlands	V	5			1960								2002	2005	2010
New Zealand	V	6				1966#	1971	1976	1981		1991		2001		2011
Norway	V	9	1950#		1960		1970	1975	1980		1990		2001	2006	2010
Portugal	V	7			1960		1970		1981		1991		2001	2006	2010
Spain	V	6					1970		1981		1991		2001	2006	2010
Sweden	V	6					1970#	1974	1979			1995		2005	2010
Switzerland	V	6			1960		1970		1980				2000	2005	2010
Turkey	V	8	1950#			1965#		1975	1980	1985		1993		2006	2009
United Kingdom	V	6	1950#		1961		1971	1976#					2001		2010
United States	V	9	1950		1960		1970		1980		1990*	1994	2002	2005+	2010

NOTES: * indicates that the census has information for total population only; # indicates that the census has information for a broad age group only; + indicates that census are from individual countries' national sources. V denotes 89 countries that are included in the complete data set—both for the 1950–2010 and the 1870–1945 periods.

Projection of Educational Attainment for 2015–2040

"it became clear that the analysis of human capital could help explain much regularity in labor markets and the economy at large. . . . The accumulating evidence on the economic benefits of schooling and training also promoted the importance of human capital in policy discussions. This new faith in human capital has reshaped the way governments approach the problem of stimulating growth and productivity."
—Gary S. Becker, *Nobel Lecture, December 9, 1992*

This chapter provides projections for educational progress over the next 30 years. These projections rely on assumptions about future population structure, school enrollments, and education policies for individual countries. Notwithstanding a number of limitations, projecting the levels of educational attainment for the total and female working-age populations provides a clear view of the educational opportunities and challenges facing individual countries in the future. These projections are useful for analysts and policymakers who design policies to improve the educational attainment of the population.

The increase in the average years of schooling for the population aged 15–64 over the next three decades, to 2040, is mainly determined by the increase in the average years of schooling for the youth population between the ages of 15 and 24, from 2010 onward. The educational attainment of these population groups would be determined by school enrollments when they are at school ages corresponding to the country-specific duration of schools at each education level. In most countries, people over 25 years old do not enter schools or attain new education. Changes in population structure are also important for the distribution of educational attainment by age.

There have been quite a few attempts to project educational attainment. Ahuja and Filmer (1996) projected educational attainment for 71 developing counties through the year 2020. Their estimation used the perpetual-inventory method, in which school enrollments for the youth population between the ages of 5 and 24 lead to increases in educational attainment of the population aged 25 and over. They used existing projections of population, provided by the United Nations, and adopted projections of school enrollment ratios by UNESCO based on the extrapolation of past enrollment ratios.

Researchers at the International Institute for Applied Systems Analysis (IIASA) have produced a number of papers that project the educational distribution of a population. The projections are based on the "demographic method of multi-state population projection," which uses data on the distribution of the population of each country by age and level of education for a baseline year and then estimates distributions for earlier and later years.[1]

Yousif, Goujon, and Lutz (1996) projected the distribution of population by age, gender, and educational attainment for six North African countries. Goujon (2002) made projections for countries in the Middle East, while Goujon and Samir (2008) provided them for Southeast Asia. Lutz and Goujon (2001) produced projections for populations of 13 world regions in the year 2030, classified by age, gender, and educational attainment.

Wils (2007), a former IIASA researcher, generated projections of the distribution of population by educational attainment for 83 developing countries from 2005 to 2025. The estimates were based on extrapolating country-specific trajectories for school enrollment ratios, using as benchmark data population data classified by age, gender, and educational level from around the year 2000. The benchmark data were from household surveys (Demographic and Health Surveys) of individual countries. The estimates were only available for three education categories: no schooling, primary, and secondary education.

The European Commission (Montanino et al. 2004) presents projections for levels of educational attainment for the population 25–64 years old for the 15 EU countries. They used population data classified by age, gender, and educational attainment from around the year 2000, collected from labor force surveys, as benchmark data, extrapolating forward to 2050. The projections for enrollment and educational attainment for the youth population were constructed with two different scenarios, which assume either constant enrollment or an increase in educational attainment of the youth population using past trends.

A recent paper by Samir et al. (2010) at the IIASA provides the most comprehensive projections for levels of educational attainment for 120 countries for the period 2005–2050. They used information from census and survey sources in 2000 as benchmark figures and made projections for educational attainment based on several different scenarios for future enrollment ratios and population structure.

Our projection methodology is built on these previous developments. We use the 2010 data on educational attainment by age group as benchmark figures to project the educational attainment of the population by age group for the next three decades.

We first estimate the distribution of educational attainment for the younger population, aged 15–24, at the five-year intervals from 2015 to 2040 and then forward-extrapolate the estimates to construct the distribution of educational attainment for the older population groups. Because the educational attainment of the younger population, aged 15–24, over the next three decades, is determined by the school enrollment ratios for the past and contemporaneous years, projections of future

school enrollment ratios are required. We make these projections for school enrollment ratios between 2015 and 2040 at five-year intervals. For the population structure, we use existing UN projections.

Our method is similar to existing work in that it uses forward extrapolation of
educational attainment estimates by age group based on actual censuses available
in 2010 and new estimates for the younger population constructed by projected
enrollment ratios. However, we improve on existing methodologies by using better,
updated benchmark data on the educational attainment of the population by age
in 2010. In addition, our projections of enrollment ratios use improved projection
methods while also utilizing a larger number of actual observations up to 2010. We
will compare our methodologies and projections with those of Samir et al. (2010)
and other existing papers.

We present the complete data set of projections for educational attainment for
the total population and female working-age population by broad age groups of
15–24 and 25–64 years. These data are available for 146 countries from 2015 to
2040 at five-year intervals. We examine the extent to which the continuous inflow
of a better-educated youth population in developing countries could help to reduce
gaps between developing and advanced countries in average years of schooling for
the total and female populations over the next 30 years. This chapter examines the
cases of five large developing countries, Brazil, China, India, Russia, and the South
African Republic.

3.1 PROJECTION METHODS

Sources of Increasing Educational Attainment

What are the factors that can cause an increase in educational attainment over time?
The advances made by the younger cohorts in educational attainment are the most
important factor for the educational progress of the overall population.

We can express the average years of schooling of the population aged 15–64 at
time t (S_t^{15-64}) as the average years of schooling across age groups (S_t^a), weighted
by that age group's corresponding share of the population, (l_t^a). The population is
divided between two major age groups, 15–24 and 25–64:[2]

$$S_t^{15-64} = l_t^{15-24} S_t^{15-24} + \left(1 - l_t^{15-24}\right) S_t^{25-64} \tag{3.1}$$

The change in educational attainment between time t and t-5 can be derived as:

$$\Delta S_t^{15-64} = S_t^{15-64} - S_{t-5}^{15-64} = l_t^{15-24} \Delta S_t^{15-24} + \left(1 - l_t^{15-24}\right) \Delta S_t^{25-64}$$

$$+ \Delta l_t^{15-24} \left(S_t^{15-24} - S_t^{25-64}\right) \tag{3.2}$$

The first term in equation (3.2) shows that the increase in educational attainment
for the youth population aged 15–24 is important for educational progress for
the overall population. It implies that the continuous inflow of a better-educated
youth population can lead to rapid growth in educational attainment among the

population aged 15–64 years. To illustrate this mechanism, consider two countries, A and B, with the same population structure and the same educational attainment among two population groups, 15–24 and 25–64 years old. If the youth population in country A becomes better educated than the youth population in country B (i.e., $S_A^{15-24} > S_B^{15-24}$), the change in educational attainment in A will be greater.

The term also shows that when the share of the youth population (l_t^{15-24}) is greater, the inflow of the better-educated youth population has a larger impact on the educational attainment of the overall population. Holding all else constant, the educational attainment in a country with a greater proportion of young people, who are assumed to have higher educational attainment, will grow faster than in a country in which youth make up a smaller proportion of the population structure. That is, assuming two countries (A and C) have the same distribution of attainment among youth aged 15–64, but country A has a relatively greater proportion of young people than does country C (i.e., $l_A^{15-24} > l_C^{15-24}$), the same increase in educational attainment by the youth population will lead to a larger change in the aggregate educational attainment in country A compared to that in country C.

The second term of equation (3.2) indicates that an increase in educational attainment for the population aged 25–64 is also important for the educational progress of the overall population. However, the increase in educational attainment for the population aged 15–24 is the driving factor for an increase in the educational attainment of the population aged 25–64, because the population over 15–24 years old will become a new inflow into the overall population as a cohort 25–34 years old in the next decade, and then as a cohort 35–45 years old in the decade after that.

The last term in equation (3.2) shows that an increase in the proportion of the population aged 15–24 within the total population can contribute to an increase in educational attainment for the overall working-age population, if the youth population is better educated than the older population. This term disappears if population structure is stable over time.

The main point is that the increase in educational attainment for the population aged 15–64 is mainly determined by the increase in the average years of schooling for the young population aged 15–24 and by the youth cohort's share of the total population. Furthermore, the educational attainment for this young-age population group is determined by school enrollment ratios.

Therefore, in generating projections of the level of educational attainment for individual countries for 2015–2040, projecting enrollment ratios and population structure are the most important factors.

Forward Extrapolation

We use the estimates of educational attainment in 2010 to project educational progress over the next 30 years. We apply forward extrapolation, using the 2010 educational attainment by age as benchmark figures, to calculate the educational attainment of the population by five-year age group from 2015 to 2040 at five-year intervals.

First, we calculate the distribution of educational attainment in four broad categories: no formal education (lu), primary (lp), secondary (ls), and tertiary education (lh). The forward-extrapolation method assumes that the distribution of educational attainment of age group a at time t is the same as that of the age group that was five years younger at time t-5:

$$h^a_{j,t} = h^{a-1}_{j,t-5} \tag{3.3}$$

where age group a denotes, a = 3: 25–29 age group, ... a = 10: 60–64 age group. This setting assumes that the educational attainment of a person who has completed her or his schooling by time t-5 remains invariant after a certain age. In other words, the educational attainment of a person who belongs to one of these age groups will remain unchanged between the ages of 25 and 64.

For the two youngest cohorts, between the ages of 15 and 24, we consider parts of the population as still being enrolled in school. Hence, for these age groups (a = 1: 15–19 age group and a = 2: 20–24 age group), we account for changes in enroll- ment ratios, $\Delta enroll^a_{j,t}$, for age group a in level j during the transition period from t to t-5[3]:

$$h^a_{j,t} = h^a_{j,t-5} + \Delta enroll^a_{j,t} \tag{3.4}$$

After estimating school attainment by broad levels of schooling—no school, some primary, some secondary, and some higher—we break down these three levels of schooling into incomplete and complete education, using completion ratio esti- mates. We do not have information pertaining to school completion or dropout ratios in the future. We have constructed the completion ratios by using forward ex- trapolation from the actual data available up to 2010 following the same procedure we applied for the estimation over 1950–2010 (see Table 2.7). To fill in the remain- ing missing observations, we have constructed completion ratios for the 15–19 and 20–24 age groups by using information on the age-specific profile of completion ratios in the nearest year. Then these estimates are forward-extrapolated to fill in missing observations for the groups over age 25 in 2015 and onward (see the for- mula in Table 2.7).

The number of years of schooling for population group a is computed using du- ration data and the attainment distribution by level of education (as shown in equa- tion 2.4 in chapter 2). The number of years of schooling for the population aged 15–64 is then constructed by aggregating the estimated years of schooling for all age groups, weighted by using the population shares (as shown in equation 2.3 in chapter 2).

3.2 POPULATION PROJECTIONS

We use our data on the distribution of educational attainment for the working-age population, by age, in the year 2010 as benchmark figures, and then apply the for- ward extrapolation to project educational attainment for the population by age for the next three decades. Projections of population structure are essential for this procedure. We use population projection data from the 2012 version of the United

Nations' *World Population Prospects*. For Taiwan, we use projections gathered by its national statistical agency.

The UN Population Division regularly publishes population projections by age and gender for individual countries of the world. The data set provides population projections, by five-year age group, for 2015–2040 at five-year intervals. The UN projections include different variants based on assumptions about mortality, fertility, and migration. We use the "medium" fertility variant that is considered as the most likely future scenario and that is widely used by the literature.

Figure 3.1 shows the structure of the population shares by age and gender in 2010 and 2040, for world and for advanced countries and developing countries groups. The projected age pyramids in 2040 show that the old-age population's share is expected to increase rapidly, particularly in advanced countries. Consequently, the share of the working-age population, aged 15–64, is expected to slowly decline in advanced countries, whereas it continues to rapidly increase in developing countries (Figure 3.1 and Table 3.2). Figure 3.1 also shows the structure of the population by age and gender in 2010 and 2040 for the US and for five large, developing countries, the so-called BRICS countries including Brazil, China, India, Russia, and the South African Republic. The share of the working-age population aged 15–64 is expected to increase in these developing countries. A notable exception is China, where the population is expected to age quite rapidly.

Figure 3.2 shows the change in the proportion of the younger population, aged 15–24, within the total population, aged 15–64, in the period from 1950 to 2050. The share of population in this age group is an important factor in determining changes in the educational attainment of the working-age population. This share has continuously declined over the past 30 years for both advanced and developing countries. The UN projections show that this share will be largely constant at approximately 19% for the group of advanced countries, while it will continue to decline, from 28% to 22%, over the next three decades, for the group of developing countries.

As an alternative scenario, we have considered Samir et al.'s (2010) projection of population structure. This projection is based on the same assumptions used in the UN projections, except that it allows educational attainment to have an impact on fertility and mortality.[4]

Fertility assumptions are a key factor in population projections. The literature shows that a strong link exists between the educational level, especially that of females, and fertility.[5] Holding all else constant, fertility tends to be higher for uneducated women than for highly educated women. In a forward projection, a higher level of female education will lower fertility rates, decreasing the size of the young population.

Samir et al. (2010) also considered that mortality rates differ among population with different levels of education. However, their results show that mortality does not make significant differences in the projections of the working-age population aged 15–64. We decide to use a constant mortality rate for the population at all education levels.[6]

Samir et al. (2010) emphasized the link between educational attainment and fertility in their population projections. An important question is how significantly further consideration of this link, beyond what is assumed in the UN projection, could alter the trajectory of fertility and population structure over the coming decades.

We compare Samir et al.'s population projections with the UN's projections to assess quantitative differences in population structure. We compute the shares of youth cohorts, aged 15–19 and 20–24, among the overall population, aged 15–64,

A. World

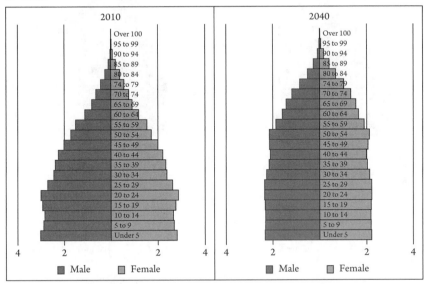

B. Advanced group

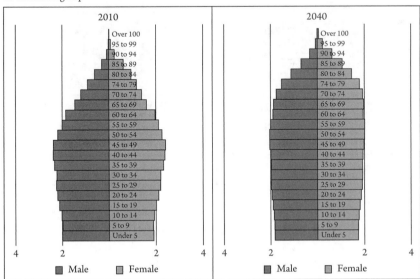

Figure 3.1 Structure of Population by Age and Sex, for the World, Advanced and Developing Groups, and Selected Countries, for Years, 2010 and 2040
NOTE: The number indicates each group's share (%) in total population.
SOURCE: Constructed from the 2012 version of the United Nation's *World Population Prospects*.

C. Developing group

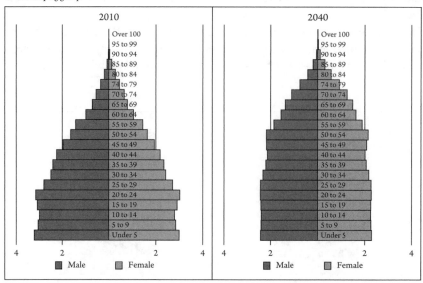

D. USA

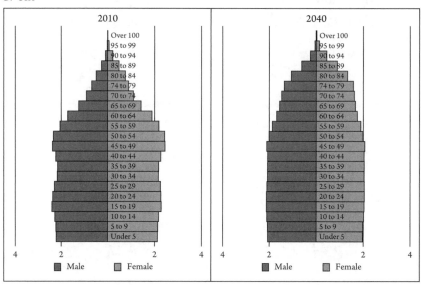

Figure 3.1 (continued)

E. Brazil

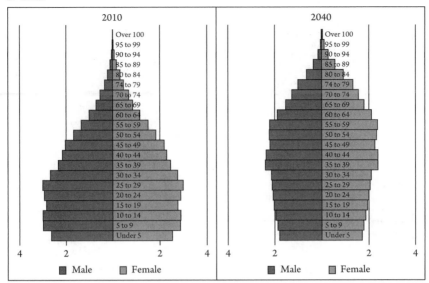

F. China

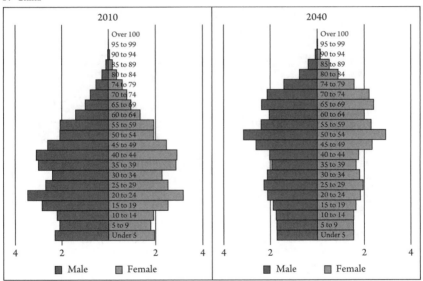

Figure 3.1 (continued)

G. India

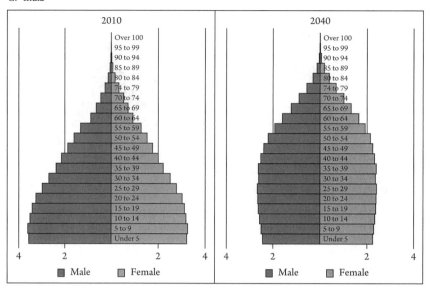

H. Russian Federation

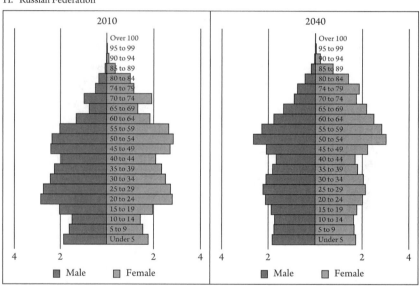

Figure 3.1 (continued)

I. South Africa

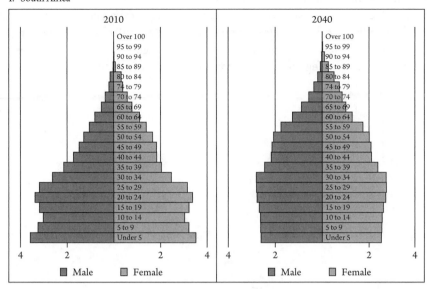

Figure 3.1 (continued)

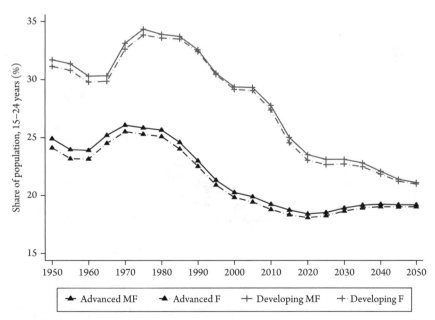

Figure 3.2 Change in the Share of Population Aged 15–24, for Advanced and Developing Groups, 1950–2050
SOURCE: Constructed from the 2012 version of the United Nation's *World Population Prospects*.

from the sample of all 146 available countries for the years 2010 and 2040. We find that the means and standard deviations of shares of the youth cohorts in the samples of advanced and developing groups are quite similar between two projections. Figure 3.3 shows that the two projections are highly correlated, although, for a number of developing countries, Samir et al.'s projections show a slightly lower

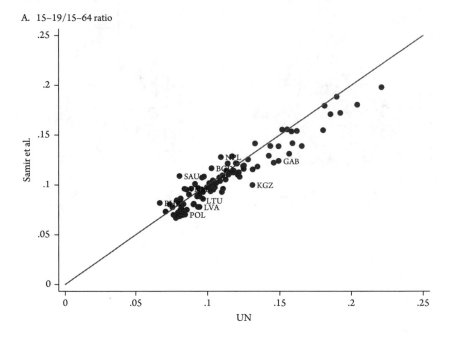

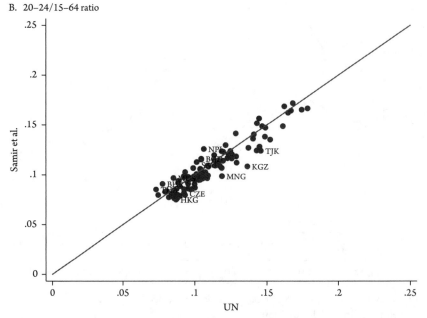

Figure 3.3 Comparison between the United Nations' and Samir et al. (2010)'s Projections for Population Shares Aged 15–19 and 20–24 in 2040

share for the population aged 15–24 compared to the UN's projections. The difference must reflect their consideration of the negative association between the level of educational attainment and fertility rates.

We also find that the use of Samir et al.'s population projections does not make any quantitatively significant difference to the final projections for educational attainment over the next decades. Since the two population projections generate similar population structures and educational attainment, we decided to use only the UN projections.

3.3 PROJECTIONS OF ENROLLMENT RATIOS

We estimate the trend in enrollment ratios at each education level for the total and the female populations from 1870 to 2010 using a logistic growth equation. Then, we use the estimated parameters to construct enrollment ratio projections for 2015–2040.

The logistic growth model assumes that the enrollment ratios ($enroll_j$) at education level j (primary, secondary, and tertiary) for each country grow logistically over time (t), until they approach the maximum ratios, $enroll_j^{max}$. That is, the enrollment ratios follow the following logistic growth time trend:

$$enroll_{j,t} = enroll_j^{max} / (1 + exp(-a_j - \beta_j time)) \tag{3.5}$$

Hence, to estimate the enrollment ratios for 2015–2040, we fit actual enrollment data, by educational level, for the 146 countries from 1870 to 2010, to the following equation:

$$\ln \left(enroll_{j,t} / (enroll_j^{max} - enroll_{j,t}) \right) = a_j + \beta_j time + \mu_{j,t} \tag{3.6}$$

where a_j is the constant term, β_j the slope coefficient, and $\mu_{j,t}$ the disturbance term. Note that the slope of the logistic curve varies over time, changing proportionally to the size of the slope coefficient, β_j.[7] The estimation uses a panel of cross-country data on the enrollment ratio at each education level for each group of advanced and developing countries, from 1820 to 2010 at five-year intervals. The dependent variable is the enrollment ratio at each education level for either the total population or female population. We adopt a country fixed-effects regression model in which the constant term in equation varies by country, considering that the unobserved, persistent characteristics of a country can influence the growth of the enrollment ratio. The slope coefficient is also allowed to differ by country.

Table 3.1 and Figure 3.4 present the results of our regressions.[8] Table 3.1 summarizes the estimates of the slope coefficients for enrollment ratios at each education level for individual countries, averaged by each group of advanced and developing countries. The mean and median values of the estimates are lower for primary enrollment than secondary and tertiary enrollments, for both the total and female populations. It implies that over the sample period of 1820–2010, secondary and

Table 3.1 SUMMARY OF THE ESTIMATED SLOPE COEFFICIENTS IN THE
REGRESSIONS FOR LOGISTIC TREND OF ENROLLMENT RATIOS

	Total			Female		
	Primary	Secondary	Tertiary	Primary	Secondary	Tertiary
Advanced (24)						
Mean	0.029	0.066	0.051	0.033	0.086	0.094
Median	0.022	0.061	0.047	0.028	0.086	0.093
Standard Deviation	0.014	0.019	0.014	0.016	0.020	0.015
Min	0.013	0.032	0.033	0.012	0.038	0.066
Max	0.073	0.106	0.075	0.078	0.113	0.123
No. of observations	**647**	**613**	**717**	**418**	**384**	**389**
Developing (122)						
Mean	0.059	0.080	0.074	0.068	0.094	0.096
Median	0.054	0.074	0.071	0.065	0.088	0.092
Standard Deviation	0.028	0.031	0.025	0.030	0.037	0.039
Min	0.014	0.014	0.010	0.017	0.012	0.021
Max	0.144	0.240	0.182	0.159	0.295	0.277
No. of observations	**1961**	**1798**	**1763**	**1426**	**1385**	**1237**

NOTES: The table presents the summary statistics on the estimates of the slope coefficients (β_j) from the regressions for enrollment ratios, averaged by each group of advanced and developing countries. The specification is the logistic time trend model (equation (3.6) in the text), in which the coefficients are allowed to vary for individual countries. Dependent variables are enrollment ratios for total and female population in each education level. The regressions use a panel set of cross-country data from 1820 to 2010 at the five-year intervals for each group of advanced and developing countries. The estimation technique with country-fixed effects is used in all regressions.

tertiary enrollment ratios have grown more rapidly than have primary enrollment ratios. The estimates are higher in developing countries than in advanced countries at all education levels for total population, implying that school enrollment ratios for the total population have grown more rapidly in developing countries than in advanced countries. On the contrary, for the female population, the estimates are broadly similar between the two groups of countries at all education levels. The estimates also show that at each education level, female enrollment ratios have grown more rapidly than enrollment ratios for the total (male) population.

Table 3.1 shows that the standard deviations of the estimated coefficients are small, compared to the mean or median values of the estimates at all education levels, for both total and female populations. That is, the estimates are quite concentrated at the mean. Figure 3.4 confirms that the estimated slope coefficients are not

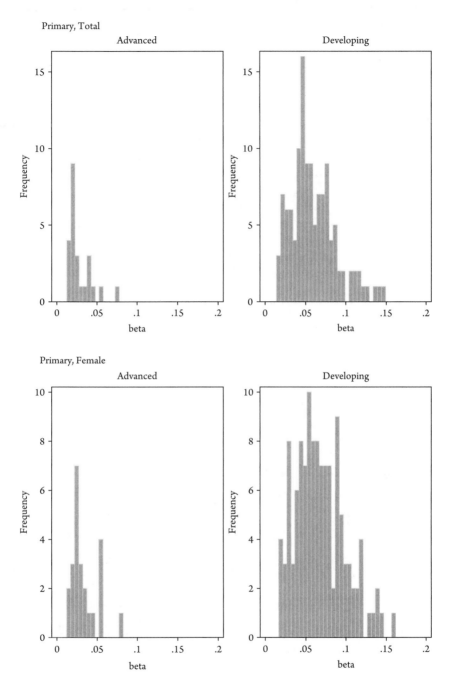

Figure 3.4 Distribution of the Estimated Slope Coefficients in the Regressions for Logistic Trend of Enrollment Ratios

Secondary, Total

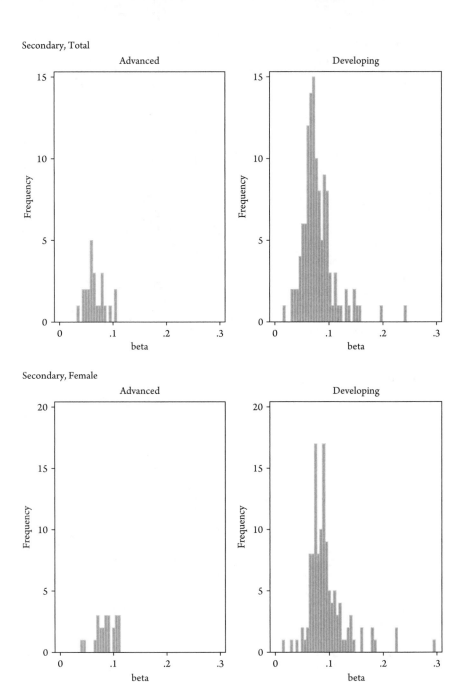

Figure 3.4 (continued)

Tertiary, Total

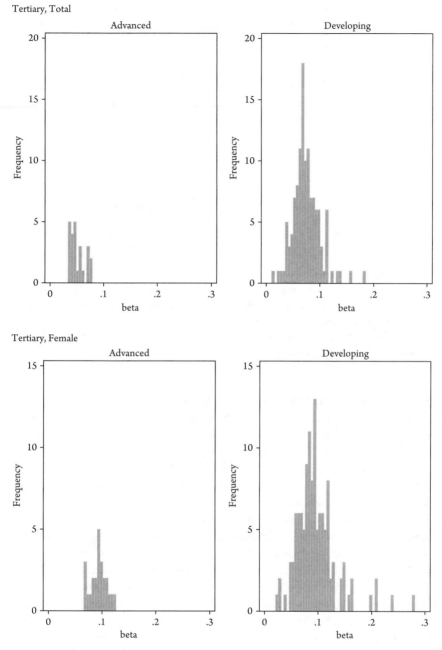

Figure 3.4 (continued)

much dispersed across countries by regional group. The results seem to indicate that the logistic growth model explains well the behaviors of enrollment ratios at each education level, for both the total and female populations for individual countries.

The growth curves for the enrollment ratios implied by the parameters β_j over the sample period 1820–2010 and the forecasting period 2015–2040 are shown in

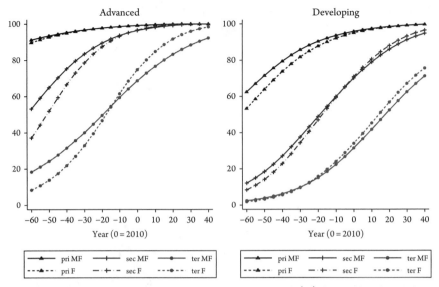

Figure 3.5 Estimates and Projections of Enrollment Ratios (%) for Total and Female Population, over the Sample Period 1850–2010 and the Forecasting Period 2015–2040
NOTE: The curves are derived from the estimated logistic trend regressions in Table 3.1. They are the average values for the individual countries that belong to each sample of advanced and developing countries.

Figure 3.5. They are the average values for the individual countries that belong to the sample of advanced or developing countries. The cubic splines explain that enrollment ratios grow over time, first in an accelerating phase of expansion and then in a decelerating phase. When only a small proportion of the school-aged cohort is enrolled, increasing enrollment would not be difficult. In contrast, once a vast majority of the cohort have already attended schools, enrolling the remaining percentage of children would become more difficult. Expanding enrollment to include hard-to-reach groups, such as children in remote rural areas and working children, would require more resources and well-targeted policies (Samir et al., 2010).

Using the logistic-trend estimates, we generate projections of enrollment ratios for 2015–2040 by five-year intervals.[9] Our projections are based on the logistic-trend scenario, in which enrollment ratios converge to the estimated logistic trends of enrollment ratios for each country. In contrast, previous researches, including that of Samir et al. (2010), assume the "global common logistic trend" model, in which enrollment ratios expand according to the slopes common to all countries. Our method, therefore, improves existing models by considering country-specific trajectories for school-enrollment ratios.

Figure 3.5 displays first the expansion of primary education, followed by that of secondary and tertiary education. This trend confirms the global trend of school-enrollment ratios, discussed in chapter 2 (see Figure 2.1). Figure 3.5 also shows that, for secondary and tertiary education, enrollment ratios for the school-aged female population are projected to increase faster than those for the overall school-aged population, in both advanced and developing countries, after a turning point.

This reflects a historical trend in the past decades, in which female enrollment in secondary and tertiary schools, including those at teachers' colleges, has increased at a dramatically greater rate than those of males. In 2010, female enrollment ratios at both the secondary and tertiary levels are higher than male enrollment ratios in advanced countries, as well as in developing regions (Table 2.2). The proportion of female population aged 15–64 that has attained a tertiary education is also higher than that of the total population aged 15–64 in advanced countries and some developing regions, including Latin America and developing Europe.

3.4 EDUCATIONAL ATTAINMENT BY EDUCATION LEVEL AND GENDER, 2010–2040

The projections show that the educational attainment of the working-age population will continue to rapidly rise over the next 30 years. The average extent of schooling for the world population is projected to increase by approximately 2.2 years, from 8.3 in 2010 to 10.5 in 2040. The source for this continuous increase is mainly the significant expansion of tertiary education in the next three decades. The proportion of the population with a tertiary education is projected to rapidly increase, from 15% in 2010 to 26% by 2040. Meanwhile, the proportion of the working-age population that is either uneducated or has attained a primary education as their highest education level is expected to steadily decline over the coming decades; the proportion of the population with no schooling is projected to decline, from 13% in 2010 to 5% in 2040, while the proportion with only primary schooling is projected to decline, from 21% to 12%. In contrast, the proportion of the population that has attained a secondary education as their highest level is expected to slightly increase, from 51% and 57% of the population, for the next 30 years.

The level of educational attainment is projected to increase at a faster rate in developing countries than in advanced countries. In developing countries, the average years of schooling for the working-age population is projected to increase from 7.7 years in 2010 to 10.2 years in 2040, while, in advanced countries as a whole, it is expected to increase from 11.9 to 12.8 over the same period. The faster educational progress predicted in developing countries over the next 30 years is expected to contribute to a narrowing of the education gap between developing and advanced countries. The difference between advanced and developing countries in terms of the average number of years of schooling of the population is projected to drop to 2.6 in 2040, declining from 4.3 in 2010. Nevertheless, the educational gap between developing and advanced countries is expected to remain at a level that is still significant over the next 30 years. The projections show that, in 2040, educational attainment for the overall population aged 15–64 in developing countries will reach a level comparable to that of advanced countries in 1990 (Table 2.8).

Over the next 30 years, the reduction in the educational attainment gap between developing and developed countries for the overall population aged 15–64 will come from the continuation of the increasing trend in educational attainment among the population under 25 years old in developing countries (see Figure 3.6). The average duration of education among the population 15–24 years old in developing countries is projected to rise, from about 8.5 years in 2010 to 10.9 years in 2040, while it is expected to increase from 11.0 to 12.1 years in advanced countries.

The gap between developing and advanced countries for the average years of schooling among 15–24 year olds is smaller than that among 25–64 year olds. As, over time, educational attainment for the population aged 15–24 leads to changes in educational attainment for the population aged 25–64, the educational attainment gap between developing economies and advanced countries for the population aged 25–64 is forecasted to narrow. The difference between the two groups in terms of the average amount of schooling among those aged 25–64 is expected to decrease to about three years (10 years in developing countries vs. 13 years in advanced countries) in 2040, from about five years (7.4 years vs. 12.2 years) in 2010.

The improvements in secondary and tertiary enrollment ratios among the younger cohorts will continuously contribute to the growth of the average years of schooling. The average years of education at the secondary and tertiary levels among the population aged 15–24 in developing countries are projected to increase at faster rates, which will narrow the gap in levels with advanced countries over the next 30 years (Figure 3.7).

The data in Table 3.2 shows that regional gaps in educational attainment are also narrowing among developing regions. Educational attainment for the population aged 15–64 in the Middle East/North African countries is expected to grow at a higher rate over the next 30 years, rising from 7.7 years in 2010 to 10.7 years in 2040. The projected educational attainment also shows strong growth for Asia/Pacific countries (from 7.4 to 10.3 years) and Sub-Saharan African countries (from 5.5 to 8.4 years) by 2040. In the developing Europe and Central Asia regions, the average number of years of schooling for the working-age population is expected to remain at the same level. The change in the average amount of schooling for the working-age population in each developing region reflects changes in both the enrollment ratios and population structures of individual countries.

Table 3.3 presents projections of educational attainment for the five BRICS economies, including Brazil, China, India, Russia, and the South African Republic. The projections for the United States are also presented for comparison. The educational attainment for the US working-age population is expected to increase only slightly, from 13.2 to 13.4 years, over the next three decades. In Russia, the average years of schooling for the working-age population is expected to decline, although slowly. By contrast, education attainment is expected to continue to rise in Brazil, China, India, and the South African Republic. The average years of schooling is expected to rise significantly, from 8.0 to about 10.9, in China, and from 6.6 in 2010 to 10.0 by 2040 in India, over the next three decades. During the same period, the average extent of schooling is expected to increase by about 1.1 years in Brazil (from 8.2 in 2010 to 9.3 years), and by 1.6 years in the South African Republic (from 9.9 to 11.5 years).

We have also constructed data on educational attainment for the female population aged 15–64. Table 3.4 presents the projections of educational attainment for the female population, by group and region. Over the next 30 years, the changes in educational attainment for the female population show patterns that are similar

Table 3.2 Projections of Educational Attainment of Total Population Aged 15–64 by Group and Region

Region (no. of countries) and Year	Population Aged 15–64 (Million)	No Schooling	Highest Level Attained (% of population aged 15–64)						Average Years of Schooling
			Primary		Secondary		Tertiary		
			Total	Completed	Total	Completed	Total	Completed	
World (146)									
2010	4248	12.9	21.1	14.8	51.4	27.2	14.6	8.2	8.34
2020	4706	9.5	17.9	13.1	56.0	31.9	16.6	8.9	9.04
2030	5044	6.9	15.1	11.5	57.6	36.0	20.4	10.8	9.76
2040	5255	4.8	12.1	9.6	57.2	38.7	25.9	13.9	10.52
Advanced (24)									
2010	651	1.2	9.9	8.5	53.1	38.2	35.8	19.9	11.94
2020	658	1.0	6.8	5.8	53.9	39.7	38.4	19.8	12.34
2030	654	0.9	5.1	4.3	53.5	41.4	40.6	20.7	12.58
2040	649	0.8	3.5	3.0	52.4	42.4	43.4	21.8	12.83
Developing (122)									
2010	3597	15.0	23.1	15.9	51.2	25.2	10.8	6.0	7.69
2020	4048	10.9	19.7	14.3	56.3	30.7	13.1	7.1	8.50
2030	4390	7.8	16.6	12.6	58.2	35.2	17.4	9.4	9.34
2040	4606	5.4	13.3	10.5	57.8	38.2	23.5	12.7	10.20
Middle East/North Africa (18)									
2010	240	21.3	22.5	14.9	42.1	23.8	14.0	8.5	7.65
2020	288	14.8	22.3	15.6	44.8	27.6	18.1	10.9	8.54
2030	334	9.5	19.9	14.6	45.1	29.3	25.5	14.8	9.63
2040	369	6.2	16.4	12.6	41.6	28.4	35.8	20.9	10.68

continued

Table 3.2 (CONTINUED)

Region (no. of countries) and Year	Population Aged 15–64 (Million)	No Schooling	Highest Level Attained (% of population aged 15–64)						Average Years of Schooling
			Primary		Secondary		Tertiary		
			Total	Completed	Total	Completed	Total	Completed	
Sub-Saharan Africa (33)									
2010	278	31.0	37.0	20.6	29.4	14.3	2.6	1.2	5.50
2020	364	21.8	38.2	22.4	36.3	18.1	3.6	1.6	6.40
2030	478	15.8	35.1	21.8	43.0	22.1	6.1	2.7	7.41
2040	612	11.4	29.7	19.4	49.0	26.1	10.0	4.5	8.44
Latin America/the Caribbean (25)									
2010	386	5.6	32.3	21.9	48.6	27.5	13.4	8.4	8.68
2020	438	3.6	26.7	19.2	53.8	33.1	16.0	9.4	9.08
2030	471	2.3	21.4	16.2	55.8	37.3	20.5	11.9	9.82
2040	489	1.4	16.8	13.4	55.4	39.3	26.4	15.4	10.52
Asia/the Pacific (26)									
2010	2454	15.4	22.1	15.8	54.5	24.5	8.1	4.6	7.39
2020	2731	11.1	17.2	13.3	60.9	31.3	10.8	5.9	8.43
2030	2892	7.8	13.3	11.0	63.4	37.4	15.6	8.4	9.38
2040	2930	5.0	9.6	8.5	63.1	41.9	22.3	12.1	10.33
Europe/Central Asia (20)									
2010	240	0.4	3.6	3.0	55.8	43.1	40.2	19.8	11.74
2020	227	0.7	3.2	2.8	51.9	41.6	44.3	21.8	11.55
2030	215	0.7	3.4	3.1	48.7	38.9	47.2	23.5	11.65
2040	206	0.7	3.6	3.2	44.2	35.9	51.6	26.1	11.82

NOTES: Regional averages are weighted by each country's school-age population. See Appendix Table for the list of countries included in each region/group.

A. 15–24

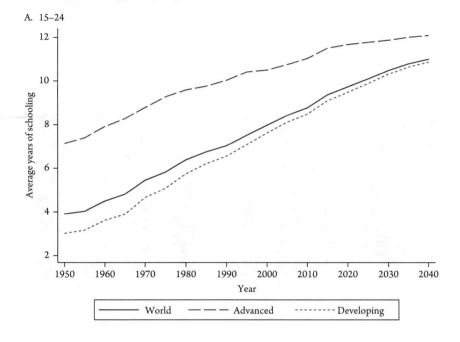

B. 25–64

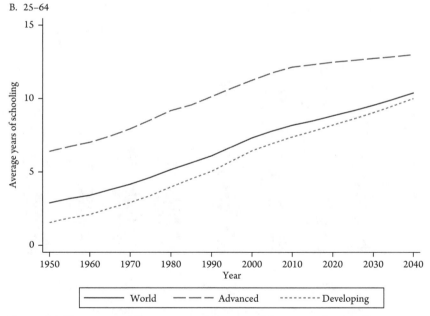

Figure 3.6 Estimates and Projections of Educational Attainment by Age Group, 1950–2040

to those for the total population. The average number of years of schooling for the worldwide female population aged 15–64 is projected to increase, from 8.0 in 2010 to 10.6 years in 2040. Over the next three decades, the proportion of those with a tertiary education among the worldwide female population is projected to rapidly increase, from 15% in 2010 to 29% by 2040. The average years of schooling of the

A. Average years of schooling, 15–24 years

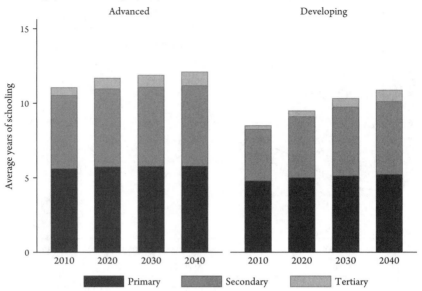

B. Average years of schooling, 25–64 years

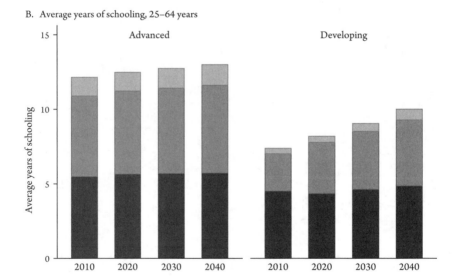

Figure 3.7 Projections of Educational Attainment by Education Level and Age Group, 2010–2040

female working-age population in developing countries is projected to increase from 7.2 in 2010 to 10.3 in 2040, compared to an increase from 11.9 to 13.0 years, over the same period, for advanced countries.

Table 3.5 shows the "gender ratio," the ratio of female-to-male attainment (expressed as a percentage), which compares the regional figures for females with the

Table 3.3 Projections of Educational Attainment of Total Population Aged 15–64, Selected Countries

Region (no. of countries) and Year	Population Aged 15–64 (Million)	No Schooling	Primary		Secondary		Tertiary		Average Years of Schooling
			Total	Completed	Total	Completed	Total	Completed	
					(% of population aged 15–64)				
USA									
2010	210	0.3	2.6	2.1	41.5	34.4	55.6	27.5	13.24
2020	217	0.4	2.1	1.5	40.8	34.5	56.8	28.1	13.32
2030	221	0.5	1.5	1.1	40.6	34.7	57.5	28.5	13.39
2040	232	0.5	0.9	0.6	41.1	35.9	57.5	28.1	13.43
Brazil									
2010	132	7.0	34.6	25.2	48.6	28.4	9.8	6.6	8.17
2020	147	4.2	30.6	24.8	54.0	32.2	11.3	6.9	8.00
2030	151	2.3	26.4	22.9	56.0	34.1	15.2	9.1	8.66
2040	151	1.0	22.5	20.8	55.4	33.7	21.1	12.6	9.31
China									
2010	978	2.6	20.8	13.1	71.8	24.7	4.8	2.6	7.96
2020	1004	1.3	12.7	7.9	74.8	30.0	11.3	6.1	8.99
2030	988	0.7	7.7	4.9	72.7	36.0	18.9	10.3	9.88
2040	909	0.4	3.1	2.0	66.4	40.6	30.2	16.9	10.92
India									
2010	762	30.1	17.2	16.0	43.9	25.6	8.9	5.3	6.59
2020	908	20.6	15.6	15.1	56.5	35.1	7.4	4.3	7.80
2030	1005	13.4	12.5	12.4	63.9	41.9	10.2	5.7	8.95

continued

Table 3.3 (CONTINUED)

Region (no. of countries) and Year	Population Aged 15–64 (Million)	No Schooling	Primary		Secondary		Tertiary		Average Years of Schooling
			Total	Completed	Total	Completed	Total	Completed	
					(% of population aged 15–64)				
2040	1072	7.9	8.8	8.8	68.6	47.2	14.7	8.1	10.03
Russian Federation									
2010	101	0.5	1.8	1.2	34.8	25.4	63.1	26.6	12.02
2020	95	1.0	1.1	0.8	30.8	23.2	67.2	29.1	11.60
2030	88	1.2	0.9	0.6	28.8	21.2	69.3	30.9	11.68
2040	84	1.2	0.8	0.6	25.7	19.5	72.3	32.7	11.80
South Africa									
2010	30	4.0	17.1	6.3	74.5	55.4	4.5	0.3	9.89
2020	36	1.9	12.4	4.9	79.8	61.2	6.0	0.3	10.47
2030	39	0.7	7.7	3.1	80.8	62.0	10.9	0.6	11.05
2040	42	0.3	4.6	1.9	76.5	58.2	18.7	1.0	11.49

Table 3.4 Projections of Educational Attainment of Female Population Aged 15–64 by Group and Region

Region (no. of countries) and Year	Population Aged 15–64 (Million)	No Schooling	Primary		Secondary		Tertiary		Average Years of Schooling
			Total	Completed	Total	Completed	Total	Completed	
			(% of population aged 15–64)						
World (146)									
2010	2100	16.9	21.0	14.4	47.7	25.5	14.5	7.8	7.95
2020	2319	12.3	17.9	13.0	51.8	30.3	18.0	9.7	8.84
2030	2477	8.6	14.8	11.4	54.3	34.9	22.3	12.1	9.72
2040	2574	5.7	11.7	9.3	54.1	37.9	28.5	15.7	10.62
Advanced (24)									
2010	324	1.5	10.2	8.5	51.2	36.9	37.2	20.3	11.94
2020	328	1.2	6.9	5.9	51.9	38.7	40.0	20.8	12.39
2030	325	0.9	5.2	4.4	50.8	39.7	43.2	22.5	12.69
2040	321	0.7	3.6	3.0	49.6	40.6	46.1	23.9	12.96
Developing (122)									
2010	1776	19.7	23.0	15.4	47.0	23.5	10.3	5.6	7.22
2020	1990	14.1	19.7	14.1	51.8	28.9	14.4	7.9	8.25
2030	2152	9.8	16.3	12.4	54.8	34.2	19.2	10.5	9.27
2040	2252	6.4	12.8	10.2	54.8	37.5	26.0	14.5	10.29
Middle East/North Africa (18)									
2010	117	27.6	19.6	14.1	39.7	23.6	13.1	8.1	7.19
2020	137	18.9	19.7	14.6	43.4	28.2	18.0	10.6	8.30
2030	159	11.8	17.5	13.4	44.7	30.7	26.0	15.0	9.60
2040	177	7.1	14.2	11.2	41.6	30.2	37.1	21.5	10.83

continued

Table 3.4 (CONTINUED)

Region (no. of countries) and Year	Population Aged 15–64 (Million)	No Schooling	Primary		Highest Level Attained				Average Years of Schooling
					Secondary		Tertiary		
			Total	Completed	Total	Completed	Total	Completed	
					(% of population aged 15–64)				
Sub-Saharan Africa (33)									
2010	140	36.4	35.2	19.3	26.2	12.7	2.2	1.0	4.99
2020	183	25.9	36.5	21.0	34.2	17.5	3.4	1.5	6.05
2030	239	18.7	33.5	20.6	41.7	22.2	6.1	2.9	7.20
2040	307	13.3	28.3	18.3	48.2	26.7	10.2	5.0	8.35
Latin America/the Caribbean (25)									
2010	196	6.0	31.2	21.1	48.5	27.9	14.3	8.8	8.73
2020	222	3.5	25.9	18.6	53.1	33.6	17.5	10.4	9.22
2030	238	2.1	20.8	15.7	53.9	37.3	23.2	13.8	10.03
2040	245	1.1	16.4	13.1	52.0	38.2	30.6	18.4	10.79
Asia/the Pacific (26)									
2010	1199	21.2	22.5	15.4	49.4	22.3	6.8	3.9	6.76
2020	1331	15.0	17.8	13.4	55.1	28.8	12.1	6.9	8.09
2030	1406	10.1	13.5	11.1	58.8	35.7	17.7	9.9	9.28
2040	1419	6.2	9.4	8.4	59.1	40.6	25.4	14.3	10.44
Europe/Central Asia (20)									
2010	124	0.4	3.5	3.0	52.0	39.9	44.1	19.5	11.82
2020	117	0.6	3.0	2.6	49.4	39.7	47.0	21.3	11.60
2030	110	0.7	3.2	2.9	47.8	38.6	48.2	22.1	11.66
2040	105	0.7	3.5	3.2	44.6	36.8	51.2	24.0	11.78

NOTES: Regional averages are weighted by each country's school-age population. See Appendix Table for the list of countries included in each region/group.

114

same for males for the next three decades. Gender equality will continue to improve, in all regions, over the next decades. For the world population aged 15–64, the ratio of the female-to-male average years of schooling is expected to rise from 91% in 2010 to 102% in 2040. The most notable increases in the ratios are expected in Asia/Pacific (85% to 102%), Sub-Saharan Africa (from 83% in 2010 to 98% in 2040), and in the Middle East/North Africa (89% to 103%). The gender-equality ratios in the advanced economies, developing Europe, and Latin American will remain at high levels, over 100%, throughout the coming decades. Notwithstanding the great extent to which gender inequality still exists worldwide, with girls at

Table 3.5 PROJECTIONS OF EDUCATIONAL ATTAINMENT BY GENDER, 2010–2040

Region (no. of countries) and Year	Average Years of Schooling (population aged 15–64)		Gender Ratio (F/M, %)
	Females (F)	Males (M)	
World (146)			
2010	7.95	8.73	91.1
2020	8.84	9.23	95.7
2030	9.72	9.80	99.2
2040	10.62	10.43	101.8
Advanced (24)			
2010	11.94	11.94	100.0
2020	12.39	12.28	100.8
2030	12.69	12.47	101.7
2040	12.96	12.70	102.0
Developing (122)			
2010	7.22	8.15	88.5
2020	8.25	8.74	94.3
2030	9.27	9.41	98.6
2040	10.29	10.11	101.7
Middle East/North Africa (18)			
2010	7.19	8.10	88.8
2020	8.30	8.77	94.7
2030	9.60	9.66	99.4
2040	10.83	10.54	102.8
Sub-Saharan Africa (33)			
2010	4.99	6.01	83.0
2020	6.05	6.76	89.6
2030	7.20	7.63	94.4
2040	8.35	8.56	97.5
Latin America/the Caribbean (25)			
2010	8.73	8.62	101.3
2020	9.22	8.93	103.2
2030	10.03	9.60	104.5
2040	10.79	10.24	105.4

continued

Table 3.5 (CONTINUED)

Region (no. of countries) and Year	Average Years of Schooling (population aged 15–64)		Gender Ratio (F/M, %)
	Females (F)	Males (M)	
Asia/the Pacific (26)			
2010	6.76	8.00	84.5
2020	8.09	8.75	92.4
2030	9.28	9.48	97.9
2040	10.44	10.24	102.0
Europe/Central Asia (20)			
2010	11.82	11.64	101.6
2020	11.60	11.49	101.0
2030	11.66	11.65	100.0
2040	11.78	11.88	99.1

a disadvantage, the disparities are expected to occur increasingly at the expense of boys for some regions.

Our projections show that the significant improvements seen in the educational attainment over the past decades will continue to occur in the future, particularly at the levels of secondary and tertiary education. Figure 3.8 presents the global maps of educational attainment for the working-age population. They present the proportions of total population who have received at least some secondary education, in 2010 and 2040.

The 2010 map shows that, in many advanced countries and former Communist countries, the proportion of working-age population that has attained at least a secondary education was over 80%, whereas in the majority of developing countries, secondary and tertiary levels of education are not yet universal. The bottom map presents our 2040 projections, in which secondary and tertiary levels of education have become more prevalent as the great majority of the working-age population, except for those in some sub-Saharan countries, has attained a secondary education.

3.5 COMPARISONS WITH EXISTING PROJECTIONS

We compare our projections for the educational attainment of the overall population aged 15–64 with the estimates projected by Samir et al. (2010). They constructed a data set for the distribution of educational attainment for the population, classified by five-year age group and by gender, for 120 countries for the period from 2005 to 2050 at five-year intervals.

Samir et al. (2010)'s methodology is similar to our forward-extrapolation projections. They used the information from the censuses/surveys available in 2000 as benchmarks, and adopted a forward-extrapolation method to construct their projections. Nevertheless, there is a significant difference in terms of the benchmark data. Our 2010 benchmark figures are entirely based on actual population censuses (or their extrapolated estimates) on attainment by age, from UNESCO and from

A. 2010

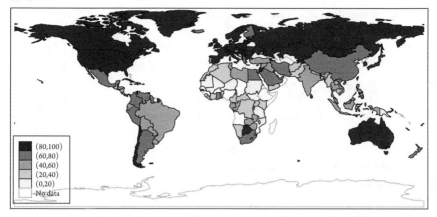

B. 2040

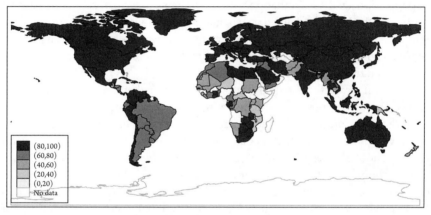

Figure 3.8 Proportions of Population Who Have Received at Least Some Secondary Education, for Selected Years, 2010 and 2040.

national sources that are broadly consistent among countries and over time. By contrast, Samir et al.'s 2000 baseline data are compiled from various sources of census and from survey data sets. Hence, the accuracy of their projections is completely dependent on whether or not the quality of the baseline data is sufficient for cross-national comparisons. Samir et al. have not explicitly stated the sources for their baseline data. However, the same group of the researchers at the IIASA used the same baseline data from the year 2000 in another paper, in which they provided the backward-extrapolation estimation for educational attainment from 1970 to 2000 (Lutz et al., 2007). According to the explanations in that paper, the baseline data from around the year 2000 are compiled from various sources, including national censuses compiled by UNESCO (35 countries), census data provided by national statistical offices (28 countries), labor-force surveys (8 countries), Demographic and Health Surveys (33 countries), and Eurostat data (16 countries).

As discussed in Barro and Lee (2013), the labor-force surveys available from the OECD are often incompatible with the national censuses in the UNESCO database. In addition, the estimates for educational attainment from the Demographic and Health Surveys (DHS) are even less compatible with the UNESCO census data. The educational attainment categories used in the DHS are not consistent with those used in the UNESCO database. DHS is based on a sample of a small number of households. Lutz et al. (2007) try to make adjustments to DHS data on educational attainment by using the results of a regression performed on a common sample of the ten countries that are present in both the UNESCO and DHS data sets. Nevertheless, the adjusted baseline data from DHS are not fully compatible with the census data from UNESCO and national sources.

Another difference between our projections and those of Samir et al.'s is the methods used for projecting educational attainment for the age groups 15–19 and 20–24. Both our projections and those of Samir et al. consider that a proportion of youth population, aged 15–24, that has completed primary or secondary education can advance to the next cycle of schooling, including upper secondary or tertiary levels of education. Samir et al. estimate country-specific values for the portions of the population aged 15–24 that transitions to the next cycle of schooling based on information from the baseline data, such as the distribution of educational attainment by cohort and school duration. By contrast, we assume that changes in the proportion of transitions to the next cycle are determined by the changes in future enrollment ratios, as explained in Section 3.1.

Samir et al. projected the distribution of educational attainment using four categories. They are not exactly matched with our seven detailed categories. We can compare their projections for the average years of schooling for populations aged 15–64 with our estimates. Samir et al. present two projected values for the average years of schooling, using different assumptions for duration. One measure, "mean years of schooling" (MYS), uses country-specific data for the duration of schooling, according to each country's specific school system. This is similar to our method. However, while we use more detailed information about country-specific durations that correspond to each level of educational attainment for seven categories, Samir et al. used their own estimates of average duration, which correspond to each of their four broadly defined categories. For example, for the second of their education categories, which includes primary education and incomplete lower secondary education, they constructed the average duration, somewhat arbitrarily, as a weighted average of the lower and upper quartile values of the total duration for the completion of primary education and for lower secondary education, while the relative weight is constructed using the proportions of population in the first and third education categories.[10]

The alternative measure by Samir et al., "mean years of schooling equivalent" (MYSE), applies the world averages for duration from 2000 to construct the average years of schooling for all the countries of the world.[11] Thus, it assumes that people in a given education category will have the same educational attainment in all countries, irrespective of country-specific variations in the minimum lengths of study according to the respective education system.

Figure 3.9 plots our projections alongside Samir et al.(2010)'s two measures for projecting the average years of schooling for a sample of observations in 2010 and 2040 that are common to both data sets. They are closely correlated, notwithstanding some discrepancies.

A. Comparison with Samir et al.'s MYS

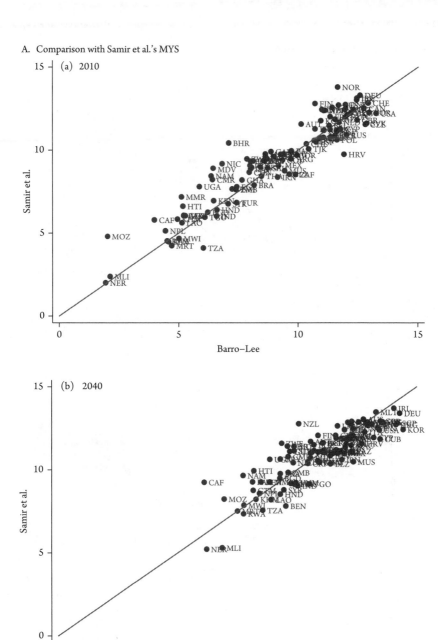

Figure 3.9 Comparison of Average Years of Schooling Projections between This Data Set and Samir et al. (2010) for Selected Years, 2010 and 2040

NOTE: MYS is average years of schooling based on the country-specific duration, while MYSE is one based on the world averages of duration.

B. Comparison with Samir et al.'s MYSE

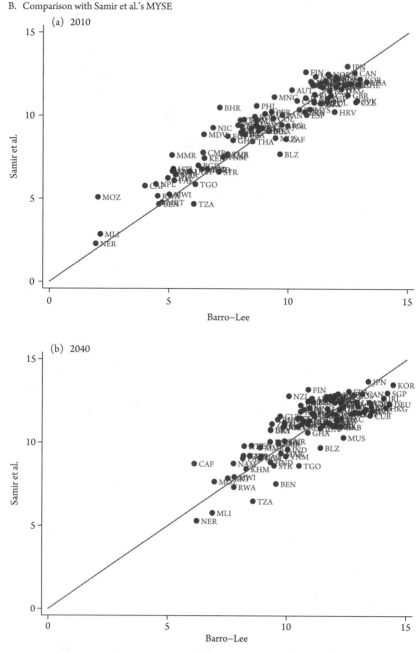

Figure 3.9 (continued)

We have compared the average years of schooling, by levels and ten-year differ-ences, for the sample of overlapping observations in the 2010–2040 period between our new data set and Samir et al.'s two measures (Table 3.6). The mean and stand-ard deviation values of the projections are broadly similar for both our projections and Samir et al.'s MYSE. By contrast, the MYSE estimates for developing countries

Table 3.6 COMPARISON OF PROJECTED AVERAGE YEARS OF SCHOOLING FOR TOTAL POPULATION AGED 15–64 BETWEEN OUR DATA SET AND SAMIR ET AL. (2010)

A. This data set and Samir et al. 2010 MYS	Obs	Correlation	This data set		Samir et al. 2010	
			2010	2040	2010	2040
World						
Levels	440	0.92	8.46 (2.76)	10.66 (1.87)	8.56 (2.60)	10.24 (1.69)
10-year differences	330	0.72	0.43 (0.22)		0.33 (0.21)	
Advanced countries						
Levels	92	0.79	11.94 (1.33)	12.82 (1.18)	11.78 (1.48	12.23 (0.89)
10-year differences	69	0.39	0.15 (0.14)		0.07 (0.22)	
Developing countries						
Levels	348	0.92	7.78 (2.70)	10.32 (1.88)	7.93 (2.44)	9.93 (1.66)
10-year differences	261	0.73	0.47 (0.21)		0.37 (0.19)	

B. This data set and Samir et al. 2010 MYSE	Obs	Correlation	This data set		Samir et al. 2010	
			2010	2040	2010	2040
World						
Levels	440	0.90	8.46 (2.76)	10.66 (1.87)	9.09 (2.39)	10.67 (1.70)
10-year differences	330	0.80	0.43 (0.22)		0.31 (0.14)	
Advanced countries						
Levels	92	0.65	11.94 (1.33)	12.82 (1.18)	11.57 (1.21)	12.32 (0.77)
10-year differences	69	0.68	0.15 (0.14)		0.13 (0.10)	
Developing countries						
Levels	348	0.90	7.78 (2.70)	10.32 (1.88)	8.61 (2.32)	10.41 (1.71)
10-year differences	261	0.76	0.47 (0.21)		0.34 (0.14)	

Obs = overlapping observations

NOTES: Figures presented in this table represent overlapping observations only. This data set consists of a total of 730 observations on average years of schooling for 146 countries at 10-year intervals from 2010 to 2040. Numbers in parentheses are standard deviations. MYS is average years of schooling based on the country-specific duration, while MYSE is one based on the world averages of duration.

SOURCE: Authors' calculations based on Samir et al. (2010) data sets and own data.

are, on average, lower than ours for the overall period, 1870–1950. Our projected values are highly correlated in levels with both MYS and MYSE, with a correlation coefficient of about 0.90, but they are less correlated in ten-year differences, with correlation coefficients of 0.72 (with MYS) and 0.80 (MYSE) for the sample of all common observations. The estimates for advanced countries are less correlated than those for developing countries, both in levels and in ten-year differences.

Educational Attainment and Economic and Political Developments, 1960–2010

"Education is the most powerful weapon which you can use to change the world."
—Nelson Mandela

This chapter explores the effects of educational capital stock on economic and political development. This examination is based on a general framework of cross-
country analysis, putting the experiences of individual countries in a global context.
We discuss a framework that relates education to economic growth, fertility, and
democracy.

For the empirical analysis, we use a panel data set comprising many variables
for a large number of countries, with the data dating back to the 1960s. This data
set has been used for cross-country regressions by Barro (2012) and is supplemented with the recently available national accounts data from the Penn World
Tables version 8.0 (PWT 8.0)[1] and our newly constructed educational attainment data.

The next chapter utilizes another data set that covers a longer period (1870–
2010) but consists of fewer countries and variables compared to the panel data set.

We begin with an introduction of the theoretical frameworks that emphasize
the role of human capital in economic development. The next three sections analyze the extent to which educational accumulation has contributed to economic
growth, by adopting a number of empirical techniques such as growth accounting, development accounting, and cross-country regressions. We then explore
the effects of human capital, measured by educational attainment, on fertility
and democracy.

4.1 THEORIES OF HUMAN CAPITAL AND ECONOMIC GROWTH

Recent studies on economic growth have emphasized the positive role of human capital in economic growth. An abundance of well-educated workers is accompanied by higher levels of labor productivity and returns to capital, and it also implies greater ability to facilitate technological innovation and adaption.

The Solow-type neoclassical growth model highlights investment rate, population growth, and human capital as important factors determining the steady-state level of per-worker output (Solow, 1956; Mankiw, Romer, and Weil, 1992). A higher investment rate of human capital accumulation allows an economy to achieve a higher level of steady-state per-worker output. During transitions, in which an economy's per-worker output converges toward its own steady state, the growth rate of per-worker output is positively related to the human capital investment rate.[2] In the long run, however, the steady-state growth rate is independent of the investment rate and is determined entirely by the rate of exogenous technological progress.

According to the endogenous growth models, which were initiated by Romer in the mid-1980s, the long-run growth rate can be determined endogenously within the model, and an economy can grow permanently due to factors other than exogenous technological progress (Romer, 1986, 1987). The standard neoclassical model assumes that, as more capital is accumulated, productivity of physical capital decreases, and thus, growth becomes slower. The initial wave of the endogenous growth models introduced a broad concept of capital—including human capital—and showed that returns to investment in a broad capital do not necessarily diminish as an economy develops. Lucas (1988) emphasized the "positive externalities" of human capital. Educated people are more productive and more innovative, and they spread external benefits to their coworkers, who learn from them and, in turn, become more productive. The positive spillovers of knowledge among skilled workers help offset the tendency of diminishing returns to capital accumulation.

In an endogenous growth model with a production function having two types of capital, physical capital (K) and human capital (H), the dynamics of economic growth during the transition period involve an adjustment of the ratio of human capital stock to physical capital stock (H/K).[3]

In the models developed by Uzawa (1965) and Lucas (1988), human capital is produced in the education sector wherein human capital stock is employed as the only input. For a given value of per-worker output, a higher level of human capital stock indicates a higher ratio of initial H/K compared to the steady-state ratio. This leads to a subsequent growth in physical capital stock, implying a higher growth rate of per-worker gross domestic product (GDP). Over time, relatively more human capital stock is allocated to the production of goods, and relatively less to human capital production. This is particularly true in times of war, which destroys a great deal of physical capital but leaves human capital relatively intact. Japan's faster growth after World War II can be cited as one such example.

On the contrary, if human capital stock is smaller relative to physical capital stock, implying a lower initial H/K ratio compared to its steady-state value, we would see slowdowns in physical capital stock accumulation and output growth rate in an attempt to eliminate the imbalance between physical capital and human capital.[4] This type of adjustment can occur in a situation like an epidemic, in which exogenous shocks destroy human capital but leave the physical capital stock intact.[5]

Thus, the endogenous growth model with two types of capital predicts that when initial human capital stock is relatively abundant compared to physical capital stock, the output growth rate tends to rise over a certain period, until the ratio between human capital stock and physical capital stock reaches its steady-state value.[6]

While the endogenous growth model with human capital stresses that the production of human capital can serve as an engine of long-term growth in the absence of technological progress, other endogenous growth models, including those in Romer (1987, 1990) and Grossman and Helpman (1991), emphasize the role of technology improvements in the process of long-term growth.[7]

In the traditional neoclassical growth theory, technology is treated as a public good freely available to anyone, and thus, it is not considered an important explanatory factor for differences in economic growth across countries. On the contrary, these endogenous economic growth models incorporate R&D theories and imperfect competition into the growth framework and show how technological progress is determined within the model.

The development of new technologies needs human capital. In particular, a high level of human skills imparted through training are often required for innovative activities. Recent papers have highlighted the complementary effects between human capital and technology. Redding (1996) and Acemoglu (1997), for instance, developed a model with multiple equilibrium growth paths in which an economy can follow either a "low-education, low-technology" or a "high-education, high-technology" growth path. Acemoglu (2002) suggested a directed technological change model in which abundant skill endowments induce more skill-biased technological progress, implying that the shift of the production technology favors skilled over unskilled labor and, therefore, increases relative demand for skilled labor.

For developing countries eager to catch up to advanced countries, technology adaptation is considered to be more important than technology innovation. Human efforts and capabilities are also necessary for imitating and adapting advanced technologies. Lack of human capacity in the facilitation of new technologies is considered to be crucial, as it points to the limited absorption capability of a nation. Nelson and Phelps (1966) showed that, for developing countries, the facilitation of new knowledge is only possible in the presence of a sufficient level of human capital. Acemoglu and Zilibotti (2001) noted that technologies invented in advanced countries are more skill-complementary. Hence, the mismatch between skills and technology results in differences in productivity, even when all countries have equal access to new technologies.

The neoclassical growth model considers population growth rate as exogenously given and predicts a negative association between population growth rate and output per-worker growth rate in the transitional period. This model does not, however, consider the effects of per-capita income, wage rates, and child-rearing costs on population growth. A strand of recent literature has incorporated an analysis of fertility choice into the growth model, so that the population growth rate becomes endogenously determined (Becker, Murphy, and Tamura, 1990). Human capital is considered to play an important role in the interactions of demographic transition and economic development. Galor and Weil (1996, 2000) and Galor (2005) presented a "unified growth theory" that explains the main features of the development process over long-term human history. In this model, human capital is a fundamental factor that generates a decline in population growth and a sustained increase in per-capita output.

4.2 HUMAN CAPITAL AND CROSS-COUNTRY INCOME DIFFERENCES

This section documents the evolution of income disparities across nations over the period 1960–2010 and examines the role of education expansion in income inequality across countries.

The disparities in per-capita income between the poor and rich regions of the world have long been a topic of interest among economists. For example, the debate over "convergence" focuses on whether the dispersion of per-capita income across countries has reduced over time (Barro and Sala-i-Martin, 2004, Chapter 1).

Figure 4.1 shows the change in the distribution of GDP per worker, using US data from 1960 as the benchmark. The sample includes 113 economies with complete observations from 1960 to 2010. The movements toward the right side of the density plots show that many countries have reduced the income gap with the United States over the past half century.

Table 4.1 shows GDP per worker relative to the United States for selected countries for 1960 and 2010. Data on GDP, adjusted by purchasing power parity in 2005, are sourced from the PWT 8.0. They are listed in descending order, in terms of their

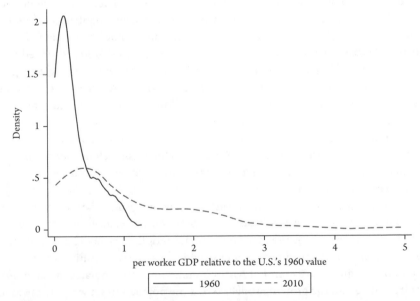

Figure 4.1 Distribution of per-Worker GDP, 1960 and 2010

Table 4.1 OUTPUT PER WORKER AND ITS COMPONENTS RELATIVE TO THE UNITED STATES FOR SELECTED COUNTRIES, 1960 AND 2010

Country	1960				2010			
	Output per worker	Physical capital per worker	Average years of schooling (S)	Human capital per worker (h)	Output per worker	Capital per worker	average years of schooling (S)	Human capital per worker (h)
United Kingdom	0.73	0.44	0.73	0.74	0.78	0.62	0.94	0.95
Germany	0.66	0.38	0.78	0.77	0.83	0.83	0.95	0.95
France	0.62	0.48	0.45	0.49	0.74	0.85	0.86	0.84
Japan	0.28	0.18	0.81	0.81	0.80	1.10	0.94	0.93
Brazil	0.17	0.18	0.26	0.47	0.21	0.24	0.62	0.62
Republic of Korea	0.11	0.05	0.46	0.61	0.63	0.74	0.98	0.98
Kenya	0.08	0.07	0.16	0.42	0.04	0.03	0.49	0.52
India	0.05	0.03	0.12	0.39	0.09	0.06	0.50	0.57
China	0.03	0.03	0.27	0.47	0.19	0.20	0.60	0.58

NOTES: The data on output and physical capital stock are sourced from the Penn World Tables (PWT) 8.0, and the data on working-age population are sourced from the United Nations (2013). Human capital per worker is measured by the average years of schooling (S) or weighted sum of the shares of workers multiplied by the relative wage rates across six education categories (h). The relative wage rates are constructed assuming that the rates of return to an additional schooling year are constant at 10%.

position in 1960. The table shows significant differences in the levels of output per worker across countries. For example, in 2010, the value of output per worker in Kenya was only 4% of that in the United States. For China and India, the values of output per worker in 1960 were 3% and 5%, respectively, of those in the United States, increasing to 19% and 9%, respectively, in 2010. The Republic of Korea had a very rapid catch-up in output per worker over time. The value of output per worker increased from 11% of the value in the United States in 1960, to 63% in 2010.

The table also shows data on physical capital stock per worker relative to the United States. It is clear that high GDP per worker is accompanied by high physical capital stock per worker. Figure 4.2 shows the strong positive relationship across countries between output per worker and physical capital stock per worker in 2010.

In this section, we investigate to what extent the gap in per-worker output can be explained by differences in human capital. We adopt "development accounting" to assess the contribution of human capital to differences in per-worker output across countries. The development accounting approach uses the aggregate production function that relates per-worker output to productive inputs, including physical and human capital.

We assume a simple Cobb–Douglas production function, such as

$$Y = AK^{(1-\alpha)}(hL)^{\alpha}, \tag{4.1}$$

where Y is value-added output (GDP), K is the physical capital, L is the number of workers, h is human capital per worker, and A is total factor productivity (TFP). The labor share of output is given by α, which varies across countries and over time.

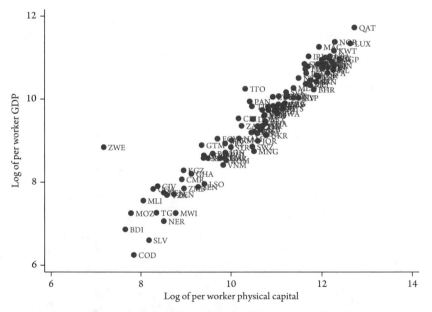

Figure 4.2 Per-Worker GDP and Physical Capital Stock per Worker, 2010

In per-worker terms, the production function can be written as

$$y = Ak^{(1-\alpha)}h^{\alpha}, \tag{4.2}$$

We want to know to what extent the variations in y are explained by the variations in the two productive inputs, k and h, and the unobservable residual, A.

To perform this task, we decompose the differences in GDP per worker across countries into differences in human capital per worker, physical capital per worker, and TFP. From (4.2), taking logs and using variance decompositions, we obtain

$$Var(\ln y) = Var(\ln \overline{h}) + Var(\ln \overline{k}) + Var(A) + 2Cov(\ln \overline{h}, \ln \overline{k})$$
$$+ 2Cov(\ln \overline{h}, \ln A) + 2Cov(\ln \overline{k}, \ln A), \tag{4.3}$$

where $\overline{k} = k^{(1-\alpha)}$, $\overline{h} = h^{\alpha}$.

Using this formula, contribution of human capital is constructed by the share of human capital dispersion in explaining the variance of log (y). Suppose that each country has the same k and A, then the fraction of the variance of (log value) per-worker GDP, explained by the difference in human capital per worker, is defined by

$$Share\ H1 = \frac{Var[\ln \overline{h}]}{Var[\ln y]}. \tag{4.4}$$

One critical issue regarding this decomposition is that the measure in (4.4) does not really answer to what extent the variation in y increases due to an increase in the dispersion of h, because A, k, and h are not independent of each other. The increase in human capital per worker can influence GDP per worker though changes in physical capital or TFP. Conversely, human capital per worker can increase in response to increases in physical capital or TFP (Klenow and Rodríguez-Clare, 1997; Hsieh and Klenow, 2010).

Hence, we define another measure for the contribution of human capital to the variance in per-worker output. We add half of the covariance terms of human capital per worker with physical capital per worker and TFP to the numerator in (4.4).

$$Share\ H2 = \frac{Var\ (\ln \overline{h}) + Cov(\ln \overline{h}, \ln \overline{k}) + Cov(\ln \overline{h}, \ln A)}{Var[\ln y]}. \tag{4.5}$$

While the measure in (4.5) has some advantages over that in (4.4), it is also subject to measurement errors, as it assumes a fixed fraction of covariance terms attributed to human capital, and relies on the estimation of TFP.

For development accounting, we need a measure of human capital per worker. We use two measures of aggregate human capital stock per worker. First, the average years of schooling (S) is defined as

$$S = \sum_a \sum_j dur_j^a l_j^a, \ j = \text{primary, secondary, tertiary}; \ a = 15\text{--}19, \ldots, 60\text{--}64,$$
$$\tag{4.6}$$

where dur_j^a is the duration of schooling at level j for population group a, and l_j^a is the fraction of population group a that has attained the educational level j. Note that this formula assumes that uneducated workers provide no human capital and that each additional schooling year contributes to human capital stock by the years of school duration. This aggregation also assumes that different types of human capital are perfectly substitutable.

An alternative measure of human capital stock assumes a Mincerian log-linear relationship between the number of years of schooling and human capital, such that

$$h = \sum_a \sum_j e^{\theta_j^a (dur_j^a)} l_j^a, j = \text{primary, secondary, tertiary}; a = 15\text{--}19, \ldots, 60\text{--}64.$$

$$(4.7)$$

In this equation, $\theta_j^a (dur_j^a)$ measures the productivity of a unit of labor for population group a with education level j relative to one without any schooling. The derivative, $\theta_j^{a\prime}(dur_j^a)$, is the marginal return to an additional year of schooling at level j. Assuming that it is a linear relation, (4.6) can be rewritten as

$$h = \sum_a \sum_j e^{\theta_j^a dur_j^a} l_j^a.$$

$$(4.8)$$

This measure indicates that human capital per worker is the sum of the shares of workers weighted by the relative wage rates $\left(\text{that is, } e^{\theta_j^a dur_j^a}\right)$ across all education categories and all age groups. If the marginal rate of return to a school year is constant for all education levels across countries, and everyone has the same level of schooling, (4.8) can be further simplified to $h = e^{\theta s}$.[8]

Note that (4.8) assumes that human capital stock for uneducated workers is constant at 1 and is equal across countries. Manuelli and Seshadri (2010) challenged this assumption of the identical productivity of uneducated workers across countries. If investments in early childhood (e.g., via medical care and nutrition) are important determinants of the early levels of an individual's human capital, human capital stock for uneducated workers can be larger in richer countries than that in poorer ones. They suggest that a six-year-old from a country in the bottom decile has less than 50% of the human capital of a six-year-old living in the United States. However, there is no strong evidence that the productivity of uneducated workers varies across countries and is higher in richer countries. Using US census data from 2000, Jones (2011) provided conflicting evidence. He showed that mean wages for uneducated workers born in the United States are about 17% lower compared to those of immigrants from the very poorest of countries. Using Mexican microdata, he also showed that this wage gap is not driven by a bias from the endogenous decision of immigrants.

The perfect substitutability assumption among different schooling levels in (4.6) and (4.8) can cause substantial bias (Jones, 2011). If skilled workers are not easily substitutable for unskilled workers, the productivity of unskilled workers can be higher when more schooling causes relative scarcity of unskilled workers over time. This potential bias leads to underestimation of true human capital differences across countries. If the elasticity of substitution is lower, the contribution of human capital in explaining per-worker output differences would increase (Jones, 2011).[9] It is, however, practically difficult to estimate the elasticity of substitution among multiple skill types, especially between non–primary educated workers and primary- or secondary-educated workers. The assumption of perfect substitutability allows for the easy calculation of the aggregate human capital measure. Despite potential measurement errors, it can still give a benchmark estimate of the contribution of human capital to variations in per-worker output across nations.

We assume that the relative wage rate of a worker with schooling S is determined by the constant marginal return rate to an additional year of schooling of 10%, the world average of return rates (Psacharopoulos, 1994).[10] Figure 4.3 shows the change in the Mincerian-type human capital stock measures over time across regions. Significant progress of human capital accumulation has taken place in both advanced and developing regions since 1960. Among the developing regions, the Asia-Pacific region and the Middle East and North Africa have shown strong progress compared to Sub-Saharan Africa and South Asia.

Table 4.1 compares the ratios of human capital stock per worker for selected countries to output per worker in the United States for the years 1960 and 2010. The gap in human capital stock per worker across economies is smaller than that in output per worker. It implies that the dispersion of human capital per worker may not explain the major portion of dispersion in output per worker. Figure 4.4 shows the relationship between output per worker and human capital stock per worker in 2010 across countries. They have a positive association, although there are many outliers.

Table 4.2 summarizes the results of the development accounting exercise using (4.4) and (4.5) and data from 2010. It presents the estimates for Shares $H1$ and $H2$. For 83 countries, the variance of log GDP per worker is 1.40, and the fractions of the variance of log GDP per worker explained by human capital per worker and measured by the average years of schooling are 11.3% by Share $H1$ and 20.2% by Share $H2$ when the average years of schooling is used. When the Mincerian-type human capital measure is used, the corresponding fractions of the variance of log GDP per worker explained by human capital per worker are 5.6% and 13.5%.

The variance decomposition method has a drawback in that it is sensitive to outliers. Caselli (2005) used a measure of the inter-percentile differentials. The contribution of human capital is measured by the 90th-to-10th percentile ratio of human capital per worker divided by the corresponding ratio of GDP per worker.

$$\frac{h^{90}/h^{10}}{y^{90}/y^{10}}, \tag{4.9}$$

where x^j denotes the value of the jth percentile of the distribution of x.

Table 4.3 shows the estimates for the measure in (4.9) for 2010. The average value of the 90th-to-10th percentile ratio of GDP per worker for the sample of 83 countries is 24.7. When the measure of average years of schooling is adopted, the corresponding ratio of human capital per worker is 2.60. Hence, the fraction of the cross-country per-worker GDP dispersion explained by human capital is 10.5%. When the Mincerian-type human capital measure is used, human capital per worker explains approximately 8.8% of variance of per-worker GDP.

A. World, and Advanced and Developing Countries

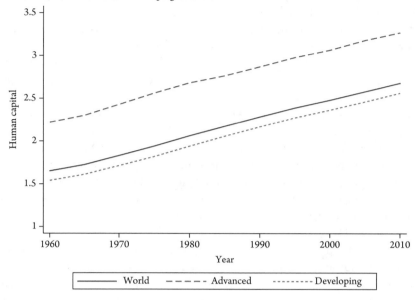

B. Major Regions

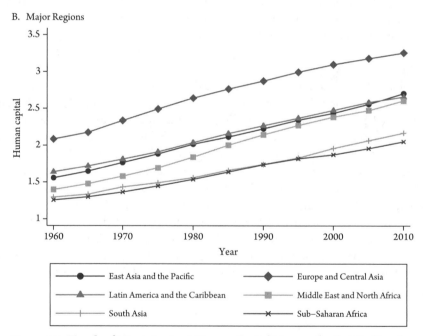

Figure 4.3 Trends of Mincerian-type Human Capital Measure for the World and by Group and Region, 1960–2010

NOTES: The measure of human capital stock is constructed based on equation (4.8), which assumes a Mincerian log-linear relationship between the number of years of schooling and human capital for the working-age population. The data for the group or region are the averages weighted by the country population size.

A. Average years of schooling

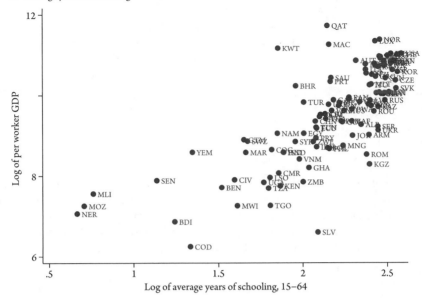

B. Mincerian-type Human capital per worker

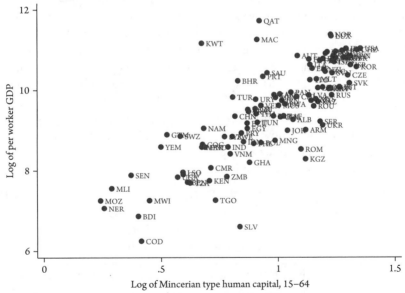

Figure 4.4 Per-Worker GDP and Human Capital Stock per Worker, 2010

In conclusion, the development accounting exercises show that human capital explains between 6% and 20% of the cross-country differences in per-worker output. Thus, it is not the most important determinant of international income disparity, which is consistent with the findings of previous papers that cross-country differences in output per worker are attributable to differences in TFP rather than to capital and labor inputs (Hall and Jones, 1999; Caselli, 2005).

Table 4.2 VARIANCE DECOMPOSITION OF CROSS-COUNTRY
DIFFERENCES IN OUTPUT PER WORKER, 2010

	Var(log(y))	Var(log($\bar{\text{h}}$))	Contribution of human capital	
			Share H1	*Share H2*
Average year of schooling(S)	1.396	0.158	11.3%	20.2%
Human capital per worker (h)	1.396	0.078	5.6%	13.5%

NOTES: Contribution of human capital is constructed by the share of human capital dispersion in explaining the variance of log GDP per worker (y). Share *H1* uses variance of human capital as a measure of human capital dispersion, whereas Share *H2* adds half of covariance terms of human capital with physical capital per worker and TFP (see (4.4) in the text). See Table 4.1 for the explanation of human capital measures.

4.3 GROWTH ACCOUNTING

This section appraises the contribution of education to output growth based on the conventional Solow-type growth accounting. The basic assumption of this approach is that an increase in educated workers raises output through the improvement of labor productivity, which is recognized by a higher earnings stream during their working lives. Using cross-country data, we can assess the contribution of education or human capital to differences in growth rates of per-worker output across economies.

Following the pioneering work of Solow (1957), the growth accounting method has long been used to break down the growth rate of aggregate output into contributions from the growth of productive inputs.

Let us assume a standard production function such as

$$Y = F(K, H, A), \tag{4.10}$$

Table 4.3 ACCOUNTING FOR CROSS-COUNTRY DIFFERENCES
IN OUTPUT PER WORKER, 2010

	90th-to-10th percentile ratio		Contribution of human capital
	Output per worker	**Human capital**	
Average year of schooling (S)	24.69	2.60	10.5%
Human capital per worker (h)	24.69	2.17	8.8%

NOTES: Contribution of human capital is measured by the 90th-to-10th percentile ratio of human capital divided by the corresponding ratio of GDP per worker. See Table 4.1 for the explanation of human capital measures.

where Y is the output (real GDP), K is the stock of physical capital, H is the labor input, and A denotes the level of technology or TFP.[11] Here, H is a concept of the overall labor input that incorporates the quality of the labor force, such as an increase in educational attainment.

The growth accounting method, decomposing the growth in output Y into each of the three productive inputs $(K, H, \text{and } A)$ can be applied to this production function (see Barro and Sala-i-Martin, 2004, Chapter 10).

$$\frac{dY}{Y} = \frac{F_K \cdot K}{Y} \cdot \frac{dK}{K} + \frac{F_H \cdot H}{Y} \cdot \frac{dH}{H} + \frac{dA}{A}, \qquad (4.11)$$

where dY/Y, dK/K, dH/H and dA/A represent the percentage rate of change of the variable Y, K, H, and A, and F_K and F_H are the marginal products of capital and labor, respectively. We generally do not measure dA/A directly, but it can be calculated as the residual. The term "TFP growth" is interpreted as a measure of technological progress.

When the marginal products can be measured by factor prices, we can rewrite (4.11) using the labor share V_H and the capital share V_K :[12]

$$\frac{dY}{Y} = V_K \cdot \frac{dK}{K} + V_H \cdot \frac{dH}{H} + \frac{dA}{A}. \qquad (4.12)$$

In practice, growth accounting is applied to data between two points in time, $T\text{-}1$ and T, using logarithmic differences.[13]

$$\ln\left[\frac{Y(T)}{Y(T-1)}\right] = \overline{v_K}\ln\left[\frac{K(T)}{K(T-1)}\right] + \overline{v_H}\ln\left[\frac{H(T)}{H(T-1)}\right] + d\ln TFP, \qquad (4.13)$$

where $\overline{v_i} = [v_i(T) + v_i(T-1)]/2$.

If the production function exhibits constant returns to scale in K and H, all the income associated with the real output Y is attributed to capital and labor. That is, $V_K + V_H = 1$. In this case, (4.13) simplifies to

$$\ln\left[\frac{Y(T)}{Y(T-1)}\right] = (1 - \overline{v_H})\ln\left[\frac{K(T)}{K(T-1)}\right] + \overline{v_H}\ln\left[\frac{H(T)}{H(T-1)}\right] + d\ln TFP. \qquad (4.14)$$

The aggregate index of labor quality is defined as $h = H/L$, where L denotes total work hours (or number of workers).

We can then write the growth accounting in per-worker terms, such that

$$\ln\left[\frac{y_{(T)}}{y_{(T-1)}}\right] = (1 - \overline{v_H})\ln\left[\frac{k_{(T)}}{k_{(T-1)}}\right] + \overline{v_H}\ln\left[\frac{h_{(T)}}{h_{(T-1)}}\right] + d\ln TFP, \qquad (4.15)$$

where $y \equiv Y/L$ and $k \equiv K/L$.

Following (4.15), the growth in output per worker is decomposed into three components. The first is the growth in physical capital per worker and reflects capital deepening. The second is the growth in human capital per worker and measures changes in labor quality, such as an increase in average years of schooling for the labor force. The third is the TFP growth. By decomposing the growth in per-worker output into these inputs, the growth accounting procedure gives a measure of human capital's contribution to per-worker output growth.

In this approach, the overall labor input is an aggregate of all labor inputs from different categories classified by schooling, gender, experience, and so on. The inputs are weighted by the relative productivity.

Our cross-country data set allows the classification of labor inputs only by educational attainment. Hence, we construct an aggregate labor input measure by combining the classified labor inputs into seven educational categories.

The growth rate of aggregate labor input is expressed as the share-weighted aggregate of the components (see Jorgenson et al. 2000).

$$\Delta lnH = \sum_l \overline{v}_l \Delta lnL_l, \, l = u, \, pi, \, pc, \, si, \, sc, \, hi, \, hc, \qquad (4.16)$$

where $\Delta lnL = \ln L(T) - lnL(T-1)$, and $\overline{v}_l = \frac{1}{2}\{v_l(T) - v_l(T-1)\}$. The weights are the shares of labor income attributed to each labor input that has attained education of level l:

$$v_l = \frac{W_l \times L_l}{\sum_l W_l \times L_l}, \qquad (4.17)$$

where L_l indicates the quantity of the labor input (such as the number of workers) in category l, and W_l, its wage rate. Thus, (4.16) and (4.17) reflect substitution among heterogeneous types of labor in different categories with different marginal products.

The growth of aggregate labor quality (human capital per worker) is defined as

$$\Delta lnh = \Delta lnH - \Delta lnL = \sum_l \overline{v}_l \Delta ln(L_l / L). \qquad (4.18)$$

From (4.18), we see that the growth in labor quality is defined as the difference between the weighted and unweighted growth of workers, while the weights are the shares of labor incomes.[14] For a given total of work hours, the labor quality improves when employment of more productive and the number of higher-wage workers increases, substituting for less-productive and lower-wage workers, respectively.[15] The quality of labor input must improve with the increase in average years of schooling of workers.

We apply the growth accounting approach to decompose the output per-worker growth rates for a broad number of countries in the period 1961–2010. We collect data on GDP and physical capital stock from the PWT 8.0. Labor shares, which vary across countries and over time, are also available from the PWT 8.0.

The working-age population, sourced from United Nations data, is used as a measure of the size of workers. The available cross-country sources of labor force or employees are less reliable than those of the working-age population. We do not have data on the number of work hours for most countries.

The constructions of the overall labor input and labor quality growth rates in (4.16) and (4.18), respectively, require data on labor income shares of all labor inputs. We do not have detailed data on wage rates for constructing the labor income shares of individual countries, but international data on the education-wage profiles derived from the Mincerian equation are available (Psacharopoulous, 1994). We assume that the wage rates of workers are determined by their years of schooling and that the marginal rate of return on an additional school year is constant at 10%, the world average of return rates (Psacharopoulous, 1994).[16] Then, we can construct the relative income shares of all labor inputs. Therefore, the human capital measure for growth accounting is equal to the Mincerian-type human capital per worker in (4.8).

For the analysis of growth accounting, we assemble data for 83 countries having complete data. It is a well-known fact that growth rates vary significantly across economies. Figure 4.5 depicts the large variations in the observed growth rates of per-worker GDP in the period 1960–2010. There are the well-known "growth miracles"—the best-performing economies, most of which are located in East Asia and Southeast Asia, include China, Republic of Korea, Taiwan, Thailand, Singapore, and Hong Kong. On the other hand, there are "growth disasters," denoted by the worst-performing countries. They include a number of nations in Sub-Saharan Africa, such as Niger, the Central African Republic, Senegal, and Zimbabwe, all of which showed negative growth in per-worker GDP over the past half century.

Nevertheless, for the whole sample of 83 countries, the growth performance of individual countries has not been strongly persistent over time. Table 4.4 shows that the correlations of growth rates across decades are weak, ranging from 0.59 to –0.17, in our sample. Thus, past performance is not a useful indicator of future growth. Interestingly, the bilateral correlations of growth rates over two consecutive decades have decreased in the sample of advanced countries and increased in the sample of developing countries.

Table 4.5 reports the results of the growth accounting decomposition for each of the five decades in the period 1961–2010 for 83 countries that have complete data. For the illustration, we compute the weighted averages for the world and subgroups/regions using each country's share in the world current-price real GDP (CGDP) sourced from the PWT 8.0. We also report the average of the estimates over the overall period of 1961–2010.

According to Table 4.5, the average annual per-worker GDP growth rates for the 83 countries, weighted by each country's population size, for the overall period was 2.6%. The growth rate was 3.6% in the 1960s, and since then, it has fallen to about 2.3–2.5%.

The average per-worker GDP growth rate over 1960–2010 was 2.2% for the sample of 24 advanced countries and 3.3% for the sample of 59 developing countries. In the advanced countries, the average per-worker GDP growth rates dropped from about 4.0% in the 1960s to about 2.0% in the 1970s, 1980s, and 1990s and then dropped further, to about 0.8% in the 2000s. The significant decline in per-worker GDP growth rate in the 2000s reflects the impacts of the global financial crisis that has hit the advanced economies more severely since 2008. In contrast, for developing countries, the average per-worker GDP growth rates accelerated from 2.5% in the 1960s, 1970s, and 1980s to 3.8% in the 1990s, rising further

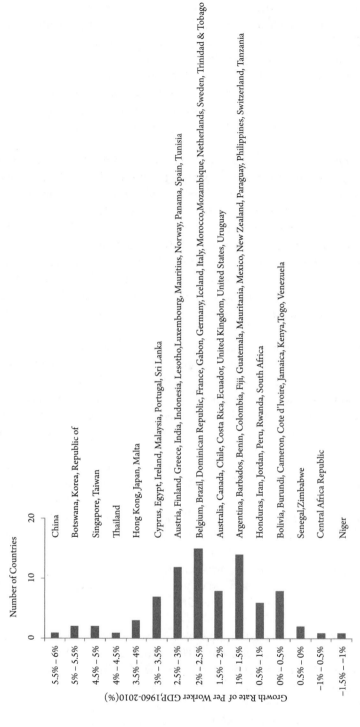

Figure 4.5 Distribution of Growth Rates of per-Worker GDP, 1960–2010

Table 4.4 CORRELATIONS OF PER-WORKER GDP GROWTH
RATES ACROSS DECADES

(A) World (83)

	1961–1970	1971–1980	1981–1990	1991–2000	2001–2010
1961–1970	—				
1971–1980	0.220	—			
1981–1990	0.277	0.470	—		
1991–2000	0.134	0.346	0.588	—	
2001–2010	−0.173	0.178	0.171	0.500	—

(B) Advanced Economies (24)

	1961–1970	1971–1980	1981–1990	1991–2000	2001–2010
1961–1970	—				
1971–1980	0.543	—			
1981–1990	0.141	0.023	—		
1991–2000	−0.191	0.039	0.268	—	
2001–2010	0.144	−0.093	−0.105	−0.152	—

(C) Developing Economies (59)

	1961–1970	1971–1980	1981–1990	1991–2000	2001–2010
1961–1970	—				
1971–1980	0.195	—			
1981–1990	0.252	0.516	—		
1991–2000	0.136	0.382	0.588	—	
2001–2010	−0.137	0.193	0.275	0.635	—

NOTES: Data are sourced from the PWT 8.0. The number of observations is in parentheses.

to 4.9% in the 2000s. This reflects strong growth in recent decades in developing countries, especially large-GDP economies such as China and India. Table 4.5 shows the rise in per-worker GDP growth rates during the recent decades in the Asia-Pacific region.

The results of growth accounting show that about 71% of the world's per-worker GDP growth during 1961–2010 can be explained by increases in factor inputs, including physical capital per worker and human capital, measured by average educational attainment per worker, while the remaining 29% of output growth can be attributed to TFP growth. The annual growth rate in TFP was about 0.8% for the 83 countries over the period 1961–2010. The TFP growth rate was highest for the Asia-Pacific region (1.4% per year), contributing to 32% of per-worker GDP growth. In contrast, the TFP growth rates were low, and at times even negative, for Sub-Saharan Africa (−0.2%) and Middle East and North Africa (−0.8%).

Physical capital per worker contributed to about 49% of per-worker GDP growth for the 83 countries. The contribution of physical capital per worker was higher in developing countries (55.0%) than in advanced countries (45.4%). This difference

Table 4.5 GROWTH ACCOUNTING FOR GDP PER WORKER, 1960–2010

Region (no. of countries)	Growth Rate of per-worker GDP	Labor Income Share	Contribution from		TFP Growth Rate
			Physical Capital	Human Capital	
World (83)					
1961–70	0.0363	0.63	0.0136 (37.4%)	0.0066 (18.2%)	0.0161 (44.4%)
1971–80	0.0233	0.62	0.0138 (59.3%)	0.007 (30%)	0.0025 (10.7%)
1981–90	0.0228	0.60	0.0097 (42.5%)	0.0057 (25.2%)	0.0074 (32.3%)
1991–00	0.0252	0.58	0.0124 (49.3%)	0.0062 (24.6%)	0.0066 (26.2%)
2001–10	0.0243	0.54	0.0154 (63.2%)	0.0038 (15.7%)	0.0051 (21.1%)
1960–2010	0.0264	0.59	0.013 (49.2%)	0.0059 (22.2%)	0.0075 (28.6%)
Advanced (24)					
1961–70	0.0400	0.66	0.0146 (36.5%)	0.0069 (17.1%)	0.0186 (46.4%)
1971–80	0.0217	0.65	0.0122 (56.3%)	0.0071 (32.7%)	0.0024 (10.9%)
1981–90	0.0217	0.63	0.0085 (39.4%)	0.0054 (24.7%)	0.0078 (35.9%)
1991–00	0.0190	0.62	0.0084 (44.3%)	0.005 (26.2%)	0.0056 (29.5%)
2001–10	0.0079	0.60	0.0064 (80%)	0.0037 (46.2%)	-0.0021 (-26.2%)
1960–2010	0.0221	0.63	0.01 (45.4%)	0.0056 (25.3%)	0.0065 (29.2%)
Developing (59)					
1961–70	0.0251	0.55	0.0105 (41.7%)	0.0058 (23%)	0.0089 (35.3%)
1971–80	0.0278	0.54	0.0183 (65.7%)	0.0067 (24%)	0.0029 (10.3%)
1981–90	0.0256	0.53	0.0125 (49.1%)	0.0067 (26.1%)	0.0063 (24.8%)
1991–00	0.0382	0.50	0.0208 (54.5%)	0.0087 (22.9%)	0.0087 (22.7%)
2001–10	0.0488	0.45	0.0289 (59.2%)	0.004 (8.3%)	0.0159 (32.6%)
1960–2010	0.0331	0.51	0.0182 (55%)	0.0064 (19.3%)	0.0085 (25.7%)

Asia and the Pacific (12)

1961–70	0.0208	0.60	0.0083 (40.1%)	0.0064 (30.7%)	0.0061 (29.2%)
1971–80	0.0297	0.58	0.0181 (61.1%)	0.0074 (25%)	0.0041 (13.9%)
1981–90	0.0481	0.55	0.019 (39.6%)	0.0064 (13.2%)	0.0227 (47.1%)
1991–00	0.0559	0.51	0.0305 (54.5%)	0.0105 (18.7%)	0.015 (26.8%)
2001–10	0.0631	0.45	0.0373 (59.2%)	0.0038 (6%)	0.022 (34.8%)
1960–2010	0.0435	0.54	0.0227 (52.1%)	0.0069 (15.8%)	0.014 (32.1%)

Latin America and the Caribbean (19)

1961–70	0.0321	0.49	0.011 (34.2%)	0.0054 (16.7%)	0.0157 (49.1%)
1971–80	0.0305	0.48	0.0171 (56.2%)	0.0058 (19%)	0.0076 (24.9%)
1981–90	−0.0113	0.48	0.0028 (24.4%)	0.007 (61.7%)	−0.0211 (−186%)
1991–00	0.0092	0.47	0.0053 (57.8%)	0.0058 (63.8%)	−0.002 (−21.6%)
2001–10	0.0160	0.45	0.0085 (53.4%)	0.0043 (27%)	0.0031 (19.6%)
1960–2010	0.0153	0.47	0.0089 (58.5%)	0.0057 (37%)	0.0007 (4.5%)

Middle East and North Africa (8)

1961–70	0.0294	0.40	0.0321 (109.1%)	0.0056 (19%)	−0.0083 (−28%)
1971–80	0.0146	0.42	0.0353 (241.6%)	0.0074 (50.7%)	−0.0281 (−192.3%)
1981–90	0.0115	0.43	0.0092 (80.2%)	0.0066 (57.6%)	−0.0043 (−37.8%)
1991–00	0.0141	0.43	0.0064 (45.8%)	0.0061 (43.1%)	0.0016 (11.1%)
2001–10	0.0230	0.36	0.0166 (72.1%)	0.0046 (20%)	0.0018 (7.9%)
1960–2010	0.0185	0.41	0.0199 (107.6%)	0.0061 (32.7%)	−0.0075 (−40.3%)

continued

141

Table 4.5 (CONTINUED)

Region (no. of countries)	Growth Rate of per-worker GDP	Labor Income Share	Contribution from Physical Capital	Contribution from Human Capital	TFP Growth Rate
Sub-Saharan Africa (20)					
1961–70	0.0261	0.60	0.0052 (20.1%)	0.0028 (10.6%)	0.0181 (69.4%)
1971–80	0.0092	0.57	0.0099 (107.1%)	0.0043 (46.8%)	−0.005 (−53.9%)
1981–90	−0.0082	0.58	−0.0028 (−34%)	0.0086 (104.5%)	−0.0141 (−170.5%)
1991–00	−0.0084	0.55	−0.0049 (−57.6%)	0.0052 (61.4%)	−0.0088 (−103.8%)
2001–10	0.0139	0.51	0.0082 (59%)	0.0067 (48%)	−0.001 (−6.9%)
1960–2010	0.0065	0.56	0.0031 (48.2%)	0.0055 (84.7%)	−0.0021 (−32.8%)

NOTES: Data are sourced from the PWT 8.0 and the new Barro-Lee human capital data (www.barro-lee.com). GDP growth is an average annual GDP growth rate over the period, weighted by country share in current price real GDP. The contribution of inputs (physical capital per labor and human capital) is the rate of growth multiplied by the average income share.

is attributed not only to the relatively higher rates of capital accumulation, but also to the higher capital income shares in developing countries than in advanced countries.

The growth accounting results show that the contribution of human capital to economic growth is sizable in the world economy. The annual growth rate of human capital (labor quality) is estimated, on average, to have been about 0.6% from 1961 to 2010 for the 83 countries. The share of overall per-worker growth explained by human capital is about 22%. The share is slightly larger in the group of advanced countries (about 25%) compared to that in the group of developing countries (about 19%). The contributions of human capital to economic growth are much larger in Sub-Saharan Africa and the Middle East and North Africa, where TFP growth rates contribute negatively to output growth.

The growth accounting exercise implies that human capital is a significant factor in economic growth, but its contribution to per-worker GDP growth is smaller than that of physical capital per worker or TFP growth.[17] This result, however, does not necessarily indicate that human capital is less important than other factors. Because the growth accounting method provides only a mechanical decomposition of growth in output into a variety of inputs and TFP, it does not explain where the growth in inputs and TFP come from. The growth accounting approach ignores the contribution of human capital to the growths in other inputs and in technological progress.

Because the marginal productivity of physical capital increases with the abundance of factors complementary to physical capital, human capital can promote the accumulation of physical capital. Benhabib and Spigel (1994) showed that the level of initial human capital stock is positively correlated with subsequent accumulation of the physical capital in cross-country data.

In addition to the stimulating effect of human capital on physical capital accumulation, human capital also has a positive effect on technological progress. TFP growth may be an outcome of the efforts and capability of technological improvements in the economy. Since the capability of technological improvements hinges on the human capital stock present in the economy, human capital also significantly affects TFP growth.

However, growth accounting also ignores the interactions of technology and physical capital accumulation with human capital growth. The endogenous growth model with two types of capital predicts that human capital changes in response to the imbalance between physical capital and human capital stocks. Skill-biased technological change can raise the relative demand for skilled workers and skill premium, thus promoting human capital investment. The influences of physical capital and technology changes on human capital growth can have the opposite effect of exaggerating the true contribution of human capital to output growth.

In the Solow-type neoclassical growth model, in which investment rates for physical capital and human capital accumulations, population growth, and TFP growth rates are exogenously given, growth accounting can provide a more accurate decomposition of growth in output into the contributions of productive inputs and TFP growth rates. However, if there are interactions among human capital, physical capital, and TFP, growth accounting provides misleading information about the sources of economic growth.

In conclusion, growth accounting as well as development accounting show that human capital plays an important role, though not a major one, in explaining the cross-country differences in both the levels and growth rates of per-worker output. However, these approaches do not necessarily indicate that there is a causal relation between human capital and output. In the next section, we adopt another approach, based on regressions, to investigate the impact of human capital on output growth.

4.4 CROSS-COUNTRY GROWTH REGRESSIONS

In this section, our analysis is based on a general framework of cross-country regressions that relate education to economic growth (Barro, 1991; Barro and Lee, 1994; Barro and Sala-i-Martin, 2004). After controlling other important explanatory variables, the framework allows us to investigate the independent role of educational attainment, measured by overall years of schooling, in economic growth. We consider not only the role of average educational attainment of the overall population, but also that disaggregated by gender.[18]

Empirical specification

The basic empirical framework, derived from the extended neoclassical growth model, as described by Barro and Sala-i-Martin (2004), is expressed as

$$Dy_{it} = f(y_{it}, y_i^*), \qquad (4.19)$$

where Dy_{it} is country i's per-worker GDP growth rate in period t, y_{it} is country i's per-worker output, and y_i^* is its own long-run (or steady-state) level of y. Dy_{it} is inversely related to y and positively related to y^*.

The inverse relation between Dy and y indicates "conditional convergence" of per-worker output: a country with a lower initial per-worker output relative to its own long-run (or steady-state) level of per-worker output grows faster than a country with higher per-worker output over time. In the cross-country context, convergence implies that relatively poorer countries would grow faster than richer countries, when controlling for the variables influencing the steady-state level of per-worker output.

For the given values of other explanatory variables, a lower level of initial real per-worker output reflects a smaller stock of initial physical capital per worker, which implies a higher level of physical capital productivity because of diminishing returns. Subsequently, it causes faster physical capital accumulation and output growth.

The value of y_i^* depends on a wide variety of external environmental variables. In the extended Solow-type neoclassical growth model, the steady-state level of per-worker output is determined by investment rate, population growth, and human capital (Mankiw, Romer, and Weil, 1992). We include investment, fertility, and human capital as fundamental growth factors. The stock of human capital is measured by the average years of schooling for the population aged 15 and over. The regression also includes the reciprocal of life expectancy at birth as a measure of health of workers in an economy.

Previous empirical research has also considered institutions and policy factors as important determinants of long-run per-worker output (Lee, 1993; Knack and Keefer, 1996; Barro, 1997). We include five variables to control for institution and policy variables: government consumption, overall maintenance of the rule of law in the economy, inflation rate, trade openness, and democracy. The regression also covers a measure for terms of trade changes as an exogenous factor.

In a reduced form, the model can be represented by

$$\mathrm{D}y_{it} = \beta_0 + \beta_1 \log\left(y_{i,t}\right) + \beta_2 h_{i,t} + \beta_3 X_{i,t} + \varepsilon_{i,t}. \tag{4.20}$$

Our regression of (4.20) applies to a panel set of cross-country data for 76 countries over ten five-year periods from 1960 to 2010, corresponding to the periods 1960–1965, 1965–1970, 1970–1975, 1975–1980, 1980–1985, 1985–1990, 1990–1995, 1995–2000, 2000–2005, and 2005–2010.[19] Some previous studies used cross-section data in which each country had only one observation. The approach using the panel data set involving country i and time period t seems to consider more information that is available from time series variations within each country. The dependent variables are the annual growth rates of real per-worker GDP over each five-year period. The regressions include period dummies to control for common shocks to (common trends in) per-worker GDP growth in all countries.

GDP data are sourced from the PWT 8.0 (2005 international dollars). Data on population structure by age, sourced from the United Nations, are used to construct per-worker real GDP. Data on the ratio to GDP of investment (private plus public), government consumption-to-GDP ratio, and openness ratio (exports plus imports relative to GDP) are sourced from the PWT 8.0. These ratio variables use current price information.

Data for life expectancy at birth and total fertility rate are sourced from the World Bank's *World Development Indicators* (WDI; 2013). Data about the law-and-order indicators (converted from seven categories to a 0–1 scale, with 1 representing the highest maintenance of law and order) are sourced from Political Risk Services' *International Country Risk Guide*.[20]

Average years of school attainment for overall population, females, and males, are sourced from our updated data set (www.barrolee.com).

Data on terms-of-trade change (growth rates over five years of export prices relative to import prices) are sourced from the International Monetary Fund's *International Financial Statistics* (IFS; Various years) and the World Bank's *WDI* (2013). This variable is interacted with openness ratio.

Inflation rate (averaged over five-year intervals) is calculated from retail price indexes from the International Monetary Fund's *International Financial Statistics* and the World Bank's *WDI*.

The measure of democracy is the Freedom House Political Rights Index (converted from seven categories to a 0–1 scale, with higher values representing the increasing presence of political rights) since 1970. It is supplemented by the related variable from Bollen (1980) for 1960 and 1965.

One concern in the empirical specification is that any effect of contemporaneous explanatory variables may reflect reverse causation from GDP growth to the explanatory variables. For example, the relationship between contemporaneous investment and growth could be interpreted as high growth causing high saving. This problem, however, can be solved by adopting the instrumental variables (IV) estimation technique. We estimate this system of ten equations by three-stage least squares. The instrumental variables technique controls for the possible simultaneity problem when X_i^s (the control variables) are endogenously determined. Instruments are mostly lagged values of the independent variables.[21] Data for lagged per-worker GDP are for 1960, 1965, . . . , 2005. Values for 1959, 1964, . . . , 2004 are used as instruments. Other regressors are averages over periods, with lagged values as instruments.

Some studies suggest estimating panel growth regressions by the fixed-effects estimation technique, considering unobserved and persistent country characteristics that influence economic growth and are also correlated with the explanatory variables. The exclusion of country fixed effects can cause biases on the estimated effects of explanatory variables on real per-worker GDP growth. However, the fixed-effects technique eliminates information from cross-section variations and does not allow estimation of the effects of variables that have little within-country time variation (Barro, 2012). It can also exacerbate measurement errors, especially if the timings of relationships are not precisely known. For the discussion below, we use the results from the IV panel estimation both with and without country fixed effects. The regression results would be most convincing if they are similar notwithstanding the inclusion of country fixed effects.

Regression results

Table 4.6 presents the regression results using the basic framework of (4.20) and the explanatory variables just described. The three-stage least-squares technique is applied to the panel data set for 76 countries.

Column 1 of Table 4.6 presents the results of the regression without country fixed effects. The first explanatory variable, the log of per-capita GDP at the start of each period, confirms the conditional convergence effect: the estimated coefficient is statistically significant at the 1% level (−0.0163, s.e. = 0.0021). The estimated speed of conditional convergence is about 1.6% per year.

The estimated coefficient on the reciprocal of life expectancy at birth (−2.04, s.e. = 0.60) is highly significant, indicating that better health is associated with higher economic growth.

The log of the total fertility rate is significantly negative (−0.026, s.e. = 0.005). The choice to have more children per adult results in a higher rate of population growth, and thereby, a lower rate of growth in output per worker.

Many government policies and institutions enter with the expected signs and statistical significances. A measure of the extent of maintenance of the rule of law

Table 4.6 Regressions for Growth Rates of GDP per
Working-age Population

	(1)	(2)	(3)	(4)
		Fixed effects		Fixed effects
Log (lagged per worker GDP)	−0.0163*** (0.00211)	−0.0338*** (0.00364)	−0.0172*** (0.00218)	−0.0359*** (0.00377)
1/ (life expectancy at birth)	−2.037*** (0.601)	−0.696 (0.897)	−2.735*** (0.684)	−1.695* (1.004)
Log (fertility rate)	−0.0261*** (0.00462)	−0.0221*** (0.00641)	−0.0253*** (0.00464)	−0.0220*** (0.00638)
Law & order (rule of law)	0.0153** (0.00599)	0.00738 (0.00826)	0.0156*** (0.00602)	0.00866 (0.00824)
Investment ratio	0.0354** (0.0161)	0.0426** (0.0203)	0.0398** (0.0164)	0.0508** (0.0208)
Government consumption ratio	0.00660 (0.0136)	0.00658 (0.0163)	0.00531 (0.0137)	0.00412 (0.0163)
Openness ratio	0.00589* (0.00323)	0.0144** (0.00604)	0.00546* (0.00327)	0.0113* (0.00625)
Terms-of-trade change	0.0737*** (0.0268)	0.0630** (0.0267)	0.0771*** (0.0268)	0.0659** (0.0267)
Democracy indicator	0.0542*** (0.0185)	0.0466** (0.0222)	0.0545*** (0.0186)	0.0442** (0.0220)
Democracy squared	−0.0512*** (0.0167)	−0.0402** (0.0200)	−0.0524*** (0.0168)	−0.0391** (0.0198)
Inflation rate	−0.0130 (0.00946)	−0.0250** (0.0127)	−0.0100 (0.00985)	−0.0229* (0.0129)
Total school years	0.000118 (0.000874)	−0.00127 (0.00169)	−0.00315* (0.00190)	−0.00522** (0.00245)
Total school years squared			0.000242* (0.000127)	0.000328** (0.000160)
No. of countries; No. of obs.	76, 722	76, 722	76, 722	76, 722

	(5)	(6)	(7)	(8)
		Fixed effects		Fixed effects
Log (lagged per worker GDP)	−0.0169*** (0.00215)	−0.0351*** (0.00367)	−0.0175*** (0.00221)	−0.0358*** (0.00378)
1/ (life expectancy at birth)	−2.124*** (0.600)	−1.273 (0.927)	−2.929*** (0.687)	−1.982** (1.007)

continued

Table 4.6 (CONTINUED)

	(5)	(6)	(7)	(8)
		Fixed effects		**Fixed effects**
Log (fertility rate)	−0.0256***	−0.0200***	−0.0238***	−0.0180***
	(0.00460)	(0.00644)	(0.00467)	(0.00656)
Law & order (rule of law)	0.0162***	0.00732	0.0161***	0.00570
	(0.00600)	(0.00824)	(0.00603)	(0.00841)
Investment ratio	0.0368**	0.0404**	0.0377**	0.0446**
	(0.0161)	(0.0202)	(0.0165)	(0.0210)
Government consumption ratio	0.00805	0.00870	0.00948	0.0119
	(0.0136)	(0.0163)	(0.0137)	(0.0166)
Openness ratio	0.00562*	0.0126**	0.00507	0.00917
	(0.00321)	(0.00613)	(0.00325)	(0.00633)
Terms-of-trade change	0.0740***	0.0647**	0.0755***	0.0641**
	(0.0268)	(0.0267)	(0.0268)	(0.0267)
Democracy indicator	0.0515***	0.0414*	0.0502***	0.0402*
	(0.0185)	(0.0222)	(0.0186)	(0.0221)
Democracy squared	−0.0499***	−0.0366*	−0.0494***	−0.0362*
	(0.0167)	(0.0200)	(0.0168)	(0.0199)
Inflation rate	−0.0135	−0.0258**	−0.0109	−0.0247*
	(0.00941)	(0.0127)	(0.00984)	(0.0129)
Female school years	0.00247	0.00528*	0.00541*	0.00857*
	(0.00157)	(0.00290)	(0.00327)	(0.00451)
Male school years	−0.00246	−0.00660**	−0.0102**	−0.0152***
	(0.00162)	(0.00300)	(0.00410)	(0.00516)
Female school years squared			−0.000342	−0.000477
			(0.000272)	(0.000325)
Male school years squared			0.000657**	0.000841**
			(0.000324)	(0.000392)
No. of countries; No. of obs.	*76, 72*	*76, 722*	*76, 722*	*76, 722*

NOTES: The panel specification uses pooled data for ten five-year periods from 1960 to 2010 (1960–1965, 1965–70, . . . , and 2005–2010) for 76 economies (see Appendix Table). Data for lagged per-worker GDP is for the initial year of each of the five-year periods (1960, 1965, . . . , and 2005). Values for 1959, 1964, . . . , and 2004 are used as instruments. Other regressors are averages over periods, with lagged values used as instruments. Period dummies are included. Standard errors are in parentheses. Asterisks denote the following significance levels: * p < 0.1, ** p < 0.05, and *** p < 0.01.

(an indicator of property-rights enforcement) is significantly positive (0.0153, s.e. = 0.006), indicating that countries with more effective law enforcement for the protection of property and contractual rights tend to have higher growth rates.

Increased openness to international trade is a positive determinant for growth, although the estimated coefficient (0.0059, s.e. = 0.0032) is marginally significant.

The ratio of government consumption to GDP enters positively, though it is statistically insignificant. This result comes partly from the new concept of government consumption in the PWT 8.0, which now includes individual education and health consumption expenditure funded by the government (Feenstra, Inklaar, and Timmer, 2013). Our conjecture is a negative effect of the net government consumption, excluding the components of education and health on growth.[22]

Higher inflation, an indicator of macroeconomic instability, has a negative effect on economic growth, but the estimated coefficient is not statistically significant (−0.0130, s.e. = 0.0095).

Like Barro (1999, 2012), the regression results confirm the nonlinear relationship between democracy and growth. The coefficients on the indicator of democracy and its square terms are positive and negative, respectively, and are statistically significant. A pattern of the coefficients demonstrates that the growth rate increases with political freedom at low levels of democracy but decreases with democracy once the society attains a certain level of political freedom. The break point between marginal effects being positive or negative occurs at a polity indicator of about 5.3.

A higher growth rate of the terms of trade (export prices relative to import prices) also has an expansionary effect on growth, as proved by the highly significant estimated coefficient (0.074, s.e. = 0.027).

Many of the variables discussed earlier also affect an economy's propensity to invest in physical capital accumulation. However, given the other explanatory variables, a higher ratio of real investment to real GDP still has a significantly positive effect on growth, as indicated by the coefficient (0.035, s.e. = 0.016).

Our main interest lies in the role of human capital, proxied by educational attainment of the working-age population, in economic growth. The estimated coefficient on the overall years of schooling (0.0002, s.e. = 0.0009) is positive but statistically insignificant, Thus, the result confirms the finding of weak or insignificant effect of overall educational attainment on output growth in the previous empirical literature based on cross-country data (Pritchett, 2001; Barro, 2012).

Column 2 of Table 4.6 adds country fixed effects. The results are quite similar to those of column 1. The estimated convergence coefficient enlarges and remains statistically significant (0.0338, s.e. = 0.0036). The estimated speed of conditional convergence is about 3.4% per year, significantly higher than 1.6% in column 1. With country fixed effects, the unobserved and omitted variables, positively related to the steady-state value of per-worker output, are likely to have a positive relation with current per-worker GDP. Therefore, the omitted variables tend to bias upward the estimated effect of lagged per-worker GDP on growth. Consequently, the inclusion of country fixed effects tends to lower the convergence rate below zero.

Column 2 also shows positive effects of life expectancy and the rule of law on economic growth. But their estimated coefficients are statistically insignificant.

The result also confirms the insignificant effect of human capital on economic growth. The estimated coefficient on the overall level of human capital is not statistically significant (-0.0013, s.e. $= 0.0017$).

Column 3 of Table 4.6 adds the square term of the overall school attainment variable to the specifications of columns 1 and 2. The coefficients on the school attainment variable and its square terms are negative and positive, respectively, and marginally statistically significant. Both of them are jointly statistically insignificant (p-value $= 0.161$).

In Column 4, with country fixed effects, the coefficients of the overall school attainments are -0.0052 (s.e. $= 0.0025$) for the linear term and 0.00033 (s.e. $= 0.00016$) for the squared term. They are significantly different from zero at the 5% level. Both the coefficients are jointly significant, though marginally, at the 10% level (p-value $= 0.079$). This coefficient configuration points to an initial fall and a subsequent increase in per-worker GDP growth with improving educational attainment. The implied breakpoint is at an average years of schooling of 8.0; hence, only the countries that have accumulated human capital above a certain threshold are able to experience a higher GDP growth induced by an increase in educational attainment for given values of the other explanatory variables. The fraction of countries included in the regressions in this range was about 34% of all observations in the sample. The fraction was much larger for the observations in 2010 (64%). Hence, the positive effects of educational attainment have become more important in recent periods for most countries in the sample. Therefore, the typical pattern in recent years indicates that the higher the education level, the higher the economic growth.

The threshold level of 8.0 years indicates that educational attainment at the secondary and tertiary levels, compared to that at the primary level, would most likely contribute positively to economic growth. According to the previous literature (Barro and Lee, 1994; Barro and Sala-i-Martin, 2004), only upper levels of schooling matter for economic growth. This effect could indicate that a workforce educated at secondary and tertiary schools facilitates technology absorption.

A higher level of educational attainment also signifies a higher ratio of human capital stock to physical capital stock. This higher ratio can stimulate physical capital accumulation and output growth. Conversely, for lower ranges of average years of schooling, the ratio can be lower than its steady-state value. It slows down physical capital accumulation and per-worker GDP growth. In addition, a higher ratio of human capital stock to physical capital stock can be closely related to higher female education relative to male education. The following paragraphs discuss the positive effect of a higher female education stock on economic growth.

Columns 5 and 6 in Table 4.6 include both female and male educational attainment, measured by overall years of schooling for female and male populations, respectively. Female attainment enters positively, and male attainment enters negatively. In column 5, which excludes country fixed effects, the estimated coefficients are not individually and jointly statistically significant. On the contrary, in column 6, which includes country fixed effects, the estimated coefficient for female education (0.0053, s.e. $= 0.0029$) is marginally statistically significant at the 10% significance level, and that for male education (-0.0066, s.e. $= 0.0030$) is significant at the 5% level; they are marginally statistically significant jointly at the 10% significance level (the p-value of joint significance is 0.088). Thus, an increase in male school attainment, with values of female educational attainment and other explanatory variables remaining constant, has a negative effect on economic growth, whereas an increase in female educational attainment, for a given value of male attainment, has a positive effect.

The point estimates on the human capital variable imply that a one-year rise in the average years of female schooling, for given values of male schooling and other variables, increases annual growth rate of per-worker GDP by about 0.53 percentage points. The pattern of coefficients implies that higher female school attainment (relative to male school attainment) enhances the long-run level of per-worker output, leading to higher output growth. It hints that a reduction in the gap between male and female school attainment improves economic and social environments more favorably for economic growth (Barro, 2012).

Columns 7 and 8 of Table 4.6 add the square terms of female and male school attainment without and with country fixed effects, respectively. In column 8, with country fixed effects, the estimated coefficients on male years of schooling and its square terms show the same patterns as those on total population. The linear term is negative (0.0152, s.e. = 0.0052), and the square term (0.0008, s.e. = 0.0039) is positive, and they are individually and jointly statistically significant. Therefore, male educational attainment, for a given value of female attainment, decreases output growth rate initially but increases it later. The implied breakpoint is at an average years of schooling of 9.1. The fraction of country-year observations included in the regressions that were above this break point is about 25%.

The pattern of coefficients for female schooling is opposite to that for male schooling. The estimated coefficients on females' overall years of schooling and its square terms are positive and negative, respectively, while only the linear term is statistically significant at the 10% level. The linear term (0.0086, s.e. = 0.0045) and the squared term (−0.00048, s.e. = 0.00033) mean that female education increases output growth rate initially, until it reaches a breakpoint level at an average years of schooling of 9.0. Thereafter, it decreases. About 77% of country-year observations in the sample belong to the range below the breakpoint. Hence, female education has a positive effect on economic growth across almost the entire range. The negative but insignificant relation between female educational attainment and output growth rate at higher values of average years of female schooling might reflect the relatively low labor-market participation rates of females who have completed upper-secondary or tertiary-level education.

The configuration of the coefficients on female and male schooling implies that the reduction in the gap between male and female school attainment is more important for economic growth when the gender gap in education is larger. But when the overall education level is above the threshold (over 9.0 years), an increase in male attainment relative to female attainment contributes to higher economic growth. Overall, the regressions support the nonlinear effects of schooling on economic growth, in which an increase in overall school years above a critical threshold level (for example, secondary and tertiary school) leads to higher growth. In addition, there is evidence for the positive contribution to long-term economic growth of enhancing school attainment for females relative to males, especially when the gender gap is higher with low female school attainment.

4.5 RELATIONSHIPS BETWEEN EDUCATION AND FERTILITY

We investigate the determinants of fertility by estimating the relationship between fertility rates and economic and social factors identified in the existing literature. We begin with a review of the existing studies on the determination of fertility and investigate the role of education in fertility rates using cross-country regressions.

Determinants of Fertility Rates

Existing theories predict mixed effects of higher income on fertility rates. The "Malthusian theory" implies that rising prosperity increases the number of children that parents and society can afford to raise. Most modern theories of demographic transition and economic growth consider children as "consumer durable goods." Thus, a higher income, other factors remaining the same, tends to increase demand for children.

However, it is costly to raise children. When the relative price of children increases with economic development, there occurs a substitution effect that makes parents reduce the desired number of children. The most crucial cost of raising children is the opportunity cost of parents' time, which is positively related with economic development. If negative substitution effects dominate positive income effects, economic development can be associated with decreasing fertility.[23]

Becker (1960), Becker and Lewis (1973), and Becker and Barro (1988) emphasized a trade-off between the quantity and quality of children. Families face the trade-off between having more children and having fewer but better-educated children. It is argued that "an increase in income should increase both the quantity and quality of children, but the quantity elasticity should be small compared to the quality elasticity" (Becker, 1960, p. 214). This implies that as income rises, the cost of nurturing and educating children becomes more expensive; in turn, the desired quantity of children falls.

The empirical evidence on the relationship between income and fertility is mixed. Most of the cross-country and cross-time evidence suggests that income and family size are negatively correlated. Becker (1960, p. 217) asserted that "indeed, most data tend to show a negative relationship between income and fertility," based on the US census data, where income is represented by father's occupation, mother's education, or monthly rental. The data show that fertility rates have declined sharply in all the regions over the recent period (Figure 4.6).

More recent empirical analyses of fertility have found evidence of a positive relationship between household income and fertility (e.g., Heckman and Walker, 1990; Schultz, 1997). Lindo (2010) found that the large and permanent income shock generated by a husband's job displacement reduces fertility, suggesting a positive causal effect of income on fertility.

The theoretical models imply an inverse relation between women's relative wage rates and fertility. Since women tend to spend more time on child-rearing than men, the rise in the relative wages of women leads to a much higher increase in the

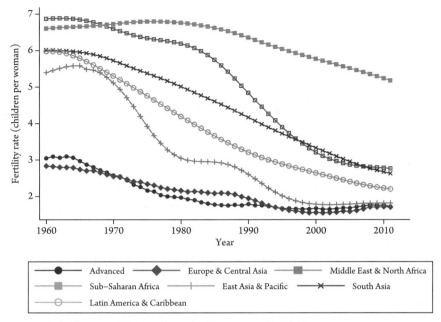

Figure 4.6 Change in Fertility Rates by Regions, 1960–2010
SOURCE: *World Development Indicator* (World Bank, 2013).

opportunity cost of women's time than in average household income (Becker 1960; Weil, 2004). In this context, a rise in women's average education causes a fall in the relative wage gap between women and men; thus, an increase in women's opportunity cost has a negative effect on fertility. An additional effect comes from the fact that educated women are aware of birth control (Barro and Lee, 1994).

Galor and Weil (1996) developed a model in which economic development is associated with a reduction of the comparative advantage of males in production, thus increasing the opportunity cost of child-rearing for females.

The empirical literature supports the strong negative effects of women's education and relative wage on fertility (Schultz, 1985; Ainsworth, Beegle, and Nyamete, 1996; Osili and Long, 2008). But some recent studies have shown that, controlling other factors, highly educated women show increased fertility, especially at older ages (Shang and Weinberg, 2013).

Demographers also emphasize a negative association between mortality and fertility when parents target at an ideal family size. A higher infant mortality rate raises the number of births required to result in a given number of survivors. Kalemli-Ozcan (2002) argued that the quantity-quality trade-off could be empirically observed by considering the uncertainty on the number of surviving children. In fact, as depicted in Figure 4.7, there have been significant reductions in infant mortality rates between 1960 and 2010 in all developing regions.

Similarly, higher life expectancy implies that not only is a smaller number of births required to generate a given number of children surviving to adulthood, but it also makes, for a given infant mortality rate, children more attractive.

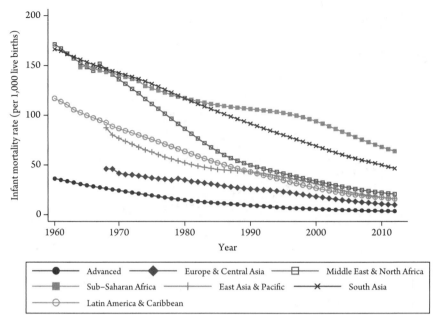

Figure 4.7 Change in Infant Mortality Rates by Region, 1960–2010
SOURCE: *World Development Indicator* (World Bank, 2013).

We have also considered democracy and the rule of law as determinants of fertil-ity. Political and social environments can influence the conditions underlying fertil-ity decisions (Przeworski, 2000). For example, democracy is more likely to support gender equality than is autocracy (Beer, 2009). Increased female labor-market participation and female wage rates in democracies are expected to lower fertility. Democratic and less-corrupt governments are also likely to provide a larger part of the public with resources for and access to family planning.

Empirical Analysis

Our empirical analysis is based on a general framework of cross-country regressions that relate education and other major determinants to fertility. We consider not only overall educational attainment but also male and female educational attain-ment separately.

Table 4.7 presents the regression results in which the dependent variable is the log of total fertility rates at period t, averaged over five-year intervals in the period 1960–2010. The regressions are applied to an unbalanced panel consisting of data from 98 countries over the ten five-year periods from 1960 to 2010. We adopt ran-dom-effects as well as fixed-effects IV estimation techniques to control for unob-served country-specific factors.

The independent variables are log of real per-capita GDP, total years of school attainment, infant mortality rate, life expectancy at birth (as a reciprocal), the

Table 4.7 REGRESSIONS FOR FERTILITY

	(1)	(2)	(3)	(4)
		Fixed effects		Fixed effects
Log (lagged per-capita GDP)	−0.743*** (0.0914)	−0.931*** (0.104)	−0.661*** (0.0944)	−0.816*** (0.111)
Log (lagged per-capita GDP) squared	0.0453*** (0.00553)	0.0573*** (0.00647)	0.0400*** (0.00575)	0.0493*** (0.00705)
Log (infant mortality rate)	0.242*** (0.0259)	0.229*** (0.0285)	0.270*** (0.0270)	0.255*** (0.0297)
1/ (life expectancy at birth)	−3.382 (4.773)	−7.799 (5.474)	−12.33** (5.437)	−14.33** (5.964)
Law & order (rule of law)	−0.208*** (0.0407)	−0.148*** (0.0444)	−0.190*** (0.0408)	−0.141*** (0.0442)
Government consumption ratio	−0.0763 (0.0805)	−0.141* (0.0840)	−0.114 (0.0810)	−0.178** (0.0850)
Democracy indicator	−0.0798*** (0.0288)	−0.0707** (0.0306)	−0.0930*** (0.0290)	−0.0823*** (0.0307)
Total school years, 15–64 aged	−0.0651*** (0.00751)	−0.0675*** (0.00964)	−0.103*** (0.0134)	−0.103*** (0.0153)
Total school years squared, 15–64 aged			0.00315*** (0.000950)	0.00292*** (0.00105)
No. of countries; No. of obs.	*98, 830*	*98, 830*	*98, 830*	*98, 830*

	(5)	(6)	(7)	(8)
		Fixed effects		Fixed effects
Log (lagged per-capita GDP)	−0.711*** (0.0914)	−0.870*** (0.104)	−0.603*** (0.0949)	−0.687*** (0.114)
Log (lagged per-capita GDP) squared	0.0436*** (0.00552)	0.0534*** (0.00645)	0.0364*** (0.00578)	0.0408*** (0.00721)
Log (Infant mortality rate)	0.212*** (0.0271)	0.179*** (0.0308)	0.240*** (0.0275)	0.202*** (0.0308)
1/ (life expectancy at birth)	0.939 (4.914)	0.371 (5.769)	−8.963* (5.417)	−7.664 (6.015)
Law & order (rule of law)	−0.195*** (0.0406)	−0.128*** (0.0441)	−0.156*** (0.0411)	−0.0975** (0.0445)

continued

Table 4.7 (CONTINUED)

	(5)	(6)	(7)	(8)
		Fixed effects		Fixed effects
Government consumption ratio	−0.0989 (0.0802)	−0.174** (0.0835)	−0.172** (0.0811)	−0.260*** (0.0851)
Democracy indicator	−0.0704** (0.0288)	−0.0596** (0.0303)	−0.0865*** (0.0287)	−0.0742** (0.0301)
Female school years, 15–64 aged	−0.0812*** (0.0149)	−0.103*** (0.0180)	−0.156*** (0.0229)	−0.182*** (0.0248)
Male school years, 15–64 aged	0.0145 (0.0146)	0.0322* (0.0172)	0.0618** (0.0287)	0.0727** (0.0302)
Female school years squared, 15–64 aged			0.00593*** (0.00179)	0.00539*** (0.00185)
Male school years squared, 15–64 aged			−0.00294 (0.00225)	−0.00169 (0.00239)
No. of countries; No. of obs.	**98, 830**	**98, 830**	**98, 830**	**98, 830**

NOTES: The dependent variables are log values of total fertility rates, averaged over ten five-year periods from 1960 to 2010 for 98 economies (see Appendix Table). Data for lagged per-worker GDP is for the initial year of each five-year period. Values for 1959, 1964, ..., and 2004 are used as instruments. Other regressors are averages over periods, with lagged values used as instruments. Period dummies are included. Standard errors are in parentheses. Significance levels: * $p < 0.1$, ** $p < 0.05$, and *** $p < 0.01$.

law-and-order indicator, government consumption, and the democracy index. The specification also includes a squared term for a log of real per-capita GDP in order to allow for a nonlinear effect of per-capita income.

Columns 1 and 2 of Table 4.7 present the regression results without and with country fixed effects, respectively. As the results in columns 1 and 2 are very similar, we focus on the results with country fixed effects in column 2.

The results provide strong evidence for nonlinear effects of per-capita income. The coefficients on per-capita GDP and its square terms are negative and positive, respectively, and they are individually and jointly statistically significant (p-value = 0.000). This configuration of coefficients indicates an initial decline and a subsequent rise in fertility with income when other variables are controlled. The linear term of −0.931 (s.e. = 0.104) and the squared term of 0.0573 (s.e. = 0.0065) imply that for low income countries operating in the range below the per-capita GDP breakpoint of $3,399 per year (in 2005 US dollars), an increase in income, with values of the other explanatory variables remaining constant, lowers fertility. The fraction of countries included in the regressions in this range was 39%. For the countries in this group, therefore, the effect of income on fertility is negative, for given values of other variables, including education and infant mortality rates.

The negative relation may reflect the increased value of parental time (for given levels of educational attainment), which results in a substitution of quality of children for quantity with rising incomes. However, it seems the substitution effect dominates only in the low-income countries. The positive income-fertility relationship in higher-income countries indicates that the positive income effect eventually surpasses the negative substitution effect. It may also reflect increasing opportunities of affordable child care and high fertility among increasing immigrants in high-income countries.

The results show positive effects of infant mortality and life expectancy on fertility. The estimated coefficient on infant mortality is positive and statistically significant at 0.229 (s.e. = 0.0285). For the reciprocal of life expectancy, the estimated coefficient (−7.8, s.e. = 5.5) is not statistically significant.

Fertility choice is negatively correlated to the maintenance of law and order and democracy. The estimated coefficients on law and order and democracy, −0.148 (s.e. = 0.044) and −0.071 (s.e. = 0.031), respectively, are negative and statistically significant. One interpretation is that better social and political environments support less gender imbalances and higher labor market participation, thereby decreasing fertility.

The result supports the notion of strong negative effects of education on fertility. The estimated coefficient on overall years of schooling (−0.0675, s.e. = 0.0096) is negative and statistically significant at the 1% level. The higher the education level, for a given income and infant mortality, the lower the fertility rate. This negative effect of the overall number of schooling years on fertility is related to the rising opportunity cost of parents' time when their education level increases, which leads to substitution of quality of children for quantity.

Columns 3 and 4 include the square term of education, and the results are similar to those we discussed previously. They show an inverse relation between fertility and variables such as infant mortality, maintenance of law and order, and democracy. Moreover, once again, we see strong nonlinear effects of per-capita income on fertility.

In columns 3 and 4, the estimated coefficient on the reciprocal of life expectancy is statistically significant. Thus, for a given income, education, and infant mortality, a higher life expectancy promotes fertility. In other words, higher longevity tends to increase the fertility rate.

Column 4 includes country fixed effects, and the estimated coefficients on overall years of schooling for the linear term (−0.103, s.e. = 0.015) and the squared term (0.0029, s.e. = 0.0011) are individually and jointly statistically significant. The pattern of coefficients implies that the effect on fertility is negative at low education levels but becomes positive when educational attainment exceeds 17.6 years. No country in our sample belongs to the range above this threshold. Thus, the effect of educational attainment on fertility is strongly negative, while its effect decreases gradually with the improvement in education level.

Columns 5 and 6 of Table 4.7 separate female and male education. The estimated coefficients on female education are negative and statistically significant regardless of the inclusion of country fixed effects. Hence, female education has a negative effect on fertility. On the contrary, fertility is estimated to be positively related to male educational attainment. However, in column 6, the estimated coefficient on male education (0.0322, s.e. = 0.0172) is statistically significant only at the 10% level.

The negative effect of female education on fertility must reflect the increased value of alternative uses of time for women and perhaps also women's increased knowledge of birth control (Barro and Lee, 1994). The positive relation between male schooling and fertility can result from an income effect dominating a negligible substitution effect on fertility from higher value of male child-rearing time. This is because males, especially in developing countries, are likely to spend a small fraction of their time on child rearing.

Columns 7 and 8 add the square terms of male and female educational attainment. In column 8, with country fixed effects, the estimated coefficients on female education confirm statistically significant nonlinear effects. The estimated coefficient on the linear term is –0.182 (s.e. = 0.025) and the squared term is 0.0054 (s.e. = 0.0019). The implication is a "U-shaped" movement of fertility, seen as an initial decline and a subsequent increase, with the improvement of female education. But no country in the sample falls above the break point of 16.9 years (for females). Thus, the effect of female education on fertility is always negative. For male education, the square term is not statistically significant. Thus, fertility is always estimated to be positively related to male education.

Overall, the regressions provide supporting evidence for a strong negative effect of female education and a positive effect of male schooling on fertility rate.

4.6 RELATIONSHIPS BETWEEN EDUCATION AND POLITICAL DEVELOPMENT

In this section, we investigate the relationship between education and political development. We begin with a brief introduction of the modernization theory and then adopt cross-country regressions to analyze the effects of educational attainment on political development measured by an index of democracy.

Modernization Theory

Over the past century, many countries have experienced democratization with economic development. Existing studies have investigated the impacts of economic development on democratic transition.

The modernization theory, articulated by Lipset (1959), suggests that economic development, measured by per-capita GDP, degree of industrialization, and level of education, promotes political development, particularly democracy as the most representative regime. Lipset emphasized the role of the intelligent middle class that participates in politics and develops the self-restraint necessary to resist dictatorships.[24] He also stressed Tocqueville's (1835) theory of "mass society," wherein private organizations and institutions act as an important source of countervailing power to inhibit the state or any single major source of private power from dominating all political resources and place checks on centralized government power. Education is also emphasized as a basic requirement of democracy that enables people to understand the need for norms of tolerance, make rational electoral choices, and support democratic practices.

Huber, Rueschemeyer, and Stephens (1993) argued that capitalism and democracy go hand in hand in the Western world, as capitalist development lowers the power of landlords and raises the power of the working and middle classes. Glaeser, Ponzetto, and Shleifer (2007) provided a theoretical model in which education improves the benefits of participation in political and social activities and draws relatively more people to advocate democracy.

Barro (1999) provided empirical confirmation of the modernization theory. Using a large sample of countries, he showed that GDP per capita and primary schooling were positive determinants of democracy for the period 1960–1995. Przeworski (2000), Glaeser, la Porta, Lopez-de-Silanes, and Shleifer (2004), and Glaeser, Ponzetto, and Shleifer (2007) also provided supporting evidence.

However, these results have been challenged by Acemoglu, Johnson, Robinson, and Yared (2005, 2008). They argued that education and per-capita GDP do not have statistically significant causal influences on democracy and that omitted country-specific factors influence democracy, education, and per-capita income together. They showed that the inclusion of country fixed effects eliminated the significance of per-capita income and education in the regressions for democracy for the period 1960–2000. However, Benhabib et al. (2011) showed that even with country fixed effects, there exists a statistically significant positive relationship between income and democracy when the censoring of the democracy variable is appropriately considered.

In sum, the debate on the validity of Lipset's modernization theory continues. In the empirical context, this debate is centered on whether the positive effects of income and education on democratization are robust to the inclusion of country fixed effects.

Empirical Analysis

In order to investigate the effect of education on political development, we set up a cross-country empirical framework such as

$$y_{it} = f(y_{i,t-1}, Z_{i,t}), \tag{4.21}$$

where y_{it} is an index of democracy in country i in period t, y_{it-1} the lagged value of the dependent variable, and Z_{it} an array of explanatory variables, such as per-capita income and education, that are considered to influence political development. The lagged dependent variable captures the persistence of a political regime, since changes in political institutions typically take a long time (Barro, 1999).

In contrast to the previous studies investigating the relationship between education and democracy and focusing on the role of overall years of schooling, we investigate the independent role of educational attainment in realizing democracy, not only in terms of the total population but also separated by gender.

The democracy index is the Polity indicator, which is constructed as democracy less autocracy (converted from a −10 to +10 scale to a 0–1 scale, with 1 representing the highest level of democracy). The results are broadly similar when we use the Freedom House measure of political rights, the data for which are available from 1970, as a dependent variable.

Figure 4.8 shows the evolution of the democracy index in terms of Polity IV by region. There was a gradual decline in political development in the 1960s and 1970s, but there have been marked improvements thereafter across regions, especially in Eastern Europe, Sub-Saharan Africa, and Latin America.

Table 4.8 contains panel regressions in which the dependent variables are the Polity indicators of democracy observed in ten five-year intervals in the period 1960–2010 for 107 countries.[25] The method of estimation, using lags of the explanatory variables as instruments, is analogous to that used for the growth regressions.

In Table 4.8, column 1 includes the lagged dependent variable, log of lagged per-capita GDP, and overall years of schooling as explanatory variables, but it excludes country fixed effects. The estimated coefficient of the lagged dependent variable is strongly positive and supports the strong persistence over five years. The estimated coefficient (0.870, s.e. = 0.014) indicates that it takes about 25 years to eliminate 50% of an initial gap between the democracy indicator and its long-run target.

The result presents mixed evidence regarding the modernization theory. The estimated coefficient on the log of lagged per-capita GDP is negative and not statistically significant (−0.0081, s.e. = 0.0051). On the contrary, the effect of the overall

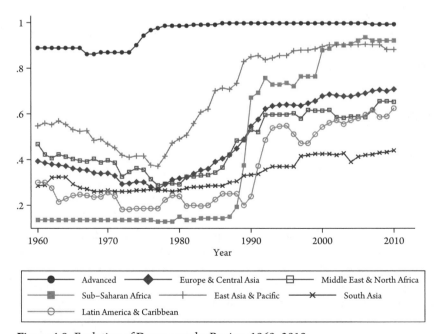

Figure 4.8 Evolution of Democracy by Region, 1960–2010

Table 4.8 Regressions for Indicators of Democracy

	(1)	(2)	(3)	(4)
		Fixed effects		Fixed effects
Lagged dependent variable	0.870*** (0.0142)	0.673*** (0.0264)	0.870*** (0.0143)	0.667*** (0.0265)
Log (lagged per-capita GDP)	−0.00811 (0.00514)	0.00399 (0.0170)	−0.00822 (0.00514)	0.0181 (0.0179)
Total school years, 15–64 aged	0.0123*** (0.00255)	0.00247 (0.00773)	0.0151*** (0.00578)	0.0227** (0.0105)
Total school years squared, 15–64 aged			−0.000218 (0.000408)	−0.00156*** (0.000601)
No. of countries; No. of obs.	*107, 892*	*107, 892*	*107, 892*	*107, 892*

	(5)	(6)	(7)	(8)
		Fixed effects		Fixed effects
Lagged dependent variable	0.866*** (0.0143)	0.672*** (0.0265)	0.867*** (0.0143)	0.662*** (0.0268)
Log (lagged per-capita GDP)	−0.0114** (0.00525)	0.000928 (0.0174)	−0.0116** (0.00526)	0.0154 (0.0181)
Female school years, 15–64 aged	0.0214*** (0.00528)	0.0124 (0.0122)	0.0276** (0.0120)	0.0395** (0.0185)
Male school years, 15–64 aged	−0.00972* (0.00544)	−0.0112 (0.0132)	−0.0136 (0.0158)	−0.0140 (0.0231)
Female school years squared, 15–64 aged			−0.000555 (0.00108)	−0.00115 (0.00147)
Male school years squared, 15–64 aged			0.000335 (0.00129)	−0.000850 (0.00184)
No. of countries; No. of obs.	*107, 892*	*107, 892*	*107, 892*	*107, 892*

NOTES: The panel specification uses pooled data for ten five-year periods from 1960 to 2010 (1960–1965, 1965–70, . . . , and 2005–2010) for 107 economies (see Appendix Table). The dependent variables are the Polity indicator, which denotes democracy less autocracy (converted from a -10 to + 10 scale to a 0–1 scale, with 1 representing the highest democracy), from Polity IV (www.systemicpeace.org). Data for lagged per-worker GDP is for the initial year of each five-year period. Values for 1959, 1964, . . . , and 2004 are used as instruments. Other regressors are averages over periods, with lagged values used as instruments. Period dummies are included. Standard errors are in parentheses. Significance levels: * $p < 0.1$, ** $p < 0.05$, and *** $p < 0.01$.

school years (0.0123, s.e. = 0.0026) is positive and statistically significant at the 1% level. Hence, while the relationship between per-capita income and democracy is not empirically supported, there is strong empirical evidence for the modernization theory concerning education.

Column 2 adds country fixed effects, which reduces the estimated persistence. The estimated coefficient of the lagged dependent variable becomes 0.673 (s.e. = 0.026). The estimated coefficient increases compared to that in column 1, implying a faster convergence toward the steady-state level in that it takes about 8.8 years to eliminate 50% of the initial gap between the democracy indicator and its long-run target. The estimated coefficient on the log of lagged per-capita GDP becomes positive (0.0040, s.e. = 0.017), but it is not statistically significant. The estimated coefficient on overall school years is positive (0.0025, s.e. = 0.0077) but not statistically significant.

Hence, the result confirms the assertion of Acemoglu et al. (2005, 2008) that it is critical to include country fixed effects in the empirical analysis of democracy. The results in column 2 do not support the modernization theory in the sense that individual countries are not likely to become more democratic when they are richer or more educated.

However, this result changes when different specifications are considered. Columns 3 and 4 of Table 4.8 add the square term of overall school attainment to the specifications in columns 1 and 2, respectively. In column 3, the coefficient on the linear term of school attainment is positive and statistically significant (0.0151, s.e. = 0.0058), but the square term is not statistically significant (−0.0002, s.e. = 0.0004). Hence, the results confirm the modernization theory in that higher educational attainment leads to a higher level of democracy over time. But there is no empirical support for the positive effect of per-capita income on political development. In chapter 6, we show that the results for per-capita income become supportive of the modernization theory, even with country fixed effects, in the panel regressions estimated with long-term data of over a century.

In column 4, with the inclusion of country fixed effects, the linear term of 0.0227 (s.e. = 0.0105) and the square term of −0.00156 (s.e. = 0.0006) are individually and jointly significantly different from zero. This configuration of coefficients indicates that educational attainment improves democracy initially but decreases it subsequently. The implied breakpoint is at an average number of years of schooling of 7.3. The fraction of countries appearing in the range below this breakpoint was 60% in the overall sample from 1960 to 2010.

The results seem to indicate that the relationship between education and political participation is not monotonic. An expansion of more-educated citizens leads to higher political participation and greater support for democracy in the less-educated countries, whereas in the better educated countries, it results in lesser political participation and smaller support for democracy. It could imply the critical role of primary education in the improvement of political rights and the roles of secondary and tertiary education in less overall political participation. The negative relation between education and democracy at a higher education level may also reflect the censoring of the democracy indicator.[26]

Columns 5 and 6 of Table 4.8 include average years of schooling for females and males, respectively. Average years of female schooling is positive and statistically significant at the 1% level (0.0214, s.e. = 0.0053). On the contrary, average years of male schooling is negative but not statistically significant only at the 10% level (−0.0097, s.e. = 0.0054). The estimated coefficients on female and male education are jointly significant at the 5% level. The pattern of coefficients implies that higher female school attainment relative to male school attainment promotes political development. That is, equal educational opportunities across genders raise the level of democracy. In other words, the disparity between male and female school attainment is a proxy for the general inequalities of schooling and income. Expanded educational opportunity for females is accompanied by a social structure that generally encourages more participation and, hence, becomes more receptive to democracy (Barro, 1999). But in column 6, with country fixed effects, the estimated coefficients on female and male education are not statistically significant.

Columns 7 and 8 of Table 4.8 add the square terms of female and male overall school years, respectively. It turns out that average years of female schooling is a significant factor of political rights only at the 5% significance level. But the estimated coefficients on female and male education (for both the linear and square terms) are jointly significant at the 1% level. In column 8, for female education, the estimated coefficients on the linear term (0.0395, s.e. = 0.019) and the squared term (−0.0012, s.e. = 0.0015) hint that democracy increases with female education in the entire sample. For male education, the estimated coefficients on the linear and square terms are all negative and not statistically significant, indicating that male education does not seem to be a significant factor of democracy.

Overall, the regressions provide strong evidence for modernization with respect to effects of schooling, particularly female schooling, on democracy. The results are broadly consistent with those of Barro (2012). This evidence is robust to the inclusion of country fixed effects. Thus, it refutes the assertion of Acemoglu et al. (2005).

Appendix Table SAMPLE OF 111 COUNTRIES USED FOR PANEL REGRESSIONS
IN TABLES 4.6–4.8

Country	Growth	Fertility	Democracy
Albania		1985–90	1975–80
Argentina	1960–65	1970–75	1965–70
Australia	1960–65	1965–70	1955–60
Austria	1960–65	1965–70	1955–60
Bahrain		1975–80	1980–85
Bangladesh	1965–70	1965–70	1980–85
Belgium	1960–65	1965–70	1955–60
Benin			1970–75
Bolivia	1965–70	1965–70	1965–70
Botswana	1965–70	1965–70	1975–80
Brazil	1965–70	1965–70	1955–60
Brunei Darussalam		1985–90	
Bulgaria		1975–80	1975–80
Burundi			1975–80

continued

Appendix Table (CONTINUED)

Country	Growth	Fertility	Democracy
Cameroon	1965–70	1965–70	1965–70
Canada	1960–65	1965–70	1955–60
Central African Republic			1965–70
Chile	1960–65	1965–70	1955–60
China	1965–70	1970–75	1955–60
Colombia	1960–65	1965–70	1955–60
Congo	1965–70	1965–70	1965–70
Costa Rica	1960–65	1965–70	1955–60
Cote d'Ivoire	1965–70	1965–70	1965–70
Cyprus	1960–65	1980–85	1975–80
Democratic Republic of the Congo		1975–80	1970–75
Denmark	1960–65	1965–70	1955–60
Dominican Republic	1960–65	1965–70	1955–60
Ecuador	1960–65	1965–70	1955–60
Egypt	1960–65	1965–70	1955–60
El Salvador	1960–65	1965–70	1955–60
Fiji			1975–80
Finland	1960–65	1965–70	1955–60
France	1960–65	1965–70	1955–60
Gabon	1965–70	1980–85	1965–70
Gambia	1965–70	1965–70	1970–75
Germany		1970–75	1955–60
Ghana	1965–70	1965–70	1985–90
Greece	1960–65	1965–70	1955–60
Guatemala	1960–65	1965–70	1955–60
Honduras	1960–65	1965–70	1955–60
Hungary		1975–80	1975–80
Iceland	1960–65	1965–70	
India	1960–65	1965–70	1955–60
Indonesia	1965–70	1965–70	1965–70
Iran (Islamic Republic of)		1970–75	1960–65
Iraq		1975–80	1975–80
Ireland	1960–65	1965–70	1955–60
Israel		1975–80	1955–60
Italy	1960–65	1965–70	1955–60
Jamaica	1960–65	1965–70	1965–70
Japan	1960–65	1965–70	1960–65
Jordan	1965–70	1965–70	1955–60
Kenya	1965–70	1965–70	1970–75
Kuwait		1975–80	1975–80
Lao People's Democratic Republic			1980–85
Lesotho			1975–80
Liberia		1965–70	1965–70

Luxembourg	1965–70	1965–70	
Malawi	1965–70	1965–70	1970–75
Malaysia	1960–65	1965–70	1965–70
Mali	1965–70	1965–70	1965–70
Malta		1965–70	
Mauritania			1965–70
Mauritius			1975–80
Mexico	1960–65	1965–70	1955–60
Mongolia			1975–80
Morocco	1960–65	1965–70	1970–75
Mozambique		1975–80	1980–85
Nepal			1965–70
Netherlands	1960–65	1965–70	1955–60
New Zealand	1960–65	1965–70	1955–60
Niger	1965–70	1970–75	1965–70
Norway	1960–65	1965–70	1955–60
Pakistan	1965–70	1965–70	1955–60
Panama	1965–70	1965–70	1955–60
Paraguay	1960–65	1965–70	1955–60
Peru	1965–70	1965–70	1955–60
Philippines	1960–65	1965–70	1955–60
Poland		1975–80	1975–80
Portugal	1960–65	1965–70	1955–60
Qatar		1975–80	1980–85
Republic of Korea	1965–70	1965–70	1955–60
Romania		1970–75	1965–70
Rwanda			1970–75
Saudi Arabia		1975–80	1975–80
Senegal	1965–70	1965–70	1970–75
Sierra Leone	1965–70	1965–70	1970–75
Singapore	1965–70	1965–70	1970–75
South Africa	1960–65	1975–80	1955–60
Spain	1960–65	1965–70	1955–60
Sri Lanka	1960–65	1965–70	1955–60
Sudan		1975–80	1980–85
Swaziland			1975–80
Sweden	1960–65	1965–70	1955–60
Switzerland	1960–65	1965–70	1955–60
Syrian Arab Republic		1965–70	1970–75
Taiwan	1965–70		1955–60
Thailand	1960–65	1965–70	1955–60
Togo	1965–70	1965–70	1965–70
Trinidad and Tobago	1960–65	1965–70	1970–75
Tunisia	1965–70	1965–70	1965–70
Turkey	1965–70	1965–70	1955–60
USA	1960–65	1965–70	1955–60
Uganda	1965–70	1965–70	1995–00

continued

Appendix Table (CONTINUED)

Country	Growth	Fertility	Democracy
United Kingdom	1960–65	1965–70	1955–60
United Republic of Tanzania		1965–70	1970–75
Uruguay	1965–70	1965–70	1955–60
Venezuela	1965–70	1965–70	1955–60
Viet Nam		1975–80	1980–85
Zambia	1965–70	1965–70	1970–75
Zimbabwe		1975–80	1985–90
No. of countries	76	98	107

Historical Evidence on the Effects of Education on Growth, Fertility, and Democracy, 1870–2010

"A jade without chiseling will not become a useful object. A man without learning will not know the way. The rulers should put education first to govern the state and manage people." (玉不琢，不成器；人不学，不知道。是故古之王者，建国君民，教学为先)

—*THE BOOK OF RITES* 《礼记·学记》

In chapter 4, we discussed the effects of educational attainment on economic growth, fertility, and democracy using the panel data set from 1960 to 2010.

This chapter investigates these relationships over longtime horizons. We construct a long-term macroeconomic panel data set consisting of internationally comparable data on per-worker GDP growth, fertility, educational attainment, and the indicator of democracy over the past 140 years since 1870.

5.1. LONG-TERM HISTORICAL DATA SET

Long-term data provide more time-series variations but tend to entail larger measurement errors. For instance, standard data on historical GDP from Maddison (2007) comprise periods and countries that were originally missing or had been inadequately treated (Ursúa, 2011). Our empirical analysis uses per-capita GDP data from the Barro–Ursúa Macroeconomic Data Set.[1] Barro and Ursúa constructed a per-capita GDP data set covering 42 countries from as far back as at least 1913, and in many cases, from 1870 or earlier.

In order to construct per-worker GDP, we use data on population structure by age from Mitchell (2003a, 2003b, 2003c), the United Nations' *Demographic Yearbook* (1955), and the League of Nations' *Statistical Yearbook* (various years).

The indicator of democracy is sourced from Polity IV, the data for which are available since at least 1901 (albeit with some gaps in data).

Data on total fertility rates are compiled from four sources: Chesnais (1992); the database of Institut National d'Etudes Démographiques; the Human Fertility Database; and *Vital Statistics of the United States*. Chesnais (1992) included data from 1855 to 1987 for 20 developed countries in Europe and from 1950 to 1987 for 14 developing countries in Asia and Latin America. The additional three sources, namely the Institut National d'Etudes Démographiques, the Human Fertility Database, and *Vital Statistics of the United States*, provide the data for 25 developed countries in Europe.

For additional demographic variables, we compile historical data on infant mortality rates, which are sourced from the data set assembled by Abouharb and Kimball (2007). Additionally, we update the data on infant mortality rates using the *World Development Indicators* (World Bank, 2013).

We combine these data with our newly constructed historical estimates of educational attainment. Using Barro and Ursúa's GDP data and the variables for democracy and education, the common sample shrinks to only 28 countries. Using Maddison's (2007) GDP data to expand the data set, we include 12 additional countries with historical data on democracy and fertility.[2] The full sample is composed of 40 countries that have at least four observations with complete data on per-capita GDP, democracy, and educational attainment between 1870 and 1950. For the fertility data, we have not imposed the same criterion, considering that fertility data are typically available since 1950. The full sample includes eighteen countries with less than four observations of fertility rates between 1870 and 1950. Table 5.1 shows the list of 40 countries in our sample.

Table 5.1 SAMPLE OF 40 COUNTRIES USED FOR LONG-TERM DATA REGRESSIONS
IN TABLES 5.2–5.4

Country	Growth	Fertility	Democracy
Argentina	1875–80	1950–55	1875–80
Australia	1905–10	1920–25	1905—10
Austria	1875–80	1925–30	1875—80
Belgium	1875–80	1925–30	1875—80
Brazil	1875–80	1955–60	1875—80
Bulgaria	1925–30	1925–30	1890—95
Canada	1875–80	1920–25	1875—80
Chile	1875–80	1945–50	1875—80
China	1890–95	1960–65	1890—95
Colombia	1900–05	1960–65	1900—05
Costa Rica	1920–25	1960–65	1920—25
Denmark	1875–80	1900–05	1875—80
Egypt	1925–30	1960–65	1925—30
El Salvador	1920–25	1960–65	1920—25
Finland	1920–25	1920–25	1920—25
France	1875–80	1875–80	1875—80
Germany	1875–80	1900–05	1875—80

Greece	1915–20	1950–55	1890—95
Guatemala	1920–25	1960–65	1920—25
Honduras	1920–25	1960–65	1920—25
Hungary	1920–25	1920–25	1890—95
Ireland	1925–30	1925–30	1925—30
Italy	1875–80	1900–05	1875—80
Japan	1875–80	1915–20	1875—80
Mexico	1890–95	1945–50	1890—95
Netherlands	1875–80	1895–00	1875—80
New Zealand	1875–80	1920–25	1875—80
Nicaragua	1920–25	1960–65	1920—25
Norway	1875–80	1905–10	1875—80
Peru	1900–05	1960–65	1900—05
Portugal	1875–80	1925–30	1875—80
Russian Federation	1875–80	1925–30	1875—80
Spain	1875–80	1900–05	1875—80
Sweden	1875–80	1875–80	1875—80
Switzerland	1875–80	1900–05	1875—80
Turkey	1875–80	1960–65	1875—80
USA	1875–80	1910–15	1875—80
United Kingdom	1875–80	1900–05	1875—80
Uruguay	1875–80	1960–65	1875—80
Venezuela	1885–90	1950–55	1885—90
No. of countries	*40*	*40*	*40*

NOTE: The sample consists of 40 countries that have at least four complete observations for GDP and the Polity democracy indicator at five-year intervals prior to 1950.

5.2. GLOBAL TRENDS IN ECONOMIC, DEMOGRAPHIC, AND POLITICAL DEVELOPMENTS

This section provides an overview of long-term historic economic and political developments in the world.

The long-term data from Maddison (2007) depicted a slow increase in per-capita income for the major countries and regions in the world before 1800. He estimated that the average global growth rates of GDP per capita were a mere 0.04% from 1500 to 1700 and 0.07% from 1700 to 1820. Much evidence shows that, over the long-run period of human history until the 18th century, income growth, population growth, and technological progress were insignificant by modern standards.[3] In this long-term human history, income growth had a positive effect on population growth, which maintained per-capita income at the subsistence level.

The long-term data depicts that the pace of income growth accelerated over the past 200 years or so. The 19th and 20th centuries witnessed a dramatic increase in the pace of income and population growth, which were accompanied as well as stimulated by the process of industrialization. After the Industrial Revolution in the middle of the 18th century, the growth rates of per-capita income increased markedly in Western Europe (Figure 5.1). The take-off into sustained growth also occurred in other regions, starting with the western offshoots (the United States, Canada, Australia, and New Zealand), and proceeding to Latin America and Asia, and finally, to the least developed countries in Africa (Figure 5.1).

During the modern economic growth era, unprecedented income growth was associated with rapid population growth in all the regions (Figure 5.2). Population growth had a negative effect on per-capita income growth. However, it was offset by the strong positive effects of technological progress and physical capital accumulation, generating persistent expansion in per-capita income (Galor, 2005).

The significant increase in population growth reflected a rapid decrease in mortality rates during this era. Crude death rates and mortality rates started to decline in France and Scandinavian countries starting from around 1800, as depicted in Figure 5.3. Significant reductions in crude death rates and infant mortality rates have also been recorded across the developing regions in the recent period (see Figure 4.7 in chapter 4).

Existing data show that crude birth rates and fertility rates increased in most of Western Europe until the second half of the 19th century.[4] The significant increase in household income led parents to desire more children. Thereafter, fertility rates declined steadily in developed countries (Figure 5.4). A similar pattern of rising fertility rates followed by a fall also appeared in developing regions. The initial phase of increasing fertility rates seemed to support the "Malthusian theory," implying that rising income increased the number of children that parents could afford to raise. However, eventually, the rising opportunity cost of parents' time, positively tied to economic development, led to parents desiring fewer children (Becker, 1960; Barro and Sala-i-Martin, 2004, section 9.2).

The driving economic forces in the 19th and 20th centuries were technological progress and physical capital accumulation. However, the process of industrialization was also associated with acceleration in human capital accumulation. As described in chapter 1, economic, social, and political changes led to significant increases in the demand for and supply of education during this period. Human capital accumulation expanded rapidly in the 19th and 20th centuries (Figure 5.5). Human capital formation, in turn, contributed to faster technological progress and sustained growth of per-capita income.

The transition to this phase of economic growth was characterized by a sharp decline in fertility rates and a gradual increase in the importance of accumulation of human capital relative to physical capital (Galor and Weil, 2000). Fertility rates began declining sharply in many Western European countries in the latter half of 19th century, and this trend was repeated in all the other regions in the next century (see Figure 4.6). A rise in the average education level, especially that of females, increased women's opportunity costs of child-bearing and brought a negative effect on fertility. The substitution effect of children's quality for quantity surpassed the income effect.

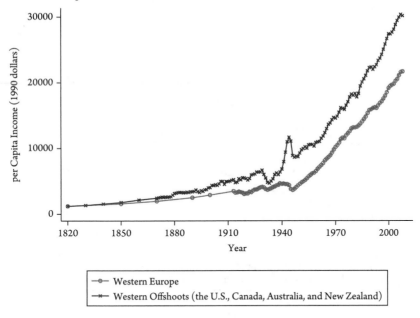

A. Western Europe and Western Offshoots

Western Europe

Western Offshoots (the U.S., Canada, Australia, and New Zealand)

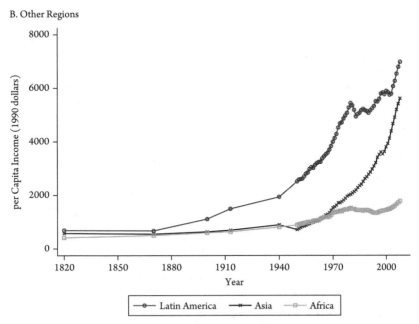

B. Other Regions

Latin America   Asia   Africa

Figure 5.1 Change in Per-Capita Income by Region, 1820–2010
SOURCE: Maddison (2010).
NOTE: Every marker in the charts indicates the availability of data for the specific year in the region.

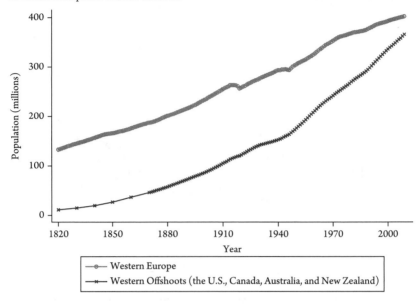

A. Western Europe and Western Offshoots

Western Europe

Western Offshoots (the U.S., Canada, Australia, and New Zealand)

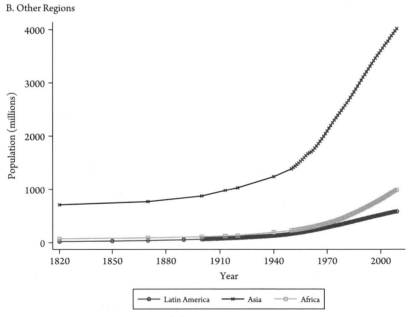

B. Other Regions

Latin America   Asia   Africa

Figure 5.2 Change in Population by Region. 1820–2010
SOURCE: Maddison (2010).
NOTE: Every marker in the charts indicates the availability of data for the specific year in the region.

A

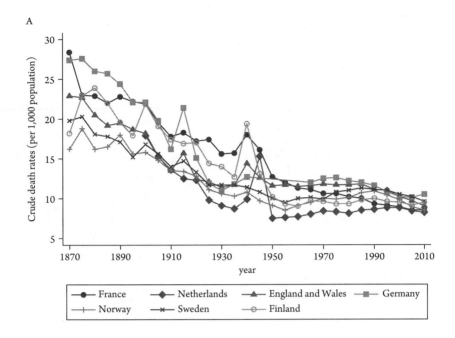

B

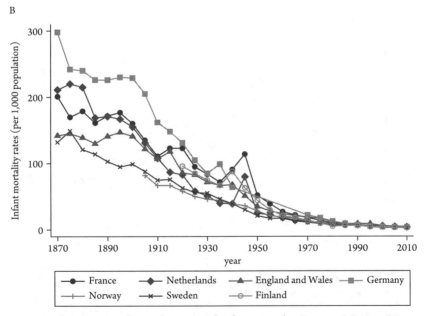

Figure 5.3 Change in Crude Death Rates and Infant Mortality Rates in Western Europe, 1870–2010

A. Crude Death Rates (per 1,000 population)

SOURCE: Reher (2004) and *World Development Indicators* (World Bank, 2013).

B. Infant Mortality Rates (per 1,000 live births)

SOURCE: Abouharb and Kimball (2007) and *World Development Indicators* (World Bank, 2013).

A

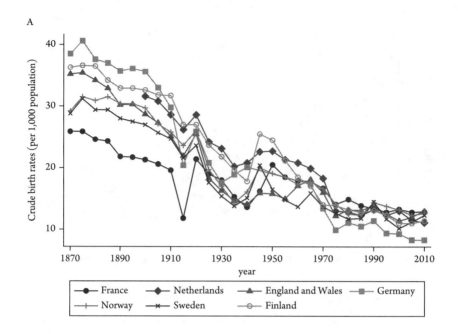

B

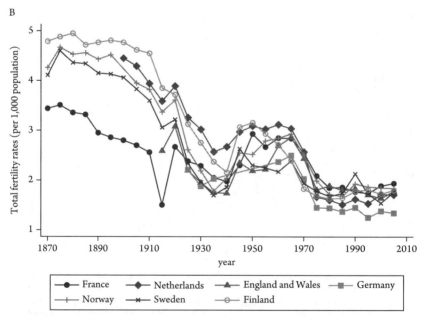

Figure 5.4 Change in Crude Birth Rates and Fertility Rates in Western Europe, 1870–2010
A. Crude Birth Rates (per 1,000 population)
SOURCE: Reher (2004) and *World Development Indicators* (World Bank, 2013).
B. Total Fertility Rates (births per woman)
SOURCE: Chesnais (1992), Institute national d'etudes database, Human Fertility Database, and *Vital Statistics of United States.*

A. World, and Advanced and Developing countries

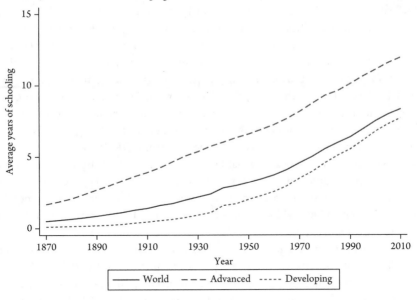

B. Major Regions

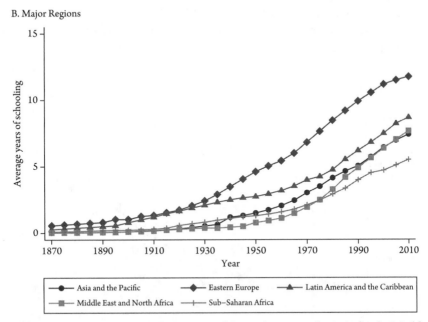

Figure 5.5 Trends of Educational Attainment for Population Aged 15–64 for the World and Across Regions, 1870–2010

Figure 5.6 shows the strong growth of per-capita income in selected countries after World War II. Japan, the Republic of Korea, and China showed remarkable growth, catching up with the advanced countries. Nevertheless, it is well known in the literature on growth that in the broader sample of countries, there is no evidence supporting "convergence" in the world income distribution over the period: that is, there is no tendency for lower-income countries to grow faster than higher-income countries. To put it another way, there is no evidence of "absolute convergence" of per-capita income in the sense of a negative relation between growth and level of per-capita income without conditioning on other variables. Figure 5.7 (A) plots the growth rate in the period 1870–1950 against real GDP per worker in 1870, the earliest year for which data are available, for the sample of 40 countries we have assembled in the complete data set. It shows the diversity of growth performance, especially at low levels of income, which does not support the notion of convergence. Figure 5.7 (B) provides evidence from the period 1950–2010, which also does not support convergence.

Cross-country data on political development is more limited than economic data. Figure 5.8 presents the democracy index sourced from the Polity IV data set for the world, by groups of developing and advanced countries. Globally, there had been a broad tendency toward progress in democracy until the 1920s, followed by a marked decrease until the end of World War II. While democracy has improved continuously across the world thereafter, the sample of developing countries shows sharp deteriorations in the 1970s and the 1980s, when many less-developed countries switched from the more democratic regimes they had adopted at the time of their independence to one-party dictatorships (Barro, 1999).

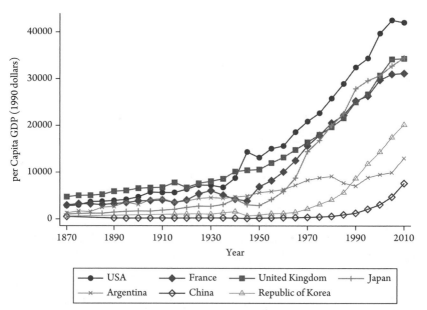

Figure 5.6 Change of Per-Capita GDP for Selected Countries, 1870~2010.
SOURCE: Maddison (2010) and Barro-Ursua Macroeconomic Data Set.

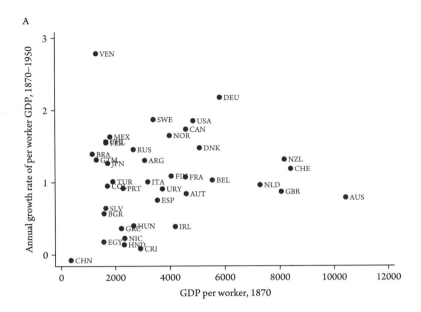

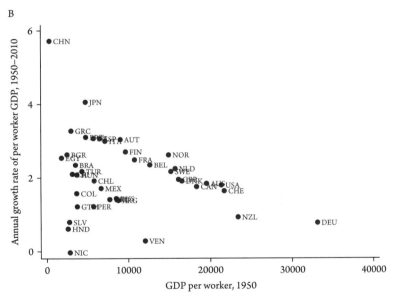

Figure 5.7 Growth versus Initial per-Worker GDP, 1870–2010.
A. 1870–1950
SOURCE: Maddison (2010) and Barro-Ursua Macroeconomic Data Set for Per-Capita
GDP, and the United Nations' *Demographic Yearbook* (1955), Mitchell (2003a,b,c), and the
League of Nations' *Statistical Yearbook* (various years) for working-age population.
B. 1950–2010
SOURCE: Maddison (2010) and Barro-Ursua Macroeconomic Data Set for Per-Capita
GDP, and the United Nations' *Demographic Yearbook 1995* (1955), Mitchell (2003a,b,c),
and the League of Nations' *Statistical Yearbook* (various years) for working-age population.

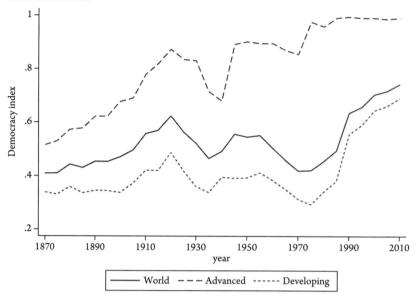

A. Unbalanced Panel

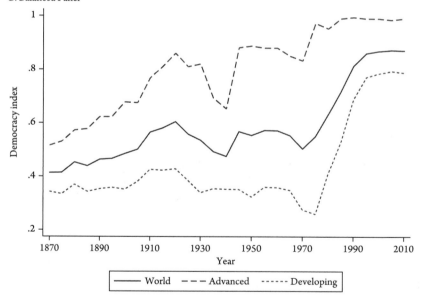

B. Balanced Panel

Figure 5.8 Evolution of Democracy for the World, 1870–2010.
SOURCE: Polity IV project (www.systemicpeace.org).
NOTES: The unbalanced panel includes the sample of 135 countries that have at least one observation for the period 1870–2010, while the balanced panel includes the sample of 49 countries that have complete data set over the whole period at five-year intervals.

5.3. REGRESSIONS FOR GROWTH RATES OF PER-WORKER GDP

In this section, our analysis adopts a general framework of cross-country growth regressions that relate education to economic growth. After controlling other important explanatory variables, the framework allows us to investigate the independent role of educational attainment in economic growth. The framework and estimation methodology are similar to those applied to a panel set for the period 1960–2010 in section 4.4. Using the long-term panel data, we analyze the growth rate of real per-worker GDP over five-year periods from 1875–1880 to 2005–2010. We estimate this system of 27 equations by three-stage least squares, both with and without country fixed effects.

Columns 1–8 of Table 5.2 present the results of the regression. These results are parallel to those in Table 4.6, except that the array of the explanatory variables is now limited to the log of initial per-worker GDP, democracy indicator and its square, and educational attainment.[5] Period dummies are added to control for time effects.

In column 1 of Table 5.2, the estimated coefficient on the log of lagged per-capita GDP (−0.0054, s.e. = 0.0020) supports conditional convergence. This value is lower than that found in column 1 of Table 4.6.

Both the estimated coefficients on the democracy indicator and its square differ significantly from zero. However, the patterns of the coefficients are opposite to those in Table 4.6. Since data availability excludes the other explanatory variables included in the regression in Table 4.6, the specific patterns in Table 5.2 may reflect the influences of the excluded variables, notably institutional quality, rather than democracy (Barro, 2012).

Column 1 of Table 5.2 shows that the estimated coefficient on the overall years of schooling is positive and marginally statistically significant at the 10% level

Table 5.2 REGRESSIONS FOR GROWTH RATES OF GDP PER WORKER WITH LONG-TERM DATA, 1870–2010

	(1)	(2)	(3)	(4)
		Fixed effects		Fixed effects
Log (lagged per-worker GDP)	−0.00536*** (0.00203)	−0.0186*** (0.00419)	−0.00533*** (0.00203)	−0.0194*** (0.00420)
Democracy indicator	−0.0471** (0.0184)	−0.0572** (0.0224)	−0.0445** (0.0187)	−0.0542** (0.0225)
Democracy squared	0.0416*** (0.0161)	0.0475** (0.0195)	0.0401** (0.0162)	0.0461** (0.0196)
Total school years, 15–64 aged	0.00128* (0.000742)	0.000161 (0.00152)	−0.0000912 (0.00141)	−0.00267 (0.00208)
Total school years squared, 15–64 aged			0.000116 (0.000102)	0.000201* (0.000108)
No. of countries; No. of obs.	*40, 966*	*40, 966*	*40, 966*	*40, 966*

continued

Table 5.2 (CONTINUED)

	(5)	(6)	(7)	(8)
	Fixed effects		**Fixed effects**	
Log (lagged per worker GDP)	−0.00535***	−0.0187***	−0.00524***	−0.0196***
	(0.00203)	(0.00419)	(0.00203)	(0.00420)
Democracy indicator	−0.0469**	−0.0558**	−0.0450**	−0.0545**
	(0.0185)	(0.0225)	(0.0187)	(0.0227)
Democracy squared	0.0414**	0.0460**	0.0403**	0.0462**
	(0.0161)	(0.0197)	(0.0163)	(0.0197)
Female school years, 15–64 aged	0.000984	0.00250	−0.00289	−0.00400
	(0.00172)	(0.00249)	(0.00353)	(0.00423)
Male school years, 15–64 aged	0.000282	−0.00236	0.00329	0.00228
	(0.00178)	(0.00250)	(0.00392)	(0.00463)
Female school years squared, 15–64 aged			0.000394	0.000649*
			(0.000340)	(0.000394)
Male school years squared, 15–64 aged			−0.000302	−0.000492
			(0.000362)	(0.000417)
No. of countries; No. of obs.	*40, 966*	*40, 966*	*40, 966*	*40, 966*

NOTES: The dependent variable is the growth rate of per-worker real GDP over five-year periods from 1875–1880 to 2005–2010. The sample consists of 40 countries that have at least four complete data points for GDP and the Polity democracy indicator prior to 1950. Lagged per-worker GDP is for 1875, 1880, . . ., 2005. Values for 1874, 1879, . . ., 2004 are used as instruments. Other regressors are averages over periods, with lagged values used as instruments. Period dummies are included. Standard errors are in parentheses. Significance levels: $*p < 0.1, **p < 0.05, ***p < 0.01$.

(0.0013, s.e. = 0.0007). The point estimates on the human capital variable imply that an increase in the average number of years of schooling by three (roughly a one standard-deviation change) raises the growth rate of per-worker output by about 0.38 percentage points a year, other variables being constant. However, column 2 in Table 5.2 shows the statistical insignificance of the human capital variable with the inclusion of country fixed effects.

One interpretation of this result is that the inclusion of fixed effects excludes much of the information that can help isolate the effects of education on growth rates (Barro, 2012). With a limited number of countries, it is unlikely that variations of years of schooling over time within countries would be sufficient to isolate the independent effect of human capital on economic growth.[6]

Column 2's estimated coefficient on the log of lagged per-capita GDP (−0.0186, s.e. = 0.0042) remains statistically significant and larger in magnitude than that in column 1. It shows a conditional convergence rate at about 1.9% per year.

Column 3 in Table 5.2 adds the squared term of the overall school attainment variable to the specification in column 1. The coefficients on the overall years of schooling variable and its squared term are negative and positive, respectively, but individually and jointly statistically insignificant (the p-value for the joint significance test is 0.122).

The results of column 4, with country fixed effects, show that the coefficients on the overall years of schooling variable and its squared term are negative and positive, respectively, but only the square term is marginally significant. The estimated coefficients, –0.0027 for the linear term (s.e. = 0.0021) and 0.00020 for the squared term (s.e. = 0.00011), indicate that educational attainment reduces per-worker GDP initially, but promotes it subsequently. The implied breakpoint occurs at an average number of years of schooling of 6.7 years.[7] Hence, as we found in the regressions based on the data from 1960 to 2010 (column 4 in Table 4.6), only the countries that have accumulated human capital above a certain threshold tend to experience higher GDP growth.

Columns 5 and 6 of Table 5.2 replace educational attainment of the total population with that of females and males. The measures are overall years of schooling for the male and female populations, aged 15–64. In column 6, female attainment enters positively and male attainment enters negatively. The estimated coefficients are individually and jointly statistically insignificantly different from zero. Hence, the long-term panel regressions do not support the positive effect on economic growth of higher female school attainment relative to male school attainment. This result differs from that for the data set from 1960 to 2010 (see column 6 in Table 4.6).

Columns 7 and 8 of Table 5.2 add the squared terms of female and male average schooling years. The configuration of the coefficients shows the nonlinear associations between male and female education and economic growth, and they are broadly consistent with those in the corresponding columns in Table 4.6: female schooling, with male schooling and other variables being constant, tends to increase per-worker GDP growth, whereas male educational attainment increases output growth rate following the initial decline. However, the estimated coefficients on human capital variables, except that for the square term of female education in column 8, are not individually statistically significant.

Overall, the regressions with long-term data of over a century do not support a strong positive effect of education on economic growth, especially when country fixed effects are included. Nonetheless, there is empirical evidence for the nonlinear effects of schooling on economic growth, wherein an increase in overall schooling years above a critical threshold level, for example the secondary and tertiary levels, leads to higher growth. The evidence also supports the positive effects of higher female school attainment relative to male school attainment, which was found from the regressions based on the data from 1960 to 2010, although it is weaker in the long-term panels.

5.4. REGRESSIONS FOR FERTILITY

Only a few studies have empirically analyzed the determinants of fertility using long-term cross-country data. Galor (2005) analyzed the changes in income and fertility over the long run. Herzer et al. (2012) examined the long-run relationship

Table 5.3 REGRESSIONS FOR FERTILITY WITH LONG-TERM DATA, 1870–2010

	(1)	(2)	(3)	(4)
		Fixed effects		Fixed effects
Log (lagged per-capita GDP)	−1.073*** (0.140)	−1.171*** (0.140)	−0.914*** (0.160)	−1.057*** (0.161)
Log (lagged per-capita GDP) squared	0.0628*** (0.00822)	0.0700*** (0.00836)	0.0531*** (0.00957)	0.0631*** (0.00965)
Log (Infant Mortality Rate)	0.225*** (0.0330)	0.209*** (0.0346)	0.220*** (0.0332)	0.204*** (0.0349)
Democracy indicator	−0.127*** (0.0363)	−0.148*** (0.0366)	−0.111*** (0.0369)	−0.138*** (0.0372)
Total school years, 15–64 aged	−0.0590*** (0.00936)	−0.0450*** (0.0112)	−0.0851*** (0.0159)	−0.0639*** (0.0168)
Total school years squared, 15–64 aged			0.00189* (0.000996)	0.00139 (0.000981)
No. of countries; No. of obs.	40, 626	40, 626	40, 626	40, 626

	(5)	(6)	(7)	(8)
		Fixed effects		Fixed effects
Log (lagged per-capita GDP)	−1.062*** (0.140)	−1.156*** (0.141)	−0.851*** (0.156)	−0.972*** (0.156)
Log (lagged per-capita GDP) squared	0.0621*** (0.00826)	0.0691*** (0.00838)	0.0493*** (0.00929)	0.0575*** (0.00938)
Log (Infant Mortality Rate)	0.224*** (0.0331)	0.207*** (0.0346)	0.204*** (0.0323)	0.190*** (0.0337)
Democracy indicator	−0.124*** (0.0365)	−0.145*** (0.0367)	−0.114*** (0.0357)	−0.140*** (0.0359)
Female school years, 15–64 aged	−0.0390** (0.0170)	−0.0409** (0.0178)	−0.248*** (0.0319)	−0.241*** (0.0321)
Male school years, 15–64 aged	−0.0203 (0.0171)	−0.00492 (0.0174)	0.203*** (0.0366)	0.213*** (0.0362)
Female school years squared, 15–64 aged			0.0195*** (0.00264)	0.0187*** (0.00262)
Male school years squared, 15–64 aged			−0.0198*** (0.00293)	−0.0194*** (0.00290)
No. of countries; No. of obs.	40, 626	40, 626	40, 626	40, 626

NOTES: The dependent variable is the log of total fertility rates averaged over 1875–1880, . . ., 2005–2010. Lagged per-worker GDP is for 1875, 1880, . . ., 2005. Values for 1874, 1879, . . ., 2004 are used as instruments. Other regressors are averages over periods, with lagged values used as instruments. Period dummies are included. Standard errors are in parentheses. Significance levels: *$p < 0.1$, **$p < 0.05$, ***$p < 0.01$.

between fertility, mortality, and income, applying panel cointegration techniques to panel data for 20 countries for over a century. Murtin (2013) investigated the determinants of the demographic transition over the course of the 20th century.

Table 5.3 analyzes the determinants of fertility rates using the long-term panel data. The dependent variable is the log of total fertility rates, averaged over five-year intervals from the period 1875–2010. The IV regressions are applied to an unbalanced panel consisting of data from 40 countries over the 27 five-year periods from 1875–1880 to 2005–2010.[8] The framework and estimation methodology are similar to those applied to a panel set for the period 1960–2010 in section 4.5.

Column 1 includes the log of lagged per-capita GDP, its square, log of infant mortality, and democracy indicator, but it excludes country fixed effects. The regression results are quite consistent with those in column 1 of Table 4.7 based on the dataset for the period 1960–2010.

The results provide strong evidence for "U-shaped" nonlinear effects of per-capita income; the coefficients on per-capita GDP and its squared terms are negative and positive, respectively, and they are also individually and jointly statistically significant (p-value = 0.000). As discussed in section 4.5, the negative relation may reflect the increased value of parental time (for given levels of educational attainment), which leads to a substitution of quality of children for quantity with rising incomes. However, the positive income-fertility relationship indicates that the positive income effect eventually surpasses the negative substitution effect, when other variables are held the same.

The estimated effect of infant mortality on fertility is notably positive. The level of democracy is negatively related to fertility. There is a strong negative effect of overall schooling on fertility, as the estimated coefficient is negative and statistically significant (−0.059, s.e. = 0.0094). This negative schooling effect on fertility is related to the rising opportunity cost of parents' time as their education level increases.

The results in column 2, which includes country fixed effects, are similar to those in column 1. Per-capita income has a nonlinear effect on fertility. The estimated coefficients, −1.171 for the linear term (s.e. = 0.140) and 0.070 for the squared term (s.e. = 0.008), imply that the breakpoint lies at a per-capita GDP of $4,309 per year (in 2005 US$). The fraction of countries in the range above this breakpoint is over 72%. Thus, for the group of high-income countries in this range, an increase in per-capita income, for given values of the other explanatory variables, leads to higher fertility. The coefficient on overall years of schooling is negative and statistically significant at the 1% level (−0.045, s.e. = 0.0112), indicating that educational attainment reduces fertility rates. This is consistent with the result in column 2 of Table 4.7 in chapter 4, which is based on the data set for the period 1960–2010.

Columns 3 and 4 add the squared term of education. In terms of the estimated coefficients on overall years of schooling, the linear term is always strongly negative and statistically significant, while the squared term is positive and marginally statistically significant in column 3 and insignificant in column 4. The point estimates on both coefficients imply the negative effect of overall schooling years on fertility over the entire range of the sample.

Columns 5 and 6 of Table 5.3 separate female and male education, respectively. The estimated coefficients on female education are negative and statistically significant, regardless of the inclusion of country fixed effects. Hence, fertility is estimated to be negatively related to female education. Male educational attainment turns out to have a negative relationship with fertility, but the estimated coefficients are not significantly different from zero. As discussed in section 4.5, the negative effect of female education on fertility reflects the higher value of women's time, which leads to substitution of quality of children for quantity.

Columns 7 and 8 of Table 5.3 add the squared terms of female and male school attainment, respectively. The estimated coefficients on female education confirm statistically significant nonlinear effects; in column 8, with fixed effects, the estimated coefficient on the linear term is -0.241 (s.e. $= 0.032$), and on the squared term, it is 0.019 (s.e. $= 0.0026$). The implication is that, for given values of male education and income, typically, fertility initially decreases with female education and then increases with it in countries with high female school attainment. The implied breakpoint is 6.5 years of schooling, and the fraction of countries in the sample that fall in the range above the breakpoint is 50%. For male education, the estimated coefficients on the linear term $(0.213, \text{s.e.} = 0.036)$ and the squared term $(-0.0194, \text{s.e.} = 0.003)$ indicate that higher male education leads to higher fertility in countries with lower male educational attainment, that is, countries below the breakpoint of 5.5 years. The fraction of countries in the sample that falls below the breakpoint is 35%. The configuration of coefficients indicates that an increase in male education relative to female education raises fertility rates in countries with lower male educational attainment but tends to reduce fertility rates in countries with higher male educational attainment. The positive relation between male schooling and fertility in the initial stage can result from the domination of a positive income effect over a negative substitution effect of schooling on quantity of children. Because the male spends a small amount of his time on child rearing, the substiton effect is negligible.

Overall, the results support the negative effects of female education on fertility, especially for countries with lower educational attainment.

5.5. REGRESSIONS FOR DEMOCRACY

A handful of studies have used long-term data to investigate the effects of income and education on democracy. Acemoglu et al. (2008) found a positive correlation between changes in income and democracy over the past 500 years. They constructed estimates for the Polity index since 1500 using estimates of the extent of constraints on the chief executive. Barro (2012) investigated the relationship between per-capita income and democracy over the long-run period since 1870 and observed a strong positive effect of per-capita GDP on democracy in the panel of 28 countries. Boix (2011) found evidence of a positive effect of income per capita on democratization using panel data over a long period from the early 19th century, even when country fixed effects are included.

Murtin and Wacziarg (2011) explored the relationship among income, education, and democracy levels during the period 1870–2000 and found evidence supporting the modernization theory, which was notably conveyed through the positive effect of primary schooling on democracy. They used average years of schooling constructed by Morrisson and Murtin (2009) for the measure of education.[9]

Table 5.4 presents regressions with the long-term data from 1870 to 2010 for 40 countries, in which the dependent variables are the Polity indicators of democracy observed in 27 five-year intervals. The framework and estimation methodology are similar to those applied to a panel set from 1960 to 2010 in section 4.6.

Column 1 of Table 5.4 shows the regression without country fixed effects. The estimated coefficient on the lagged dependent variable is strongly positive and holds the persistence of a political regime over five years. The estimated coefficient (0.773, s.e. = 0.016) indicates that it takes about 13 years to eliminate 50% of an initial gap between the democracy indicator and its long-run target.

The regression includes per-capita GDP and education, both of which are stressed in the recent literature on modernization. The estimated coefficient on the log of lagged per-capita GDP (0.0395, s.e. = 0.0074) is positive and statistically significant at the 1% level. This result contrasts with the finding based on the 1960–2010 data (see column 1 of Table 4.8 in chapter 4). However, the significantly positive effect of per-capita income on democracy supports the findings of Barro (2012).

The effect of overall school years (0.0056, s.e. = 0.0028) is also positive and statistically significant at the 5% level. Therefore, the results in column 1 confirm, in the systems of equations estimated over time frames of more than a century, the modernization hypothesis—namely, the positive effects on democracy of economic development, measured by higher income and educational attainment.

Column 2 of Table 5.4 shows results upholding the assertions of Acemoglu et al. (2005, 2008). The introduction of country fixed effects reduces the estimated effect of income and schooling on political rights. With fixed effects, per-capita income and educational attainment variables do not have statistically significant effects on democracy.

Columns 3 and 4 of Table 5.4 add the squared term of overall school attainment to the specifications of columns 1 and 2, respectively. The results are broadly consistent with those from the panel regressions based on the data for 1960–2010 in chapter (see columns 3 and 4 of Table 4.8). The coefficients on the linear and

Table 5.4 REGRESSIONS FOR INDICATORS OF DEMOCRACY WITH LONG-TERM DATA, 1870–2010

	(1)	(2)	(3)	(4)
		Fixed effects		Fixed effects
Lagged dependent variable	0.773*** (0.0164)	0.642*** (0.0228)	0.762*** (0.0166)	0.631*** (0.0229)
Log (lagged per-capita GDP)	0.0395*** (0.00735)	0.0263 (0.0160)	0.0378*** (0.00730)	0.0318** (0.0160)
Total school years, 15–64 aged	0.00561** (0.00279)	−0.00829 (0.00604)	0.0275*** (0.00538)	0.0196** (0.00821)
Total school years squared, 15–64 aged			−0.00180*** (0.000384)	−0.00196*** (0.000423)
No. of countries; No. of obs.	*40, 952*	*40, 952*	*40, 952*	*40, 952*

continued

Table 5.4 (CONTINUED)

	(5)	(6)	(7)	(8)
		Fixed effects		Fixed effects
Lagged dependent variable	0.770***	0.642***	0.757***	0.630***
	(0.0165)	(0.0228)	(0.0167)	(0.0230)
Log (lagged per-capita GDP)	0.0400***	0.0261	0.0383***	0.0317**
	(0.00736)	(0.0160)	(0.00732)	(0.0160)
Female school years, 15–64 aged	0.0140**	0.000824	0.0240*	0.0198
	(0.00643)	(0.00974)	(0.0132)	(0.0162)
Male school years, 15–64 aged	–0.00908	–0.00909	0.00447	0.000113
	(0.00681)	(0.00988)	(0.0148)	(0.0180)
Female school years squared, 15–64 aged			–0.000487	–0.00113
			(0.00128)	(0.00153)
Male school years squared, 15–64 aged			–0.00144	–0.000868
			(0.00137)	(0.00163)
No. of countries; No. of obs.	*40, 952*	*40, 952*	*40, 952*	*40, 952*

NOTES: The dependent variable is the Polity democracy indicator averaged over 1875–1880, . . ., 2005–2010. Lagged per-worker GDP is for 1875, 1880, . . ., 2005. Values for 1874, 1879, . . ., 2004 are used as instruments. Other regressors are averages over periods, with lagged values used as instruments. Period dummies are included. Standard errors are in parentheses. Significance levels: $^*p < 0.1$, $^{**}p < 0.05$, $^{***}p < 0.01$.

squared terms of school attainment are positive and negative, respectively, and they are individually and jointly statistically significant at the 5% level. In column 4, with country fixed effects, the coefficient 0.0196 on the linear term (s.e. = 0.0082) and the coefficient –0.0020 on the squared term (s.e. = 0.0004) are individually and jointly significantly different from zero. This configuration of coefficients underscores the fact that educational attainment improves democracy initially, but subsequently deteriorates it. The implied breakpoint occurs at an average number of years of schooling of 5.0. The fraction of countries in the range below this breakpoint is 53% in the overall sample from 1875 to 2010.

This finding indicates that an expansion in the number of educated citizens leads to higher political participation and greater support for democracy in countries with lower educational attainment (and in less-democratic countries). This result might also imply that primary education, compared to secondary and tertiary education, matters most for democracy improvement (Mutin and Wacziarg, 2011).

The results in columns 3 and 4 also support the strong positive relationship between per-capita income and democracy. In column 3, the estimated coefficient on the log of lagged per-capita GDP is positive and statistically significant at the 1% level. In the specification of column 4, even with country fixed effects, the estimated coefficient on the log of lagged per-capita GDP (0.0318, s.e. = 0.0159) is positive and statistically significant at the 5% level.

Column 5 distinguishes between female and male education. Only the estimated coefficient on female education is individually statistically significant at the 5% level. However, the coefficients are jointly significant (p-value = 0.028). The estimated coefficients, 0.0140 for female school years (s.e. = 0.0064) and –0.0091 for male school years (s.e. = 0.0070), imply that higher female school attainment relative to male school attainment enhances political rights.

In column 6, the addition of country fixed effects reduces the estimated effect of schooling on political rights. With fixed effects, educational attainment variables do not have a statistically significant effect on political rights.

Columns 7 and 8 of Table 5.4 add the squared terms of overall school years for females and males, respectively. It turns out that the estimated coefficients on the linear and squared terms of male and female schooling are not individually statistically significant. However, they are jointly statistically significant at the 1% level. The configuration of the coefficients indicates that for all observations in the sample, democracy increases with female education, while the opposite is true for male education.

In column 8, with country fixed effects, the estimated coefficient on the log of lagged per-capita GDP is positive and statistically significant at the 5% level.

Overall, the regressions with the long-term panel data of over a century provide strong evidence for modernization with respect to the effects on democracy of per-capita income and schooling—in particular, female schooling. The results refute the findings of Acemoglu et al. (2005), who argued that the modernization hypothesis (concerning the effect of education on democracy) was not empirically supported in the cross-country panel data with country fixed effects.

Educational Attainment—Quantity and Quality of Schooling

"The philosophy of the school room in one generation will be the philosophy of government in the next."

—Abraham Lincoln

This chapter discusses indicators of educational quality. The estimates of average years of schooling provide a reasonable proxy for the stock of educational capital for a broad group of countries. However, this measure does not take account of differences in the quality of schooling across countries and over time. This chapter provides new data on educational quality based on internationally comparable test scores for a broad number of countries from 1965 to 2010.

We discuss various indicators of school outcomes, including internationally comparable test scores at the primary and secondary levels, such as the Third International Mathematics and Science Study (TIMSS) and the Program for International Student Assessment (PISA). We compile all the available test scores for primary and secondary students. By utilizing all the available test scores from international and regional assessments, we construct a panel data set of test scores in mathematics, science, and reading, and compare the performance of primary and secondary students across countries as well as over time, from 1965 to 2010 in five-year intervals.

We then construct a complete data set of educational quality, as measured by an aggregate test score combining mathematics and science scores for primary and secondary schooling at five-year intervals from 1965 to 2010 for 134 countries. The estimation uses information from the data set on international test scores for primary and secondary school students from 1965 to 2010. We interpolate and extrapolate the values using the estimated growth rates to fill in missing observations. For countries without any secondary test scores, we obtain the estimates by transforming the quality of primary education into that of secondary education based on the estimated relation between the test scores for the primary and secondary students from the common sample of actual observations.

We then investigate the determinants of school outcomes based on student-level data from the 2009 cycle of the PISA test in mathematics for 15-year-olds for 70 countries.

This chapter also discusses various measures of workforce skills. Workforce skills may be measured directly through the International Adult Literacy Survey (IALS), Adult Literacy and Life Skills Survey (ALLS), and Programme for the International Assessment of Adult Competencies (PIAAC). We discuss how the direct measures of adult skills are related to the test scores.

We then explain how various indicators of school quality and labor skills are related to average years of schooling. We attempt to construct an aggregate human capital stock measure that combines average years of schooling and quality of schooling. The quality-adjusted human capital stock for the working-age population is constructed by taking account of the differences in quality of education people attained in each schooling year.

6.1 INTERNATIONAL DATA ON STUDENT OUTCOMES

Data on International Test Scores

Education influences various dimensions of cognitive achievement, including numeracy, literacy (reading and writing), the ability to solve problems, as well as a general scientific understanding of the world (Lockheed et al. 1991). These cognitive skills affect an individual's productive behavior.[1]

Conceptually, the quality of educational output can be measured by the cognitive skills attained by students and graduates. One indicator is students' scores on internationally comparable tests.

International tests administered to samples of students of the same age or belonging to the same school grade assess the cognitive skills of students in specific areas, especially mathematics, science, and reading. While such tests typically ask students questions that reflect their respective country's national curriculum, they also include questions common to the curricula of all the participating countries. The tests designed to ensure international comparability can capture cross-country variations in cognitive achievement of the students and thereby measure differences in the quality of the future labor force (Lee and Barro, 2001).

Hanushek and Kimko (2000) compiled a cross-sectional data set of international test scores in science and mathematics for 39 countries. We (Lee and Barro, 2001) constructed scores for tests held by the International Association for the Evaluation of Educational Achievement (IEA) and the International Assessment of Educational Progress (IAEP) for various years in science, mathematics, and reading for up to 58 countries. These tests involve primary or secondary students of the same age or grade (such as ages 9 and 13) and on students in the last year of secondary education. Hanushek and Woessmann (2012) updated data on international tests in mathematics, science, and reading by including test scores up to 2003 of the IEA's TIMSS as well as the OECD's PISA.

Since its establishment in 1959, the IEA, a nongovernmental international organization, has conducted international comparative studies of student achievement
focusing on primary and secondary school subjects (see Table 6.1). The IEA's first
international study of educational achievement in primary and secondary school
mathematics was conducted in 11 countries during 1963 and 1964 for two age
groups—age 13 (equivalent to the 8th grade in the United States), and students
in the last year of secondary education (equivalent to the 12th grade in the United
States). The latest IEA surveys include the five waves of the TIMSS in 1995, 1999,
2003, 2007, and 2011 and the Progress in International Reading Literacy Study
(PIRLS) in 2001, 2006, and 2011. The TIMSS aims at evaluating the mathema-
tical and science-based knowledge of students in grades four and eight, while the
PIRLS is a test of reading skills for grade four. The latest waves of the TIMSS and the
PIRLS, conducted in 2011, involved 63 and 55 countries, respectively.

The IAEP conducts tests in mathematics and science for 9- and 13-year-old students. The first IAEP project in 1988 was only experimental, involving 13-year-olds
in six countries. The second project in 1991 was much more extensive, involving 20
countries.

The PISA, launched in 1997, has assessed the skills of 15-year-old students at
lower secondary schools every three years since 2000. Until now, five rounds of the
PISA have been conducted (2000, 2003, 2006, 2009, and 2012). The first survey
was conducted for 32 participating countries and economies in 1997, but the latest
survey in 2012 involved 65 countries and economies.

Recently, Altinok and Murseli (2007), Altinok, Diebolt, and De Meulemeester
(2014), and Angrist, Patrinos, and Schlotter (2013) constructed international data-
bases on test scores. Notably, these studies expanded country coverage by including
more developing countries that participated in regional achievement tests during
the 1990s and in recent years.

Three major regional assessments have been conducted in Africa and Latin
America.[2] Two tests focus on Africa, namely the Southern and Eastern Africa Consortium for Monitoring Educational Quality (SACMEQ) and the Programme
d'Analyse des Systèmes Educatifs (PASEC or "Education Systems Analysis Program"). The SACMEQ focused on the achievement levels of grade-six students
from 1995 to 1999, 2000 to 2002, and in 2007. The first survey from 1995 to 1997
covered seven African countries and assessed students' performance in reading. The
second and third surveys conducted tests in reading and mathematics, involving 13
and 14 countries, respectively.

The regional tests under the PASEC assess academic performance in mathematics and French for grade-two and grade-five students in the French-speaking countries of Sub-Saharan Africa. They involved 13 countries in the first round between
1996 and 2003 and 14 countries in the second round between 2004 and 2010.

The network of national education systems in Latin American and Caribbean
countries, known as the Latin American Laboratory for Assessment of the Quality
of Education (LLECE), was established in 1994. The LLECE conducted two waves
of assessments focusing on learning achievements in reading, mathematics, and science in 13 countries of the subcontinent, the first for grades three and four in 1997,
and the second for grades three and six in 2006.

Table 6.1 International Student Achievement Tests

No.	Year	Study	Organization	Subject	Countries/ Regions	Grade/Age	Region
1	1964	First International Mathematics Study	IEA	M	13	Aged 13, FS	World
2	1970–71	First International Science Study	IEA	S	19	Aged 10, 14, FS	World
3	1970–72	First International Reading Study	IEA	R	15	Aged 10, 14, FS	World
4	1980–82	Second International Mathematics Study	IEA	M	20	Aged 13, FS	World
5	1983–84	Second International Science Study	IEA	S	24	Aged 10, 14, FS	World
6	1988, 90–91	International Assessment of Educational Progress	NCES	M, S	6, 20	Aged 9 and 13 (1990–91 only)	World
7	1991	Second International Reading Study	IEA	R	31	Aged 9 and 14	World
8	1995, 1999, 2003, 2007, 2011	Trends in International Mathematics and Science Study	IEA	M, S	40, 38, 47, 58, 62	4th and 8th graders	World
9	1997, 2006	Latin American Laboratory for Assessment of the Quality of Education	UNESCO	M, S, R	11, 16	3rd, 4th (1997 only), and 6th graders	Latin America
10	1995, 2000, 2007	Southern and Eastern Africa Consortium for Monitoring Educational Quality	UNESCO	M, R	6, 13, 14	6th graders	Anglophone Africa
11	2000, 2003, 2006, 2009, 2012	Programme for International Student Assessment	OECD	M, S, R	42, 40, 57, 69, 64	Aged 15	World
12	2001, 2006, 2011	Progress in International Reading Literacy Study	IEA	R	32, 35, 41	4th graders	World
13	2002–2003	Monitoring Learning Achievement	UNICEF, UNESCO	M	11	8th graders	Africa
14	2004–2010	Program for the Analysis of CONFEMEN Education Systems	CONFEMEN	M, R	13	5th graders	Francophone Africa

NOTES: The number of observations included in this study is denoted by the number of participating countries/regions (excluding unavailable). FS, M, S, and R indicate final secondary, mathematics, science, and reading, respectively.

There exists another regional assessment that was not utilized by Altinok, Diebolt, and De Meulemeester (2014) and Angrist, Patrinos, and Schlotter (2013). The United Nations Organization for Education, Science and Culture (UNESCO), in collaboration with the United Nations Children's Fund (UNICEF), conducted another major regional assessment, titled Monitoring Learning Achievement (MLA), which involved 72 developing countries, including 46 African countries. Between 1992 and 2003, this joint UNESCO-UNICEF project conducted assessments for grades four and five in literacy, numeracy, and essential life skills, and for grade eight in mathematics and science (Chinapah et al., 2000).

Table 6.1 summarizes the details of international tests that have been conducted in mathematics, science, and reading since 1964. Our self-compiled database of international test scores is an extension of the database of Altinok et al. (2014) and Angrist et al. (2013). Our data sets also include additional observations from the recent international assessments of the TIMSS 2011, the PIRLS 2011, and the PISA 2012, and from the regional MLA assessment. Because the data set does not include data the survey organizations considered less internationally comparable (and, consequently, not made public), the number of observations is often smaller than the number of countries that participated in the assessments.

Methodology for Constructing the Panel Data Set

We construct a data set of international test scores to compare the performance of students across countries and over time, utilizing all the available test scores. We aim to construct separate panel data sets of test scores for primary and secondary students across countries and over time, from 1965 to 2010 in five-year intervals.

One shortcoming of the available test-score data, however, is that different tests have different participating countries, student samples, subjects, and testing techniques. In addition, the observations apply to different years and are most abundant for the 1990s and the 2000s.

The original test scores are reported in various formats, such as the number of correct items, correct percent, and proficiency scales (scales ranging from 0 to 1000, with a mean of 500 and a standard deviation of 100). For comparability of data, we transform all test scores to a common scale between 0 and 100.

Unfortunately, the IEA assessments prior to 1995 in mathematics and science and prior to 2001 in reading are not directly comparable among the tests, due to different samples and testing techniques. We need to adjust these IEA assessments to be comparable over time. Following the approach by Hanushek and Kimko (2000), we anchor them on an external assessment that provides comparable data over time. We use the time trend of the performance of US students at the National Assessments of Educational Progress (NAEP) as an anchor. Since 1969, the NAEP has periodically conducted national assessments of achievement for students aged 9, 13, and 17 in a number of subjects, including reading, mathematics, and science. Student performance in each subject is summarized as an average score on a scale of 0 to 500. Since the United States has consistently participated in all assessments, it is possible to use the pattern of its NAEP scores to compare test-score levels across time. Although there are differences between the NAEP and other international assessments in terms of assessment purpose, content, target population, and administration, the scores are considered to be comparable. Indeed, the recent NAEP assessments for mathematics, reading, and science were coordinated with the TIMSS, the PIRLS, and the PISA assessments for better comparisons.

Figure 6.1 shows the available NAEP mean scores in the three subjects and for the abovementioned age groups from 1970 to 1999. These scores are sourced from long-term NAEP trend assessments in mathematics, science, and reading, which were conducted every four years since their first administration around 1970. Long-term trend assessments have maintained comparability across assessment instruments over time (Campbell, Hombo, and Mazzeo, 2000).

We scale the level of each international test score relative to the comparable test scores of assessments conducted by the United States. This method is applied to international test scores from the assessments administered by the IAEP and IEA, from their first test up to the TIMSS in 1995 and the PIRLS in 2001, thus allowing us to construct consistent international test scores over time. Because the long-term trend assessments of the NAEP are available only after 1970, we match the test scores from the first International Mathematics Study in 1965 to the estimates of the NAEP scores for 1965, which are extrapolated from the trend of NAEP mathematics scores.

We also adjust the variances of individual tests. In order to adjust international variations in test scores across different tests, Hanushek and Kimko (2000) and

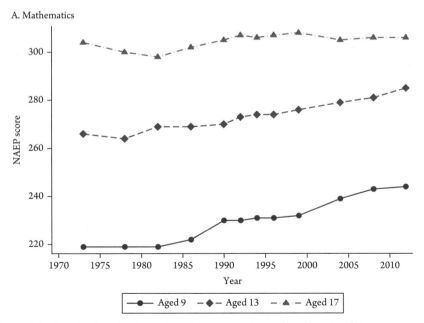

Figure 6.1 Trends of NAEP Long-term Assessment Scores by Subject and Age, 1970–2010
SOURCE: Campbell, Hombo, and Mazzeo (2000) and updated data from US Department of Education. National Center for Education Statistics (http://nces.ed.gov/nationsreportcard/naepdata/).

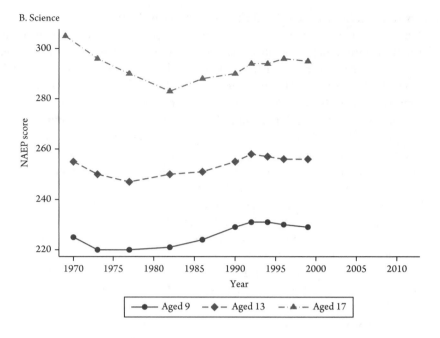

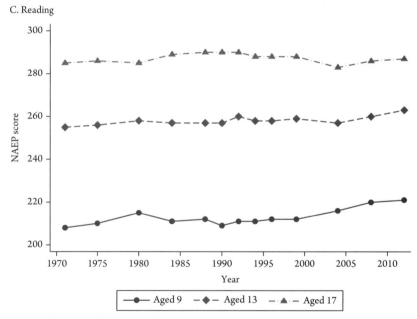

Figure 6.1 (continued)

Hanushek and Woessmann (2012) used information on cross-country variations among the 13 "OECD Standardization Group" (OSG) of countries. They assumed that the standard deviation of test scores among the OSG countries that participated in any particular international test would not vary much over time by subject. We use the same methodology to adjust cross-country variations in earlier international tests for the variance in the 1995 TIMSS. Hence, the mean scores of individual countries in earlier international tests are adjusted twice: first, when the US scores in the international tests are transformed by anchoring on the corresponding US NAEP scores; and second, when the dispersions of the test scores from the anchored US scores are adjusted to equalize the variances of test scores among the OSG over time.

Because recent IEA tests (that is, those after the TIMSS 1995 and the PIRLS 2001 assessments) are designed to allow intertemporal comparison of achievement levels, we do not link them with the US NAEPs, nor do we adjust the variances. Instead, we link them to the benchmark data from the TIMSS 1995 and the PIRLS 2001, using the trends of test scores for individual countries in the actual series of the TIMSS and the PIRLS surveys. Hence, our measures reveal exactly the same trends as found in the international reports of the IEA on students' performance between 1995 and 2011 for mathematics and science, and between 2001 and 2011 for reading.

Our data set also includes test scores from the PISA assessments. We transform the PISA test scores by anchoring them to the TIMSS results of students in the same project and the same year until 2003 for mathematics and until 2006 for science. Then, we transform the later surveys using the time trend of student performance in the PISA series.[3]

We adjust the regional assessments to internationally comparable measures utilizing the information on the countries that appear in both the international and the regional achievement tests. We adopt this approach, which has also been used in previous studies (Altinok et al., 2014 and Angrist et al., 2013). Given the absence of the US-based assessments, the regional tests cannot be anchored on the NAEP. Instead, we use the relation between the scores in a regional survey and a corresponding IEA survey conducted for the same specific grade and same specific subject in the same year. We compute the averages of the scores from the common sample of countries that participated in both the international and the regional assessments; to match the average scores, we rescale the regional test scores.[4] More specifically, Colombia and El Salvador participated in both the LLECE and the TIMSS mathematics and science tests in 2007. Botswana participated in both the SACMEQ and the TIMSS in 2007. For the PASEC, because no member country participated in another IEA survey, the scores are first rescaled to the SACMEQ based on the test scores of Mauritius, which participated in both the PASEC and the SACMEQ. Then, they are converted to the TIMSS scores in 2007. For the MLA, the scores of Botswana, Morocco, and Tunisia are used for the transformation of the MLA scores to the 1999 TIMSS scores in mathematics.

Our constructed database includes adjusted test scores for each subject (mathematics, science, and reading) by each grade level (primary or lower secondary) for every five-year period. The underlying data are applied to the nearest five-year value. By making all available test scores consistent, we are able to compare the test scores for primary and secondary students in the same subject across years. If countries participated in multiple comparable tests in or around a specific year, we use the simple average of the results from the respective surveys.

Table 6.2 NUMBER OF AVAILABLE TEST-SCORE OBSERVATIONS
BY YEAR, 1965–2010

A. Primary Education

Survey Year (to the nearest 5-year value)	Group of Countries								
	All			Advanced			Developing		
	M	S	R	M	S	R	M	S	R
1965	0	0	0	0	0	0	0	0	0
1970	0	14	12	0	9	7	0	5	5
1975	0	0	0	0	0	0	0	0	0
1980	0	0	0	0	0	0	0	0	0
1985	0	15	0	0	9	0	0	6	0
1990	13	12	26	7	7	18	6	5	8
1995	36	25	17	13	13	0	23	12	17
2000	13	0	45	0	0	11	13	0	34
2005	75	47	71	13	13	13	62	34	58
2010	58	51	48	18	18	16	40	33	32
Total	195	164	219	51	69	65	144	95	154

B. Secondary Education

Survey Year (to the nearest 5-year value)	Group of Countries								
	All			Advanced			Developing		
	M	S	R	M	S	R	M	S	R
1965	11	0	0	10	0	0	1	0	0
1970	0	16	0	0	11	0	0	5	0
1975	0	0	0	0	0	0	0	0	0
1980	17	0	0	11	0	0	6	0	0
1985	0	17	0	0	10	0	0	7	0
1990	19	16	30	9	9	18	10	7	12
1995	40	37	0	21	20	0	19	17	0
2000	67	57	41	24	24	22	43	33	19
2005	84	85	66	24	24	24	60	61	42
2010	87	85	67	24	24	24	63	61	43
Total	325	313	204	123	122	88	202	191	116

NOTES: The table refers to the number of available actual test scores for the indicated survey year (or the nearest five-year value). M, S, and R indicate mathematics, science, and reading, respectively.

Table 6.2 presents the distribution of countries by the numbers of adjusted test-score data available since 1965 for mathematics, science, and reading for primary and secondary students at five-year intervals. For primary education, we compile a total of 195 observations for mathematics, 164 for science, and 219 for reading test scores. For secondary education, we compile 325 observations for mathematics,

313 for science, and 204 for reading. The table in the appendix provides information about the availability of the adjusted test scores from 1965 to 2010 at five-year intervals for individual countries. We find that 115 and 116 countries have at least one test score for the primary and the secondary level of schooling, respectively, in the three subjects mentioned above.

One issue is whether the test scores for different subjects can be aggregated. Figure 6.2 plots the test scores in mathematics and science from the sample countries that participated in assessments of both subjects via the TIMSS, the PISA, and

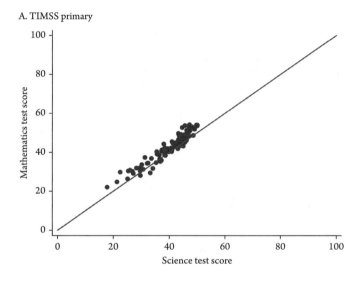

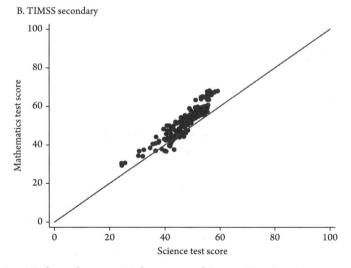

Figure 6.2 A Relation between Mathematics and Science Test Scores
NOTES: The samples are the countries that participated in assessments of both mathematics and science in the TIMSS, the PISA, or the LLECE surveys.

C. PISA secondary

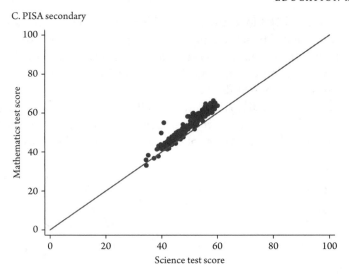

D. LLECE primary

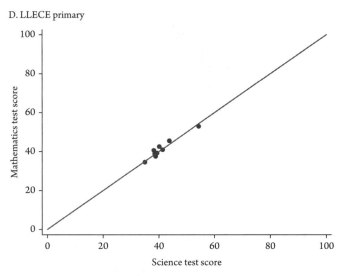

Figure 6.2 (continued)

the LLECE surveys at the primary- or secondary-school level. They are highly correlated. Using the estimated relation between the mathematics and science test scores
from the common sample of observations at the primary- or secondary-school level,
we construct the aggregate of these test scores. The regression results are reported in
Table 6.3.

We can also construct an aggregate of all test scores for the three subjects. However, because reading scores are slightly less comparable to mathematics and science
test scores, we decide not to combine reading with mathematics and science. The
differences in the languages spoken in each country may make the evaluation of
reading competence less comparable across countries. Studies show that family and
school factors determining reading performance are not the same as those determining performance in mathematics and science (Lee and Barro 2001).

Table 6.3 Regressions for Mathematics Test Scores
for Primary and Secondary Students

	(1)	(2)
	Primary students	**Secondary students**
Science test scores	0.9681***	1.1518***
	(0.0260)	(0.0184)
Constant	3.3548***	−3.3652***
	(1.0787)	(0.9152)
R-squared	0.90	0.89
No. of obs.	149	483

NOTES: Dependent variables are the adjusted mathematics test scores of primary students in column 1 and secondary students in column 2. The regressions use a panel set of cross-country data from 1965 to 2010 at five-year intervals. The regressions are estimated by the panel ordinary least squares (OLS) technique. *** indicates statistical significance at the 1% level.

Completed Data Set of the Adjusted Test Scores

We construct the aggregate measures of the adjusted test scores for the primary and secondary levels of schooling from 1965 to 2010 at five-year intervals. The constructed aggregate test scores consist of observations for 134 countries, either for primary or secondary students. The constructed database has many missing observations. We fill these in through interpolation and extrapolation of the available data.

First, when feasible, we use a linear interpolation estimate in situations in which the missing observation is located between two actual test scores.

When interpolation is not feasible, we use forward- or backward-extrapolation estimates based on the time trend of test scores in the region each country belongs to. We estimate the longitudinal patterns of test scores from 1965 to 2010 at five-year intervals by regressing the log value of test scores separated by age group (education level) on a time variable:

$$\ln(Test\ Score)_{j,t} = \alpha + \beta_R time + \mu_{j,t} \tag{6.1}$$

where α is the constant term, β_R is the slope coefficient, and $\mu_{j,t}$ is the disturbance term for country j at time t. The regression allows the slope coefficient to vary by region. The regression does not allow for country-specific slope estimates, because the numbers of available observations for many countries are too small to generate reliable country-specific estimates. We estimate the specification with country fixed effects so the intercept in equation (6.1) varies by country, considering that the unobserved and persistent characteristics of a country can influence the level of test scores. The regressions use separate adjusted test scores for primary and secondary students.

Table 6.4 REGRESSION FOR AGGREGATE TEST SCORES

	(1)	(2)
	Primary students	**Secondary students**
Advanced × year	0.0025***	0.0027***
	(0.0006)	(0.0003)
Asia and the Pacific × year	0.0044***	0.0028***
	(0.0012)	(0.0008)
Eastern Europe × year	0.0018	0.0005
	(0.0013)	(0.0009)
Latin America and the	0.0085***	0.0031***
Caribbean × year	(0.0015)	(0.0012)
Middle East and	0.0079***	-0.0003
North Africa × year	(0.0017)	(0.0009)
Sub-Saharan	0.0065*	0.0043
Africa × year	(0.0039)	(0.0047)
Constant	−5.7826***	0.0270
	(1.6824)	(0.6948)
R-squared	0.47	0.05
No of countries; No. of obs.	*107, 224*	*106, 353*

NOTES: Dependent variables are aggregate test scores constructed using adjusted test scores in mathematics and science of primary students in column 1 and secondary students in column 2. The regressions use a panel set of cross-country data from 1965 to 2010 at five-year intervals. The regressions are estimated by the panel fixed-effects technique. *** and * indicate statistical significance at the 1% level and 10%.

Table 6.4 presents the results of our regressions. It summarizes the estimates of the slope coefficients for the test scores of the primary- and secondary-school students by region.

The estimated coefficients for the test scores in the primary schools range from 0.0085 for the Latin American and Caribbean countries to 0.0018 for the Eastern European countries. The estimated slope coefficient for the Latin American and Caribbean countries implies that average test scores have grown by 0.85% per year (which is about 0.3 points at the mean value of 35 points) over the sample period 1965 to 2010. The estimated growth rates for the secondary test scores are, in general, lower than those for the primary test scores.[5] We use the estimated parameters to extrapolate the estimates for the test scores.

The final data set provides the estimates of international data on student achievements at the primary and secondary school levels. The data set allows both cross-country and over-time comparisons for the period 1965–2010 at five-year intervals.[6]

Figure 6.3 presents the evolution of the unweighted average adjusted test scores for the world and major regions by level of schooling. The results show that the

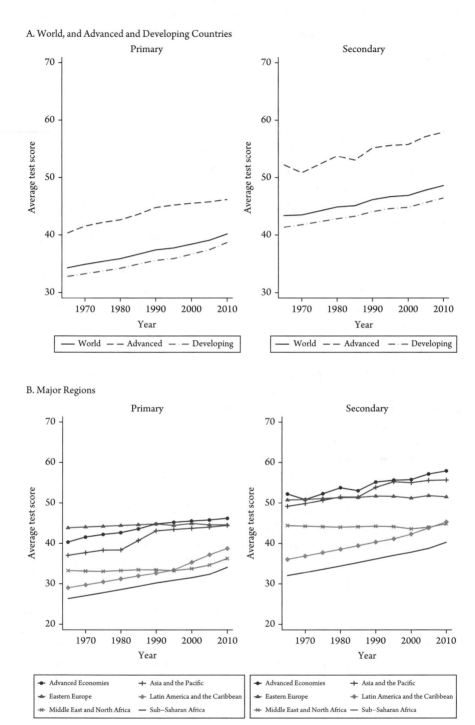

A. World, and Advanced and Developing Countries

Primary

Secondary

— World − − Advanced − · − Developing

— World − − Advanced − · − Developing

B. Major Regions

Primary

Secondary

- ● Advanced Economies ＋ Asia and the Pacific
- ▲ Eastern Europe ◆ Latin America and the Caribbean
- ✳ Middle East and North Africa — Sub−Saharan Africa

- ● Advanced Economies ＋ Asia and the Pacific
- ▲ Eastern Europe ◆ Latin America and the Caribbean
- ✳ Middle East and North Africa — Sub−Saharan Africa

Figure 6.3 Trends of Average International Test Scores by Level of Education, 1965–2010
NOTES: The data are unweighted averages.

advanced economies performed considerably better than the developing countries throughout the period. In 2010, the average test scores for the advanced economies were 46.2 for the primary and 57.9 for the secondary school levels. These scores exceeded the corresponding average test scores of 38.7 and 46.5 for the developing economies.

The Asian countries performed well by world standards: their average test scores increased from 37.1 to 44.5 and from 49.2 to 55.7 for primary and secondary students, respectively, for the period 1965–2010. The Eastern European countries, on average, maintained quite high test scores both at the primary- and the secondary-school levels, comparable to or exceeding those for the advanced countries. However, their scores do not show improvement over time. In contrast, the average test scores of the Sub-Saharan countries rose rapidly, from 26.3 in 1965 to 34.1 in 2010 for primary students, and from 32.0 to 40.3 for secondary students.

Figure 6.4 shows the time trend of test scores by level of education for individual countries from 1965 to 2010. We have complete estimates of the test scores for a total of 134 countries over the period in five-year intervals for at least one level (either primary or secondary). The data set has 108 and 109 countries with complete estimates for primary and secondary test scores, respectively.

Some earlier studies have tried to combine primary and secondary test scores using a simple average (for example) in order to generate a single measure of academic achievement. Unfortunately, the test scores for primary and secondary students in the same subject—mathematics, for instance—are not directly comparable. Figure 6.5 plots the adjusted primary and secondary test scores for the sample of 169 observations that are commonly available from the original international and regional assessments. Though closely correlated, there are considerable discrepancies between them. Although the average test scores of the primary students are lower than those of the secondary students for a country, the gap between the two test scores does not measure the difference in educational quality between the primary and secondary schools in the country.[7] The estimated growth rates for the primary and secondary test scores, as shown in Table 6.4, are not the same, either. Accordingly, we do not combine the primary and secondary test scores into a single measure.

Instead, we use the primary test scores to construct estimates for secondary test scores for a limited sample of countries that do not have any observation for the latter but have observations for the former. In our sample, 25 countries, of which 16 are from Sub-Saharan Africa and 9 are from Latin America, have only participated in international or regional assessments at the primary level and never at the secondary level.[8] We predict adjusted secondary test scores based on adjusted primary test scores from a common sample of 169 actual observations. Based on the estimated relation, reported in Table 6.5, we obtain the predicted values of the adjusted secondary test scores for 25 countries. These estimates are reported in Figure 6.4, in which the results for these additional countries are noted separately.

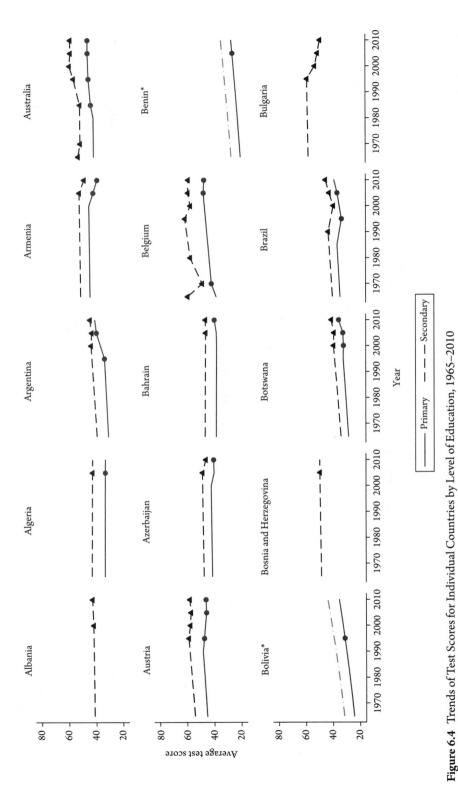

Figure 6.4 Trends of Test Scores for Individual Countries by Level of Education, 1965–2010

NOTES: Every marker in the charts indicates the availability of a test score for the specific year in the individual countries. For the 25 countries that have only primary test scores, we estimate the secondary test scores using primary test scores based on the regression in Table 6.5. These countries are demarcated by *.

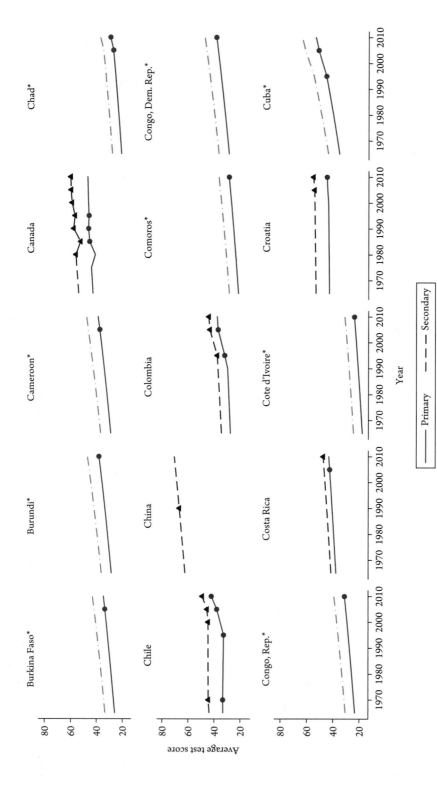

Figure 6.4 (continued)

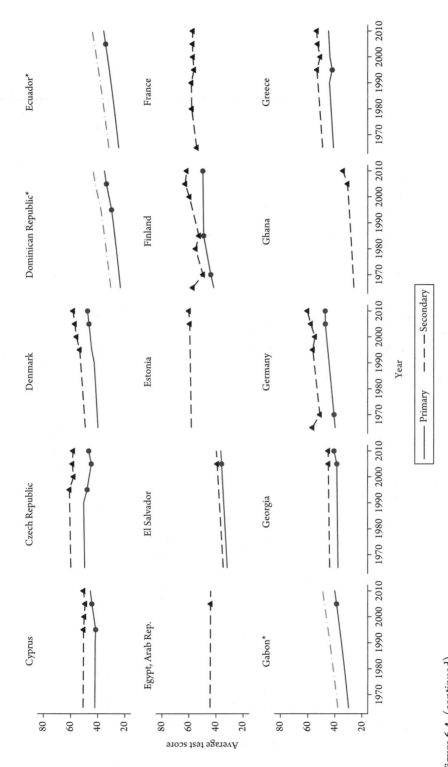

Figure 6.4 (continued)

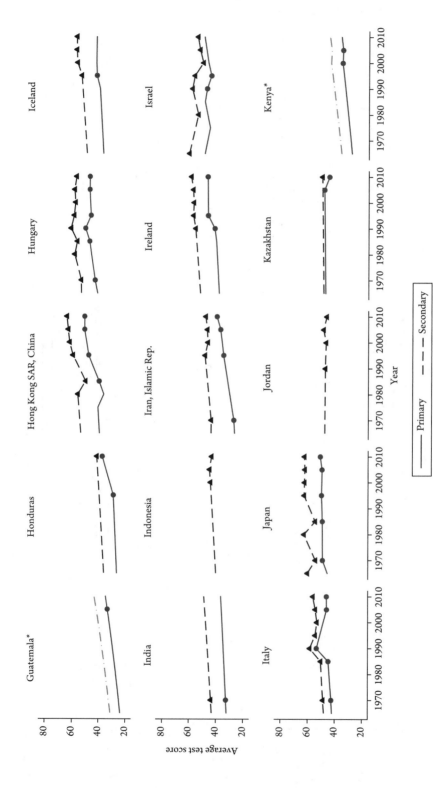

Figure 6.4 (continued)

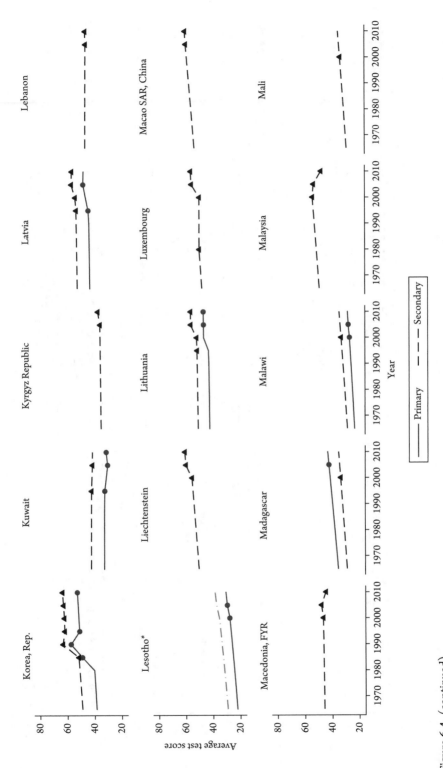

Figure 6.4 (continued)

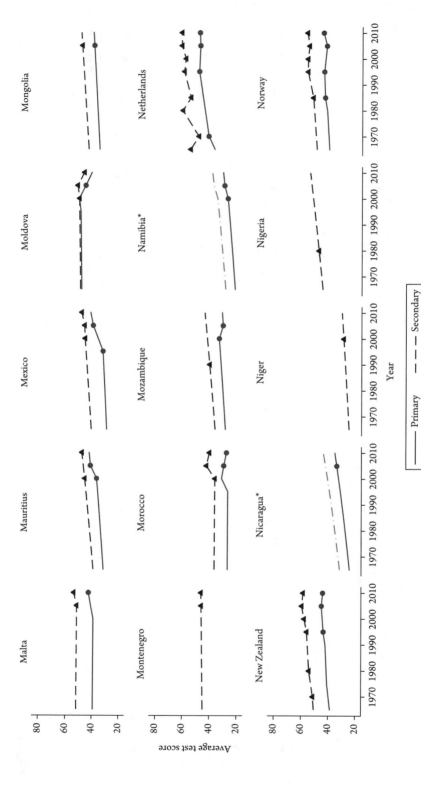

Figure 6.4 (continued)

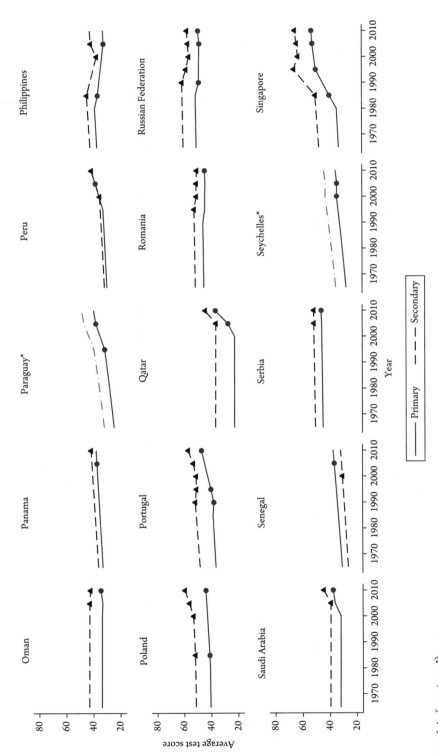

Figure 6.4 (continued)

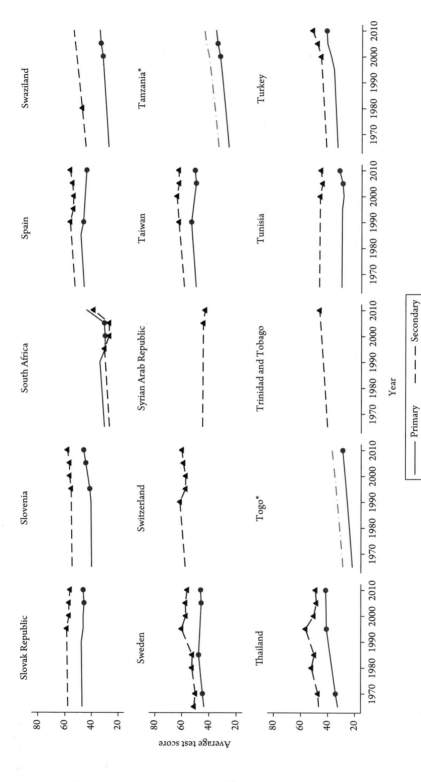

Figure 6.4 (continued)

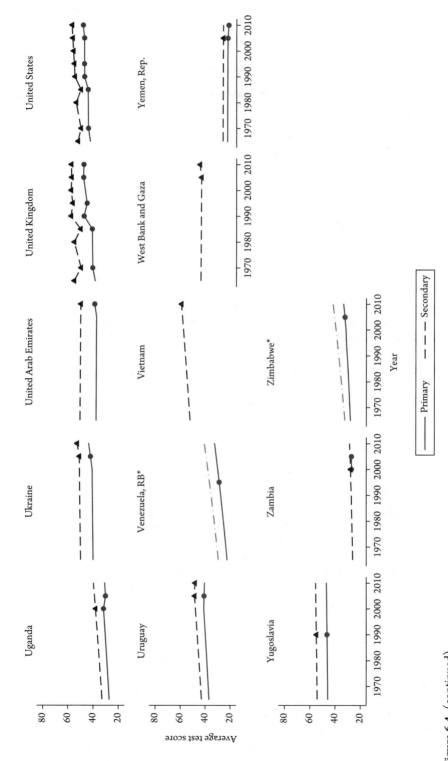

Figure 6.4 (continued)

211

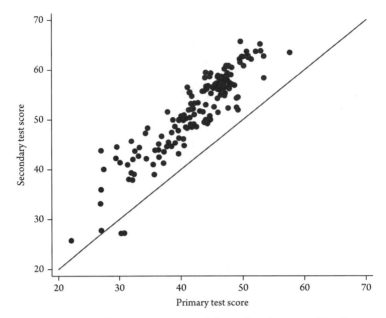

Figure 6.5 A Comparison between Primary and Secondary Aggregate Test Scores
NOTES: Aggregate test scores are constructed by combining mathematics and science test scores based on the estimated relation between test scores in the two subjects in Table 6.3.

Table 6.5 RELATION BETWEEN PRIMARY AND SECONDARY
AGGREGATE TEST SCORES

Primary test scores	1.1076***
	(0.0446)
Constant	4.6830***
	(1.8798)
R-squared	0.83
No of countries; No. of obs.	75, 169

NOTES: Dependent variables are the aggregate test scores for secondary students. The regression uses a panel set of cross-country data from 1965 to 2010 at 5-year intervals. The regression is estimated by the panel random effects technique. *** indicates statistical significance at the 1% level.

6.2 DETERMINANTS OF EDUCATIONAL QUALITY

Literature Survey

Many studies have investigated the relationship between test scores and inputs from schools, families, and communities.[9] These studies are mostly based on cross-section data on test scores within a country. Recent empirical studies have also used information from students' performance in internationally comparable tests.

The relationship between school inputs and outputs can be analyzed with an education production function that relates the output of education to various inputs, both school and nonschool:

$$Q = Q(F, R, I), \tag{6.2}$$

where Q is the outcome of education, F denotes, family factors, R denotes school inputs, and I represents the student's characteristics, including "innate ability." The outcome of education can be measured by students' scores of academic achievement.

The academic performance of students is largely affected by nonschool factors and their family background. Both of these influences not only the students' basic required schooling activities, such as enrollment, attendance, and completion, but also their learning at school (Lockheed et al. 1991). A student living in a home environment with a higher ardor for studying is likely to learn more quickly at school.

In many earlier studies, family background and children's innate abilities are important determinants of student achievement in national tests.[10] Using student-level data from international tests, recent studies have also confirmed the positive association of student achievement with family background and the student's innate abilities within individual countries.[11]

There are three key indicators concerning the family background: family income; parents' education levels; and father's occupation (Psacharopoulos and Woodhall, 1985). Demand for education is determined by family income. Rich households provide better nutrition for their children, increasing their ability to learn. Children's educational achievement and attainment are positively related to parents' socioeconomic status. The education level of parents has a strong impact on student achievement. It means that parents with higher schooling are likely to have a stronger demand for education, which drives them to provide more materials and school-related activities for their children. Children with fathers engaged in managerial/professional occupations tend to have higher educational achievement.

In addition to family inputs and children's innate ability, student achievement can be influenced by the amount of resources available to them in schools. These resources can be measured by various indicators, such as student-teacher ratio, teacher quality, expenditure per student, availability of teaching materials, instruction time, and so on.

The student-teacher ratio is expected to have a negative relationship with student achievement. This is because students involved in more frequent interactions with teachers in smaller classes tend to learn faster. Despite the effectiveness of certain teaching strategies, even for very large classes, it is often hard to control and manage students as the subjects of education in these settings. Moreover, with larger classes, teachers tend to focus more on rote learning rather than on problem-solving skills.

Some empirical studies on microdata within a country indicate the beneficial effects of having a smaller class size. According to Glass, Cahen, Smith, and Filby's (1982) meta-analysis on class size, a smaller class size leads to an improvement in student test scores. Randomized trials in Tennessee and Ontario provide evidence that randomly assigned reductions in class size improve test scores for students attending small classes (Finn and Achilles, 1990; Krueger, 1999). Angrist and Lavy (1999) also confirmed class-size effects by identifying significant differences in test scores among Israeli students who were subject to different class sizes by the exogenously given Maimonides' rule, which allows a maximum of 40 students to enroll in a class. A recent study by Fredriksson, Öckert and Oosterbeek (2013), using data from Sweden, showed that smaller classes in the primary school improve student achievement and have persistent effects on labor-market outcomes over the long run.

In contrast, in a survey of the literature, Hanushek (2006) concluded that there is no convincing evidence for the positive effect of smaller class size on student performance. He argued that the random-assignment experiment conducted in Tennessee is inconclusive because of the problems concerning the trial's design features and implementation.

Teacher quality can be identified with information about the teacher's education, experience, and qualification certificate. Highly qualified and productive teachers can contribute more effectively to student achievement. This is supported by several studies that have shown the strong effect of teacher quality on students' academic performance (Behrman and Birdsall, 1983; Card and Krueger, 1992; Goldhaber and Brewer, 1999). While the teacher's choice of school suggests the possibility of an endogeneity bias, Kane and Steiger (2008) and Chetty et al. (2013) confirmed, based on experimental or quasi-experimental data, the causal impacts of teachers on student test scores.

Total educational expenditure per student is expected to have a positive effect on student achievement. Higher educational expenditure represents more plentiful school resources, notably instructional materials, for students. According to a review of previous studies by Fulle (1986), the greater the availability of textbooks and other instructional materials at school, the higher the student achievement. However, the relationship between school resources and student achievement remains controversial. Hanushek's (1986, 2006) summaries of results from all econometric studies concluded that student performance is weakly or insignificantly related to school resource measures such as expenditure per student, student-teacher ratio, and teacher salary. Several studies have challenged his conclusion. Altonji and Dunn (1996) and Card and Krueger (1996) asserted a strong positive relation between school resources and student outcomes in the United States, disclaiming Hanushek's argument. Furthermore, Hedges, Laine, and Greenwald (1994) and Kremer (1995) criticized Hanushek's methodology, in that he had equally weighted all the reviewed studies with positive, negative, or insignificant results and had then drawn a conclusion on the effects of school inputs on student achievement based on the fraction of the studies that had shown insignificant results. According to them, it is not correct to employ a simple aggregation of the studies, as most of them were statistically designed to give a higher probability of obtaining an insignificant result. This indicates the possibility that a more accurate aggregation of the information from these studies may reveal a strong positive effect of school inputs on school quality.

Another dimension of schooling input is the intensity of operation, which can be measured as the amount of time students spend in schools. This varies across countries. The length of a school term cannot only indicate how intensively a school is operated, but can also signal the extent of emphasis placed on education in a certain society. One should also note that the length of a school term can also be influenced by natural and weather conditions. Like the other inputs of schooling, according to Lavy (2010), instruction time tends to be significantly related to student achievement.

In recent studies, institutional features of educational systems have been highly emphasized as one important set of determinants of student achievement. Institutions tend to influence the quality of education by providing motivation and incentives for the actors, especially students and teachers, in the education process. Institutional features having a large effect on the quality of education include public versus private financing and provision; school autonomy in curricular, budgetary, and personnel decisions; and external monitoring and assessment mechanisms. The impact of institutional measures on student performance has been well described by Hanushek and Woessmann (2011) in their summary of the literature on this subject.

Recent empirical studies have also used information from cross-country data on students' performance. Using 31 observations in cross-country regressions, Hanushek and Kimko (2000) found that the conventional measures of school resources, such as teacher-student ratios and educational expenditures, do not have strong effects on the test performance of students. In contrast, Lee and Barro (2001) analyzed cross-country panel data and found a close relation between school resources and student performance in internationally comparable tests. More school resources—especially a smaller class size, but probably also higher teacher salaries and longer school terms—enhance educational outcomes of students. Moreover, they also reported that student performance is highly associated with family characteristics, such as income and education of parents.

Due to the availability of more-extensive data, a number of subsequent studies have been based on student-level data across countries. For instance, Woessmann (2003) used the TIMSS 1995 data, and Fuchs and Woessmann (2007) employed the PISA 2000 data. In student-level studies, measures of family background, school inputs (especially teacher quality), and institutional factors tend to show a positive association with student achievement.[12]

Estimation of the Educational Production Function

We estimate the educational production function of equation (6.2) based on student-level data. The educational production function that relates test scores to inputs in a broad panel of countries can be specified as follows:

$$Q_{ijk} = \alpha + \beta_1 * I_{ijk} + \beta_2 * F_{ijk} + \beta_3 * R_{ijk} + \beta_4 * C_k + \varepsilon_{ijk} \qquad (6.3)$$

where Q_{ijt} denotes the international test scores of student i in school j of country k, I denotes individual factors, F denotes family factors, R denotes school inputs, C

denotes country-specific factors, and ε_{ijk} denotes unmeasured factors influencing test scores.

We use data for 70 countries from the 2009 cycle of the PISA test in mathematics for 15-year-old students as the dependent variable. The individual factors indicate the student's own characteristics, such as age, gender, immigration status, pre-primary education attendance, and language. The family background factors include parental education and occupation, family status, and the number of books at the student's home. The model includes school inputs, such as class size, shortages of teachers and materials, teacher education, instruction time, and school location. It also consists of institutional measures related to funding sources and school autonomy. At the country level, this basic model includes the country's per-capita gross domestic product (GDP). In addition, we estimate the other specifications with country-specific dummies to control for country-level heterogeneity that affects student performance.

The specification assumes equal slope coefficients for each input measure across schools and countries. The regressions apply to a total of over 240,000 observations. Each country has a varying number of observations, depending on the availability of test scores and data on inputs.

The estimation of the educational production function is subject to some methodological challenges, such as possible endogeneity of some right-hand-side variables, omitted variables, and sample selection.

Sorting out the direction of causation is always a concern in the assessment of relationships between school inputs and outcomes. It may be unclear, for example, how to interpret a positive association between test scores and school inputs, due to the endogeneity of the input choice when residents move in response to school quality.[13]

Recent studies have made some progress in dealing with this problem by adopting natural experiments, randomized trials, or instrumental variables techniques. Unfortunately, these techniques are not applicable to this panel data setting.

The endogeneity can result from some omitted country-specific factors that affect both the inputs and the outputs of schools. For example, country-specific factors, such as unexplained social and cultural features, can cause parents to provide strong support for children's education and thereby increase school inputs and student performance at the same time. The empirical specification, including the country-specific dummies, can control for the influences of omitted country-specific factors. This method allows us to see whether the estimated links between school inputs and outcomes are attributable solely to unobserved country-specific factors. Nevertheless, the results presented here are considered to be illustrative, and the interpretation of the causal relationship between school inputs and student outcomes should be cautious.

Table 6.6 provides an idea of the PISA data set via descriptive statistics of all the variables employed in the estimation. Although the PISA 2009 reports more explanatory variables related to the student, family, school, and institutional characteristics, many of these variables are not available for all the observations in the sample. Although some existing studies included these variables by adding imputed values for the missing observations, we do not add any imputed values and exclude

Table 6.6 DESCRIPTIVE STATISTICS OF THE PISA 2009

Variables	Mean	Standard Deviation	Min	Max
STUDENT CHARACTERISTICS				
Age (years)	15.77	0.29	15.17	16.42
Female	0.51	0.50		
Preprimary education (more than 1 year)	0.62	0.49		
School staring age	6.21	0.77	4.00	10.00
Grade (Grade 13 = 0)				
Grade 7	0.00	0.07		
Grade 8	0.03	0.18		
Grade 9	0.30	0.46		
Grade 10	0.57	0.50		
Grade 11	0.09	0.29		
Grade 12	0.00	0.05		
Immigration background				
First-generation student (parents only born in other country)	0.04	0.19		
Nonnative student (parents and siblings born in other country)	0.02	0.15		
Language spoken at home				
Not use the language of test	0.15	0.36		
FAMILY BACKGROUND				
Educational level of mother (no schooling = 0)				
Primary	0.12	0.32		
Secondary	0.46	0.50		
Tertiary	0.38	0.48		
Educational level of father (no schooling = 0)				
Primary	0.10	0.30		
Secondary	0.47	0.50		
Tertiary	0.39	0.49		
Living with (others = 0)				
Single mother or father	0.13	0.34		
Both Parents	0.82	0.39		
Parents' working status (unemployed or others = 0)				
Both full-time	0.37	0.48		
One full-time, one half-time	0.16	0.36		
At least one full-time	0.30	0.46		
At least one half-time	0.07	0.25		
Highest parents' job (blue collar low skilled = 0)				

continued

Table 6.6 (CONTINUED)

Variables	Mean	Standard Deviation	Min	Max
Blue collar high skilled	0.17	0.37		
White collar low skilled	0.22	0.41		
White collar high skilled	0.50	0.50		
Books at home (0–10 books = 0)				
11–25 books	0.22	0.41		
26–100 books	0.30	0.46		
101–200 books	0.15	0.35		
201–500 books	0.11	0.31		
More than 500 books	0.06	0.23		
SCHOOL INPUTS				
School's community location (fewer than 3,000 = 0)				
Town (3000–100,000)	0.46	0.50		
City (100,000–1,000,000)	0.26	0.44		
Large city with > 1 million people	0.16	0.36		
Shortage of math teachers (strongly or to some extent; not at all or very little = 0)	0.19	0.39		
Shortage of instructional materials (strongly or to some extent; not at all or very little = 0)	0.31	0.46		
Teacher education (share at school)				
Fully certified teachers	0.78	0.37	0.00	1.11
Student-Teacher ratio	16.54	9.28	0.16	326.60
Teacher absenteeism (strongly or to some extent; not at all or very little = 0)	0.16	0.37		
Instruction time (hours per week)	3.86	1.95	0.00	45.00
Standardized Tests	0.84	0.37		
Ability grouping between classes	0.69	0.46		
INSTITUTIONS				
Funding Source (%)				
Student fees or school charges paid by parents	17.91	29.36	0.00	100.00
Government	75.60	33.06	0.00	100.00
Autonomy				
Autonomy in formulating budget	0.70	0.46		
Autonomy in establishing starting salaries	0.38	0.49		
Autonomy in determining course	0.78	0.41		
Autonomy in hiring teachers	0.66	0.47		
GDP per-capita, PPP ($1,000)	21.13	13.86	2.06	67.31

explanatory variables with too many missing observations. In addition to the PISA data at the student and school levels, we add country-level per-capita GDP in 2009 measured in purchasing power parity.

The PISA sampling procedure employs a two-stage sampling technique. The first stage draws a random sample of schools, and the second stage randomly samples 15-year-old students in each of these schools, with each 15-year-old student in a school having equal selection probability. This stratified sampling design within each country produces varying sampling probabilities for different students. To obtain nationally representative estimates from the stratified survey data at the within-country level, we employ the weighted least squares (WLS) estimation, using the sampling probabilities as weights.

Column 1 of Table 6.7 presents the results of the basic regression. The model accounts for 42% of the variation in the test scores. Regarding the student characteristics, it is noteworthy that boys perform significantly better (by 16.5 points) than girls in mathematics. In contrast to the result in mathematics, girls outperform boys in reading, according to the other available studies (see, for instance, Fuchs and Woessmann, 2007). Pre-primary education shows a strong positive association with academic performance for 15-year-old secondary-school students.

The results show the strong effects of family inputs on student achievement. All family background variables are statistically significant at the 1% level. Holding other factors influencing student achievement as fixed, the educational levels of parents—which we consider separately for the mother and the father—have significantly positive effects on children's test scores. The father's education tends to have a larger influence on student performance than does the mother's education.

The coefficients on the parents' jobs and working statuses indicate strong effects of parents' income and occupation on children's academic performance. The achievement of students with at least one parent working full-time is statistically significantly better than in the case of students without working parents or with part-time working parents. Children with parents occupying white-collar and high-skilled jobs perform significantly better.

Students' test scores are also positively associated with the number of books at home, which is suggested as a powerful proxy for the educational, social, and economic backgrounds of students' families in the sociological literature (Hanushek and Woessmann, 2011). The strong impact of family background on student achievement represents the persistence of intergenerational transmission of education in a society.

The regression also consists of a number of school input measures. The student-teacher ratio has a strong negative relation to test scores, confirming that smaller class sizes are associated with better student achievement. The coefficient on teacher quality, measured by the share of fully certified teachers, is positive and statistically significant at the 1% level. The shortage of instruction materials is negatively associated with student performance. The regression confirms a strong positive effect of instruction time on test scores. On the other hand, teacher absenteeism and shortages of mathematics teachers turn out to be insignificant. Interestingly,

Table 6.7 ESTIMATION OF AN INTERNATIONAL EDUCATION PRODUCTION
FUNCTION USING THE PISA 2009 IN MATHEMATICS

Variables	(1)		(2)	
	Coefficient	Standard error	Coefficient	Standard error
STUDENT CHARACTERISTICS				
Age (years)	−0.27	(0.74)	−4.07***	(0.74)
Female	−16.53***	(0.64)	−16.86***	(0.61)
Preprimary education (more than 1 year)	15.42***	(0.57)	9.58***	(0.62)
School staring age	6.97***	(0.41)	−0.03	(0.45)
Grade (Grade 13 = 0)				
Grade 7	−98.48***	(9.05)	−103.1***	(9.53)
Grade 8	−73.70***	(7.39)	−81.36***	(8.02)
Grade 9	−37.64***	(7.18)	−49.95***	(7.74)
Grade 10	−16.41**	(7.17)	−18.53**	(7.67)
Grade 11	−12.46*	(6.96)	3.45	(7.18)
Grade 12	−9.43	(7.87)	4.67	(9.42)
Immigration background				
First-generation student (parents only born in other country)	−11.16***	(1.84)	−9.24***	(1.70)
Nonnative student (parents and siblings born in other country)	−3.01	(1.99)	−2.84	(1.87)
Language spoken at home				
Not use the language of test	−11.71***	(1.19)	1.22	(1.13)
FAMILY BACKGROUND				
Educational level of mother (no schooling = 0)				
Primary	5.00***	(1.20)	0.88	(1.16)
Secondary	7.25***	(1.46)	4.8***	(1.47)
Tertiary	8.94***	(1.46)	11.96***	(1.47)
Educational level of father (no schooling = 0)				
Primary	9.07***	(1.61)	3.63**	(1.61)
Secondary	11.31***	(1.71)	5.24***	(1.72)
Tertiary	20.72***	(1.82)	17.07***	(1.88)
Living with (others = 0)				
Single mother or father	23.01***	(1.33)	19.9***	(1.26)
Both Parents	38.35***	(1.17)	30.87***	(1.07)
Parents' working status (unemployed or others = 0)				
Both full-time	8.65***	(0.83)	4.81***	(0.81)
One full-time, one half-time	10.02***	(0.92)	7.18***	(0.91)

At least one full-time	7.16***	(0.84)	6.28***	(0.79)
At least one half-time	−3.57***	(1.08)	1.49	(1.11)
Highest parents' job (blue collar low skilled = 0)				
Blue collar high skilled	2.24***	(0.80)	−1.16	(0.81)
White collar low skilled	6.21***	(0.81)	2.24***	(0.81)
White collar high skilled	21.99***	(0.78)	19.33***	(0.82)
Books at home (0–10 books = 0)				
11–25 books	10.49***	(0.82)	8.47***	(0.83)
26–100 books	32.37***	(0.83)	24.26***	(0.81)
101–200 books	51.17***	(0.86)	39.77***	(0.86)
201–500 books	70.07***	(1.03)	56.61***	(0.97)
More than 500 books	71.25***	(1.27)	58.17***	(1.18)
SCHOOL INPUTS				
School's community location (fewer than 3,000 = 0)				
Town (3000–100,000)	10.14***	(1.29)	3.88***	(1.21)
City (100,000–1,000,000)	21.52***	(1.48)	10.54***	(1.41)
Large city with > 1 million people	33.81***	(1.65)	10.16***	(1.56)
Shortage of math teachers	−1.18	(1.41)	−5.86***	(1.27)
Shortage of instructional materials	−7.83***	(1.10)	-6.25***	(1.00)
Teacher education (share at school)				
Fully certified teachers	11.44***	(1.50)	6.25**	(2.43)
Student-Teacher ratio	−0.50***	(0.04)	−0.18***	(0.04)
Teacher absenteeism	1.80	(1.28)	−5.73***	(1.05)
Instruction time (hours per week)	1.81***	(0.23)	3.47***	(0.25)
Standardized Tests	−7.83***	(1.24)	−0.75	(1.16)
Ability grouping between classes	−4.71***	(1.03)	−0.98	(1.02)
INSTITUTIONS				
Funding Source (%)				
Student fees or school charges paid by parents	0.14***	(0.04)	0.11***	(0.04)
Government	−0.00	(0.04)	−0.08**	(0.03)
Autonomy				
Autonomy in formulating budget	0.81	(1.09)	1.45	(1.01)
Autonomy in establishing starting salaries	−13.52***	(1.08)	−4.21***	(1.09)
Autonomy in determining course	4.56***	(1.06)	1.69	(1.07)
Autonomy in hiring teachers	6.36***	(1.04)	0.20	(1.13)
GDP per-capita, PPP (1,000$)	1.68***	(0.04)		

continued

Table 6.7 (CONTINUED)

Variables	(1)		(2)	
	Coefficient	Standard error	Coefficient	Standard error
Country fixed effects	No		Yes	
Students (total = 515,958)	241,426		241,426	
Schools (total = 18,641)	11,791		11,791	
Countries (total = 73)	70		70	
R-squared	0.417		0.978	

NOTES: Dependent variables are the PISA 2009 international mathematics test scores. The estimation adopts least squares regressions weighted by students' sampling probability. Robust standard errors adjusted for clustering at the school level are reported in parentheses. Significance levels (based on clustering robust standard errors): ***1% **5%, and *10%.

regular standardized testing is statistically significant and negatively related to student achievement in mathematics.[14]

The estimation results support the argument that institutions of the school system are important for student achievement (Hanushek and Woessmann, 2011). Student performance is positively associated with the share of funding schools receive from parents. Students in schools that have autonomy in determining courses and hiring their teachers tend to represent statistically significantly better academic performance. By contrast, there is a negative association between school autonomy in establishing teachers' starting salaries and student performance after controlling other school and institutional factors. These results seem to indicate that school autonomy in such areas as operations and personnel management decisions may be conducive to student performance, as they would possibly use local knowledge to increase teaching effectiveness. By contrast, school autonomy in areas that allow for strong local opportunistic behavior, such as budget setting, may be detrimental to student performance (Bishop and Woessmann, 2004).

Column 2 of Table 6.7 includes dummy variables to capture fixed country effects. This estimation excludes the country-specific variable per-capita GDP. Family factors and school inputs continue to remain significant in this country fixed-effects estimation. This result indicates limited accountability of unobserved country factors for the relationship between educational inputs and suggests that within-country variations as well as between-country variations are important explanatory factors for the relationship. The variables for teacher absenteeism and shortages of mathematics teachers are negative and statistically significant in this specification, supporting the theoretical predictions. By contrast, regular standardized testing and school autonomy in determining courses and hiring teachers become statistically insignificant, thus indicating that their significant effects on student performance in equation (6.3) reflect mostly cross-country variations.

We estimate the extent to which a group of family-background factors explain the variation of test scores in individual countries. The figures are constructed by multiplying the test scores predicted by the mean values of family background (or

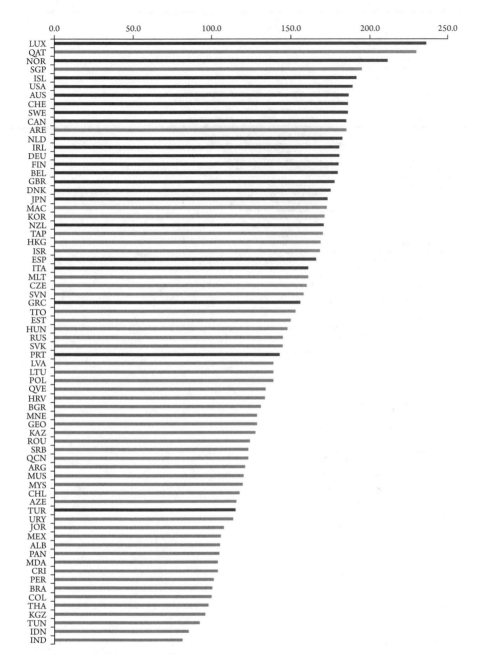

Figure 6.6 Family-background Effects on PISA Test Scores

NOTES: The values indicate the extent to which a group of family background factors explain the variations in the 2009 PISA test scores of individual countries. The figures are constructed using the test scores predicted by the mean values of family background factors in each country, based on the coefficient estimates in the student-level regression in column 1 of Table 6.3.

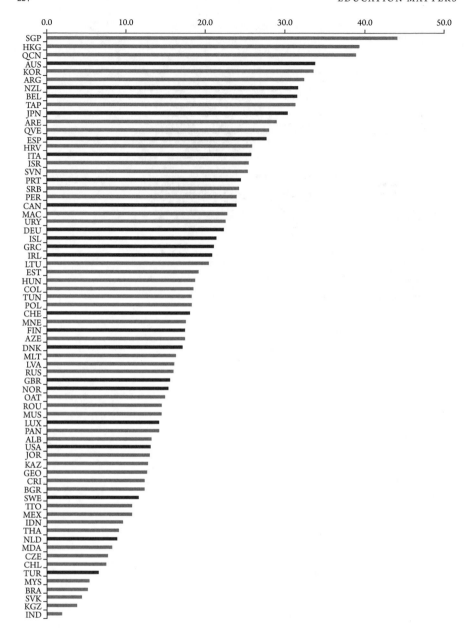

Figure 6.7 School Effects on PISA Test Scores
NOTES: The values indicate the extent to which a group of school and institutional factors
explain the variation of the 2009 PISA test scores for individual countries. See also Figure 6.6.

school-related and institutional factors) in each country with the corresponding coefficient estimates in column 1 of Table 6.7.

Figures 6.6 and 6.7 depict that a much larger portion of the test scores for each
country is explained by family background rather than by school-related factors.
Both family background and school-related variables contribute to higher test scores
in many advanced countries compared to the developing countries. Interestingly,

the East Asian economies, including Singapore, Hong Kong, Korea, Taiwan, and Japan, show the largest contribution of school and institutional factors to their children's test scores among the participating countries.

6.3 MEASURES OF ADULT SKILLS

We analyze economic growth by measuring the skills of the labor force. Although the test scores of students reflect the quality of schooling, and hence indicate the quality of the labor force, they do not directly measure the educational capital held by a country's working-age population.

The measure of students' educational attainment does not take account of the skills and experience gained by individuals after their formal education. Knowledge can be also lost after the completion of formal education. Ideally, tests of cognitive ability would be administered to adults rather than to students.

There have been attempts to directly measure the skills of the labor force across countries. On a multi-country level, as mentioned in the first section of this chapter, there are three adult literacy surveys: the IALS, the ALLS, and the PIAAC.

The IALS, conducted in 1994 for the first time, provided a direct comparison of certain work-related skills in adult populations across countries. Literacy was measured in three domains: prose literacy, document literacy, and quantitative literacy. The results were reported on a scale of 0 to 500 in each of the three domains. Literacy skills were evaluated in each country through detailed interviews with a sample of 2,000 to 8,000 persons in the working-age population. In 1994, nine countries, namely Canada, France, Germany, Ireland, the Netherlands, Poland, Sweden, Switzerland, and the United States, participated in the first survey. In total, the IALS includes literacy data pertaining to 23 countries, most of which are OECD member countries, or regions (see OECD and Statistics Canada, 1995; OECD and Human Resources Development Canada, 1998; OECD, 2000). In addition to the limited data coverage, the IALS study has been criticized because of measurement errors and problems in modeling techniques (Blum, Goldstein, and Guérin-Pace, 2001).

The ALLS, modeled on the IALS, measured prose literacy, document literacy, numeracy, and problem-solving skills of a nationally representative sample of 16- to 65-year olds. The surveys were conducted between 2003 and 2008 and involved only 10 countries.

The PIAAC measures key cognitive and workplace skills. The survey has involved 33 countries in two rounds since 2008.[15] The first results from the survey were released in October 2013.

All participating countries in the PIAAC follow the quality-assurance guidelines for survey design, assessment implementation, and reporting of results set by the OECD consortium.

Studies based on IALS data show that these measures of literacy have significant relation with gross earnings of individuals within a country and are independent of the effects of education (OECD and Human Resources Development Canada, 1998; Hanushek and Woessmann, 2011). A recent paper by Hanushek et al. (2013)

A. IALS 1994–1998 and Aggregate Secondary Test Score 1995

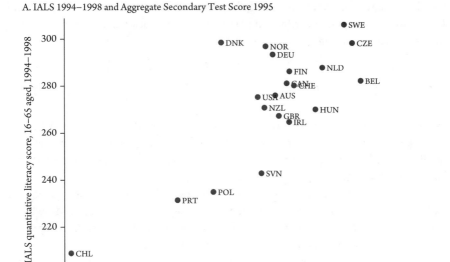

B. PIAAC 2012 and Aggregate Secondary Test Score 2010

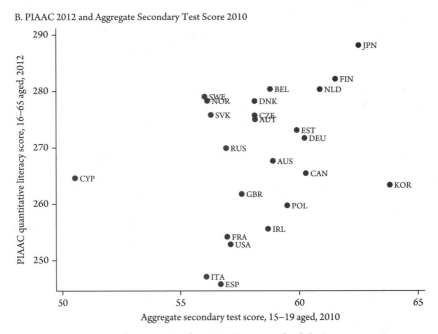

Figure 6.8 Comparisons between Student Test Scores and Adult Quantitative Literacy Scores

using international PIAAC data showed that there are considerable returns, measured by an increase in earnings over a lifetime, to adult skills.

Figures 6.8 A and B compare the aggregate mathematics and science scores for secondary students with the IALS and the PIAAC quantitative literacy scores, respectively. There is significant discrepancy in achievement between students and adults. The scatter plots of Figures 6.8 A and B reveal that Nordic countries, such as Demark, Norway, and Sweden, have an exceptionally large gap between the two test scores. The adults in these countries were among the best performers in the IALS and the PIAAC quantitative literacy tests, but grade seven students scored relatively low in mathematics in 1995 and 2010. This is in contrast to the results for Korea; it had the best performance by secondary-school students, while the adults did not perform very well. This fact suggests that students can attain a significant amount of additional quantitative skills at higher levels of education as well as in workplaces.

6.4 RELATIONS BETWEEN EDUCATIONAL ATTAINMENT AND EDUCATIONAL QUALITY

Average Test Scores and Average Years of Schooling

The correlation of average years of schooling with the aggregate mathematics and science test scores of secondary students in 2010 is positive (the correlation coefficient is 0.70) (Figure 6.9). One group of countries shows higher levels of years of schooling and educational quality. They include Finland, Japan, Republic of Korea, Singapore, and Taiwan. In contrast, both years of schooling and educational quality are low in many African countries, such as Côte d'Ivoire, Malawi, Mali, Niger, Senegal, and Yemen.

Table 6.8 lists top-performing economies in educational attainment quantity versus quality. Table 6.8A shows the top 15 economies in average number of years of

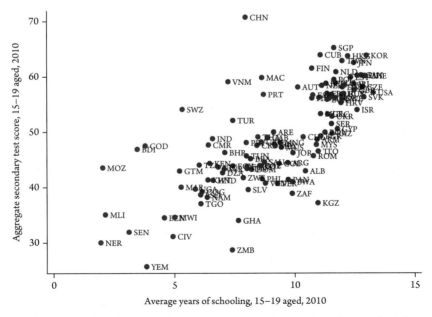

Figure 6.9 Average Test Scores and Average Schooling Years of Secondary Students in 2010

Table 6.8. Top 15 Economies in Average Years of Schooling
and Test Scores in 2010

A. Top 15 Economies in Average Years of Schooling

Economy	Average Years of Schooling	Rank	Test Score	Rank
USA	13.2	(1)	57.1	(26)
Switzerland	12.9	(2)	60.1	(12)
Czech Republic	12.8	(3)	58.1	(23)
Republic of Korea	12.6	(4)	63.8	(4)
Germany	12.6	(5)	60.2	(11)
Israel	12.5	(6)	54.0	(42)
Canada	12.4	(7)	60.3	(10)
United Kingdom	12.4	(8)	57.6	(25)
Japan	12.4	(9)	62.5	(7)
Estonia	12.3	(10)	59.9	(13)
Hong Kong, China	12.1	(11)	63.7	(5)
Ireland	12.1	(12)	58.7	(19)
Slovenia	12.0	(13)	58.5	(20)
Russian Federation	12.0	(14)	56.9	(28)
Finland	12.0	(15)	61.5	(8)

B. Top 15 Economies in Secondary Aggregate Test Score

Economy	Test Score	Rank	Average Years of Schooling	Rank
China	70.7	(1)	8.0	(85)
Singapore	65.2	(2)	11.4	(26)
Cuba	63.9	(3)	11.0	(39)
Republic of Korea	63.8	(4)	12.6	(4)
Hong Kong, China	63.7	(5)	12.1	(11)
Taiwan	62.9	(6)	12.0	(17)
Japan	62.5	(7)	12.4	(9)
Finland	61.5	(8)	12.0	(15)
Netherlands	60.9	(9)	11.7	(21)
Canada	60.3	(10)	12.4	(7)
Germany	60.2	(11)	12.6	(5)
Switzerland	60.1	(12)	12.9	(2)
Estonia	59.9	(13)	12.3	(10)
Macao, China	59.8	(14)	8.6	(71)
Poland	59.5	(15)	11.6	(23)

NOTES: Figures presented indicate aggregate test scores for secondary students and average years of schooling for working-age population. The ranks are among the sample of 117 economies in which we have constructed complete data for both average years of schooling and test scores.

schooling. The United States, Switzerland, Czech Republic, Republic of Korea, and Germany are the best-performing economies in terms of average number of years of schooling, but they are not always the top performers in test scores. As presented in Table 6.8B, the top 5 economies in secondary aggregate test scores are China, Singapore, Cuba, Republic of Korea, and Hong Kong, China.

We also show the relationship between the adult literacy measure from the PIAAC and average years of schooling of the labor force in Figure 6.10. The correlation is much lower (0.15). The sample size becomes much smaller because of the limited availability of adult literacy measures.

Hanushek and Kimko (2000) and Hanushek and Woessmann (2012) argued that educational achievement, measured by internationally comparable test scores, is a better measure of human capital stock. Hanushek and Woessmann (2012) argued that "focusing directly on cognitive skills to measure human capital has advantages such that (a) it captures the variation in knowledge and ability that schools produce which are in turn related to future economic success and (b) learning outcomes incorporate skills from family, school, and ability."

However, there are several concerns over using measures of international test scores as a measure of human capital stock. First, Hanushek and his coauthors employed the test scores of students who currently attend secondary schools. Conceptually, the measure of test scores for the population aged 15 to 64 should be a better measure of adult skills than the test scores for secondary students aged 15. However, it is not easy in practice to construct a measure of skill attainments for the population aged 15 to 64 using the average secondary test scores for students aged 15.

Another serious related concern is that the test score measure for secondary students employed by Hanushek and his coauthors does not capture the differences in the sizes of the population attaining schooling. For example, in a country where

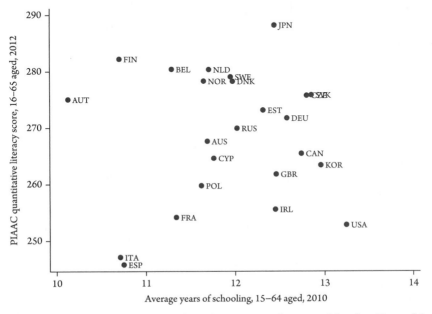

Figure 6.10 Adult Literacy Measures from the PIAAC and Average Schooling Years of the Labor Force in 2010

only a tiny fraction of the young-age population completes good quality secondary schooling and earns higher test scores, the majority of the young-age population does not attend even primary schools; thus, in such cases, the average test scores of the secondary-school students cannot adequately measure the cognitive skills of the overall school-age population or the labor force. Therefore, we need to gauge the skill levels for those who are uneducated and primary and tertiary educated.

For simplicity, we may assume that those who are uneducated or primary and tertiary educated among the population aged 15 to 24 have the same level of skills attained by the students at secondary schools. If test scores are determined only by individual ability and family factors, rather than by school inputs, the assumption that everyone in the school-age population attains the same skill level in each country could be justified. Moreover, by further assuming that a person's cognitive skills obtained at school remain unchanged over time (after the age of 25), we could construct an estimate of skill attainments for the population aged 15 to 64. However, the estimation based on this assumption must overestimate the skill levels attained by the uneducated and primary-educated populations and underestimate the skill levels attained by tertiary-educated students.[16]

A better approach is to construct a measure of human capital that includes both the quantity and the quality of schooling. The next subsection describes this procedure and discusses the estimation of education quality-adjusted human capital stock measures.

Construction of Quality-Adjusted Human Capital Stock

Average years of schooling and test scores variables turn out to be statistically significant in individual-earning regressions as well as in cross-country growth regressions.[17] This result suggests that both variables provide useful information about a country's educational capital stock.

We attempt to construct an aggregate human capital measure that combines the test scores for quality of schooling and the average years of schooling for quantity of schooling. The average years of schooling is defined as

$$S = \sum_a \sum_j dur_j^a l_j^a, j = \text{primary, secondary, tertiary}, a = 15-19, \ldots 60-64.$$

$$(6.4)$$

where dur_j^a is the duration of schooling at level j for population group a, and l_j^a is the fraction of population group a that has attained educational level j. If the marginal rate of return on an additional school year is constant for all education levels and all age groups, equation (6.4) is a good measure of human capital. Note that this formula assumes perfect substitutability among different schooling levels. It is practically difficult to estimate the elasticity of substitution among multiple skill types.

An alternative measure of human capital stock is related to the number of years of schooling by the Mincerian equation, such as

$$h = \sum_a \sum_j e^{\theta_j^a dur_j^a} l_j^a, j = \text{primary, secondary, tertiary}; a = 15-19, \ldots, 60-64.$$

$$(6.5)$$

As explained in chapter 4, this specification suggests that the human capital per worker across all education categories is the weighted sum of the shares of workers multiplied by the relative marginal products (or relative wage rates, i.e., $e^{\theta_j^a dur_j^a}$) compared to that of the uneducated worker. It contrasts the "average years of schooling" measure of equation (6.4), which uses the duration of education as the weight for the shares of workers.

We attempt to construct an aggregate human capital measure that uses test scores to gauge quality of schooling by extending equations (6.4) and (6.5).

We assume that the marginal return on an additional year of schooling increases with the quality of education. Then, a measure of the quality-adjusted average years of schooling is constructed as

$$S_q = \sum_a \sum_j \left(q_j^a\right)^\lambda dur_j^a l_j^a \tag{6.6}$$

In this equation, $\left(q_j^a\right)^\lambda$ measures the quality of the education level j that is attained by the population group a. It indicates that the higher the education quality, the higher the rate of return on an additional year of schooling. The parameter λ measures the return on educational quality or test scores at each educational level.

Alternatively, we can extend equation (6.5) by assuming that not only the number of years of schooling but also the quality of schooling is important for human capital accumulation. Then, a measure of the Mincerian-type quality-adjusted human capital stock is constructed as

$$h_q = \sum_a \sum_j e^{\left(\theta_s dur_j^a + \theta_q q_j^a\right)} l_j^a \tag{6.7}$$

This equation provides a second measure of average quality-adjusted human capital stock for the working-age population. The specification shows that, for fixed-quality differentials between educational systems, the logarithmic human capital differential (or logarithmic wage differential) increases proportionally with the years of schooling by θ_s, and for given school years, the logarithmic human capital differential increases with the quality of education by θ_q. In this form, school quality influences the log of human capital independently of the number of years of schooling.[18]

Using equations (6.6) and (6.7), we construct two measures of average quality-adjusted human capital stock for the population aged 15 to 64 at five-year intervals from 1950 to 2010. We first need to estimate the parameters in the specifications.

International data on the education-wage profiles derived from the Mincerian equation are available (Psacharopoulos, 1994). It is often assumed that the marginal rate of return on an additional school year (measured by the wage rate) is constant at 10%, the world average of return rates (Psacharopoulos, 1994). However, this specification does not control for the quality of education.

Bratsberg and Terrell (2002) and Schoellman (2012) used the estimated returns on schooling of immigrants in the United States to measure educational quality across countries. The country-specific return on schooling of foreign-educated immigrants would be associated with the quality of schooling in their birth countries. For a sample of 130 countries, using the 2000 US census data, Schoellman (2012) measured the average rate of return as 11.1%, which is close to the world average return. However, the estimates vary across countries. Figure 6.11 plots the estimated returns on school-ing of immigrants in 2000 against international test scores for secondary students in 1990. We use ten-year lagged values of international test scores, considering the time lag between completing education in their source country and securing employment in the United States. The result shows that immigrants from countries having high education quality tend to have higher returns in the US labor market. Although the estimates are subject to selection bias due to endogenous immigration decisions, the result indicates the important role of educational quality on earnings.

The effect of educational quality on earnings relative to schooling years can be drawn from existing studies. Hanushek and Woessmann (2008) surveyed various studies that assessed the impacts of cognitive skills on individual earnings after con-trolling for years of schooling within individual countries. Recent US studies provide consistent estimates of the impact of test performance on earnings after allowing for differences in the quantity of schooling, experience of workers, and other factors that might influence earnings (Mulligan, 1999; Murnane et al., 2000; Lazear, 2003). Because the units of measurement differ across tests, it is convenient to convert test scores into measures of distribution of achievement across the population. After stan-dardizing the scores, Murnane et al. (2000) suggested that an increase of one standard deviation of test performance translates into 15% and 10% higher annual earnings for males and females, respectively. Mulligan (1999) and Lazear (2003) provided es-timates of 11% and 12%, respectively. Many studies support the positive impacts of cognitive skills in other countries, including developing countries. The estimates show

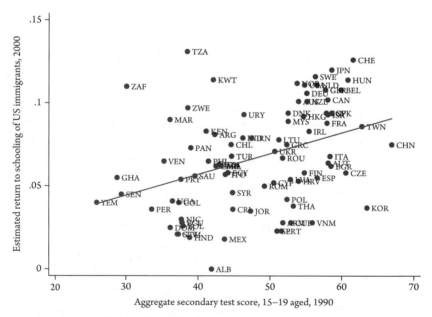

Figure 6.11 Returns on Schooling of US Immigrants and International Test Scores
NOTES: The estimated returns to schooling of foreign-educated immigrants in the United States, based on the US census in 2000, are sourced from Schoellman (2012). The international test scores are aggregate test scores for secondary students' test scores between 1965 and 2010. The regression line is y = 0.0078 + 0.0013*x, the t-values are 0.41 and 3.76, and R-squared = 0.14.

considerable heterogeneity across countries: the impact of a one-standard-deviation increase in measured test performance on earnings ranges from 5 to 7% in Ghana and from 34 to 48% in South Africa (Hanushek and Woessmann, 2008, Table 1).

Recently, Hanushek et al. (2013) used the new PIAAC survey data to show that adult skills have a significant impact on lifetime earnings. When years of schooling and other determinants are controlled, a one-standard-deviation increase in adult numeracy skills is associated with a 10.1% wage increase among prime-age workers, on average, in 22 countries. However, the estimates vary widely, ranging from 5.7% in Italy to 17.3% in the United Kingdom. In contrast, an additional year of schooling is associated, on average, with a 5.9% wage increase among prime-age workers.

Considering all the available evidence, we assume that the marginal rate of return on an additional school year is constant at 7%, given the educational quality. Then, we assume that an increase of one standard deviation of educational quality measured by aggregate test scores is associated with a 10% increase in earnings, given the average years of schooling.[19]

We construct the quality-adjusted human capital stock measure based on this information. In equation (6.6), we assume that $\lambda = 1.5$. In equation (6.7), we calibrate the parameters to make the average rate of return ono an additional year of schooling equal to 7% and the average rate of return on a one-standard-deviation increase of educational quality (independent of average years of schooling) equal to 10%. This implies that $\theta_s = 0.07$ and $\theta_q = 0.10$.

We then make several additional assumptions. First, we assume that the educational quality obtained by secondary students at age 15 is the same as the educational qualities obtained by primary and tertiary students who enroll in schools at the same time in each country. As discussed in section 6.1, there is no internationally comparable assessment that quantitatively measures the difference in educational qualities at the primary or tertiary levels relative to that at the secondary level across countries and over time.[20]

Second, we assume that a person's cognitive skills that are obtained at the secondary- and tertiary-school levels before the age of 25 remain unchanged over time. This assumption implies that graduates from tertiary schools do not obtain further cognitive skills at their workplaces.

Third, we extrapolate the test scores prior to 1965 using the estimated growth rates in Table 6.4 and project forward these figures for the older-age population groups with an appropriate time lag. This assumption is necessary, because we do not have data on test scores of the older age groups who attended schools before 1965.

The final data set contains the estimates of average educational quality-adjusted human capital stock for the population aged 15 to 64 at five-year intervals from 1950 to 2010. Figure 6.12 depicts the evolution of quality-adjusted average years of schooling (S_q) and quality-adjusted human capital stock (h_q) across regions as measured by equations (6.6) and (6.7). Since 1960, human capital accumulation has recorded significant progress in both advanced and developing regions. Among the developing regions, the Asia-Pacific region has shown strong progress compared to that of Sub-Saharan Africa.

Figure 6.13 A plots the estimated quality-adjusted average years of schooling (S_q) against average years of schooling (S) across countries in 2010. While the results

A. Quality-adjusted Average Years of Schooling

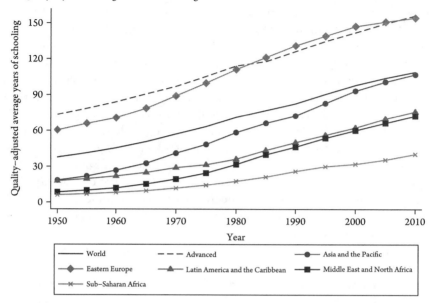

B. Quality-adjusted Human Capital

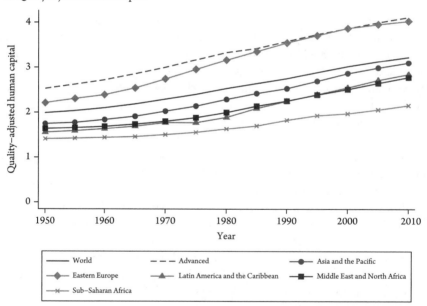

Figure 6.12 Trends of Quality-adjusted Human Capital of the Working-age Population by Group and Region, 1950–2010

NOTES: The measure in (A) is an estimate of average quality-adjusted years of schooling for the working-age population based on equation (6.6), and the measure in (B) is an estimate of average quality-adjusted human capital stock based on the Mincerian relationship in equation (6.7). The data for the group or region are the averages weighted by the country population size.

A. Quality-adjusted Average Years of Schooling

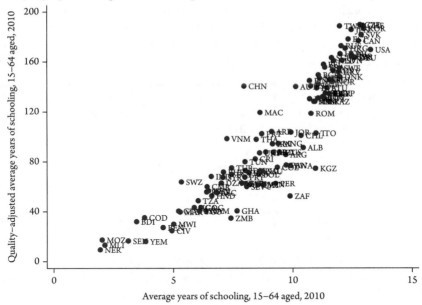

B. Quality-adjusted Human Capital

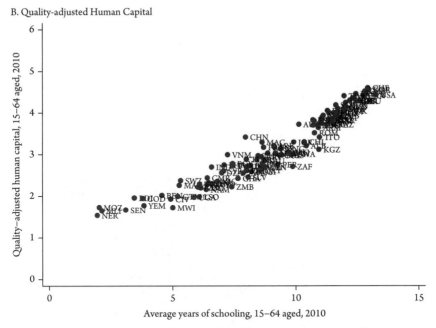

Figure 6.13 Quality-adjusted Human Capital Stock Measure and Average Years of Schooling across Countries, 2010
NOTE: See Figure 6.12

show a positive association, there is no one-to-one relation. Figure 6.13 B plots the quality-adjusted human capital stock (h_q) against average years of schooling (S): the results show a much stronger relationship. This closer relationship reflects that differences in educational quality have much larger influences for the quality-adjusted human capital stock measure (h_q) in (6.7), compared to the quality-adjusted average years of schooling (S_q) in (6.6).

Additionally, we have constructed a measure of educational quality for the working-age population by dividing each quality-adjusted educational attainment measure by its corresponding educational quantity measure:

$$Q_s \equiv S_q / S = \left(\sum_a \sum_j \left(q_j^a \right)^\lambda \mathrm{dur}_j^a 1_j^a \right) / \left(\sum_a \sum_j \mathrm{dur}_j^a 1_j^a \right) \qquad (6.8)$$

$$Q_q \equiv h_q / h = \left(\sum_a \sum_j e^{(\theta_s \mathrm{dur}_j^a + \theta_q q_j^a)} 1_j^a \right) / \left(\sum_a \sum_j e^{\theta_j^a \mathrm{dur}_j^a} 1_j^a \right) \qquad (6.9)$$

Figures 6.14. A and B plot each educational quality measure against average years of schooling across countries in 2010. In panel A, educational quality measure based on (6.8) has a positive association with quantity of schooling, but the relationship is much weaker with the educational quality measure based on the Mincerian equation.

A. Education Quality based on (6.8)

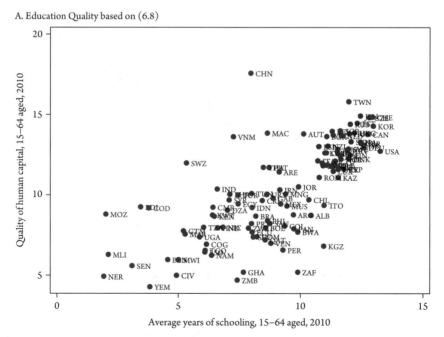

Figure 6.14 Educational Quality and Average Years of Schooling for the Working-Age Population Across Countries, 2010

B. Education Quality based on (6.9)

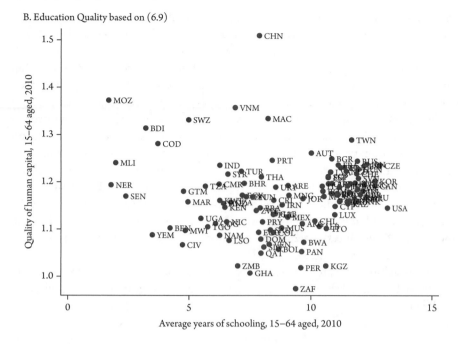

Figure 6.14 (continued)

6.5 EDUCATIONAL QUALITY, HUMAN CAPITAL, AND ECONOMIC GROWTH

Hanushek and Kimko (2000) and Hanushek and Woessmann (2012) found that the test-score measure is more significantly linked to economic growth than to average number of years of schooling in cross-country regressions. Using the updated test-score data for 77 countries that have participated at least once in any of the mathematics and science tests, Hanushek and Woessmann (2012) showed that the positive relationship between cognitive skills and economic growth is robust to alternative specifications and to the use of different subsamples. However, almost all empirical results are based on cross-section data that rely on the average test score and growth rate of each nation. Potential biases from endogeneity and missing variables are more serious in this framework: the educational quality for secondary students can increase with investment in resources by parents and the government, which are influenced positively by economic growth. In addition, unidentified country-specific factors can influence both educational quality and economic growth.[21]

Subsequent researches observe a more significant role of average schooling year on economic growth in the regressions where both average years of schooling and a test score are included. Breton (2011) pointed out the reverse causality from the average test score to the average growth rate and suggested that overall years of schooling explains a larger portion of the differences in GDP per capita across countries than test scores do. Castelló-Climent and Hidalgo-Cabrillana (2012) found a nonlinear relation between test scores and economic growth, indicating that the contribution of educational quality to economic growth increases at higher levels of educational quality, and they also confirmed a positive impact of average schooling year on economic growth, when the average test score is controlled. Islam, Ang, and Madsen (2014) constructed a composite indicator of education quality based on the method of principal component analysis, an approach that is often used to reduce a set of possibly correlated variables into a smaller set of linearly uncorrelated variables. Their set of educational quality variables includes nonrepetition rates at the primary and secondary levels; test scores in mathematics, science, and reading at the primary and secondary levels; and the number of universities per worker listed in the top 500 rankings of the Shanghai Jiao Tong University's Academic Ranking of World Universities. Their results indicate a positive effect of the quality-adjusted human capital measure, defined as the average years of schooling multiplied by an educational quality composite indicator, on total factor productivity growth across countries.

In this section, we extend the panel growth regression in chapter 4 to investigate the impact of schooling quality and quantity on economic growth. The specification is as follows:

$$Dy_{i,t} = \beta_0 + \beta_1 \log(y_{i,t}) + \beta_2 S_{qi,t} + \beta_3 X_{i,t} + \varepsilon_{i,t} \qquad \textbf{(6.10)}$$

In this specification, Dy_{it} represents the annual growth rate of real per-worker GDP over each five-year period. The variable S_q is a measure of quality-adjusted average years of schooling in (6.6).[22] Our empirical strategy differs from those in the previous studies: we control a set of other important factors for economic growth (X_{it}) and adopt an instrumental-variable technique to control for the possible endogeneity of the control variables. In addition, a fixed-effects estimation technique is used to control for unobserved, persistent country characteristics that influence economic growth.

Our regression in the form of equation (6.10) applies to a panel of cross-country data for 70 countries over ten five-year periods from 1960 to 2010, corresponding to the periods 1960–1965, 1965–1970, 1970–1975, 1975–1980, 1980–1985, 1985–1990, 1990–1995, 1995–2000, 2000–2005, and 2005–2010.

Table 6.9 presents the regression results using the basic framework of equation (6.10). Since the results for most of the other explanatory variables are similar to those in Table 5.5, we focus on human capital variables, instead of reporting all of the results.

Column 1 of Table 6.9 presents the results of the regression that includes only the average years of schooling. Column 2 adds the square term of the average schooling years variable. The specifications in columns 1 and 2 replicate columns 2 and 4 of Table 5.5. Column 1 of Table 6.9 shows a negative, but statistically insignificant, coefficient of the overall number of years of schooling, −0.0013 (s.e. = 0.0017). The estimated coefficients of the overall school attainment in column 2, −0.0052 (s.e. = 0.0025) for the linear term and 0.00033 (s.e. = 0.00016) for the squared term, are significantly different from zero at the 5% level. These results imply an initial fall and a subsequent increase in per-worker GDP growth

Table 6.9 REGRESSIONS FOR GROWTH RATES OF GDP PER WORKING-AGE
POPULATION

	(1)	(2)	(3)	(4)
Average schooling years	−0.00127 (0.00169)	−0.00522** (0.00245)		
Average schooling years squared		0.000328** (0.000160)		
Quality-adjusted human capital			0.000273* (0.000152)	0.0000408 (0.000228)
Quality-adjusted human capital squared				0.000000988 (0.000000757)
No. of countries; No. of obs.	76, 722	76, 722	70, 666	70, 666
	(5)	**(6)**	**(7)**	**(8)**
Average schooling years	−0.00174 (0.00169)	−0.000364 (0.00266)	−0.00741*** (0.00221)	−0.0131*** (0.00500)
Average schooling years squared		−0.0000198 (0.000176)		0.0000234 (0.000272)
Educational quality	0.00138 (0.00301)	−0.0226*** (0.00695)		
Educational quality squared		0.00127*** (0.000346)		
Quality-adjusted educational attainment			0.000719*** (0.000202)	0.00161*** (0.000489)
Quality-adjusted educational attainment				−0.00000245 (0.00000153)
No. of countries; No. of obs.	70, 666	70, 666	70, 666	70, 666

NOTES: The panel specification uses a panel data for ten 5-year periods, 1960–65, . . . , 2005–2010. Columns 1 and 2 replicate columns 2 and 4 of Table 5.5. The results for other explanatory variables are not reported. Quality-adjusted educational attainment is constructed by specification (6.6), while educational quality is constructed by specification (6.7). Standard errors are in parenthesis. * p < 0.1, ** p < 0.05, *** p < 0.01.

with improving educational attainment. The implied breakpoint is at the average number of years of schooling of 8.0.

Columns 3 and 4 replace the average years of schooling variables with the quality-adjusted educational attainment variables. The sample shrinks to 666 observations for the 70 countries for which data on schooling quality are available on schooling quality for the period from 1960 to 2010.

In column 3, the coefficient on quality-adjusted educational attainment turns out to be positive, though marginally significant at the 10% level. The point estimate on quality-adjusted educational attainment, 0.00027 (s.e. = 0.00015), implies that an increase in quality-adjusted average years of schooling by one standard deviation of 45.4, for given values of the other explanatory variables, increases the growth rate of per-worker GDP by about 1.2 percentage points a year.

In column 4, the estimated coefficients on quality-adjusted educational attainment and its square terms are positive, showing a different pattern from those on average schooling years in column 2. They are not individually statistically significant, but jointly statistically significant, though marginally so at the 10% level (p-value = 0.10).

Column 5 includes average schooling years and educational quality. The estimated coefficient is positive for educational quality, but negative for average number of years of schooling, although both are statistically insignificant. Column 6 adds their square terms and presents the statistically insignificant coefficients of the linear and square terms of overall school attainments individually and jointly. In contrast, the coefficients of educational quality, −0.0226 (s.e. = 0.0070) for the linear term and 0.00127 (s.e. = 0.00035) for the squared term, are significantly different from zero, suggesting an initial fall and a subsequent increase in per-worker GDP growth with improving educational quality. The educational quality of 8.9 is an implied breakpoint. Above this breakpoint were about 53% of the country-year observations in the regressions.

Column 7 includes average schooling years and quality-adjusted educational attainment. The estimated coefficient is positive, 0.00072 (s.e. = 0.0002), for quality-adjusted educational attainment and negative, −0.0074 (s.e. = 0.0022), for average schooling years. Both of them are individually statistically significant at the 1% level. Thus, an increase in quality-adjusted educational attainment, for given values of overall schooling years and other explanatory variables, has a positive effect on economic growth. In this specification, the effect of an additional schooling year on growth, controlling for the level of quality-adjusted educational attainment, is negative. Given quality-adjusted educational attainment, an increase in average number of schooling years means that quality-adjusted attainment is due less to quality and more to quantity. Therefore, the negative coefficient of average schooling years in this specification reflects the positive effect of educational quality on economic growth. The patterns of the coefficients on quality-adjusted educational attainment and average schooling years also indicate that the increase in average years of schooling can influence economic growth through two channels: by its own impact, and by the increase in quality-adjusted educational attainment. The patterns also indicate the net effect can be positive when the second channel dominates the first channel.

Column 8 adds the square terms of average schooling years and quality-adjusted educational attainment. Like the results in column 7, the linear term of quality-adjusted educational attainment enters positively, while that of average schooling years enters negatively. The coefficients are individually statistically significant at the 1% level. In contrast, the square term of quality-adjusted educational attainment is negatively related, while that of average number of schooling years is positively related. But their estimated coefficients are individually statistically insignificant.

Overall, the regressions support a positive effect of educational quality or quality-adjusted human capital stock on economic growth, when average number of schooling years is controlled.

Appendix Table Availability of Test Scores

A1. Primary Test Scores

Country	No. of obs.				Year									
	M	S	R	Total	1965	1970	1975	1980	1985	1990	1995	2000	2005	2010
Advanced Economies (24)														
Australia	3	4	1	4					s				ms	ms
Austria	3	3	2	3							ms		ms	ms
Belgium	2	3	2	4		s				r			ms	ms
Canada	2	3	2	4					s	ms	ms			r
Denmark	2	2	3	3						r			ms	ms
Finland	1	3	3	4		s			s	r			ms	ms
France	0	0	4	4						r		r	r	r
Germany	2	3	4	5		s				r		r	ms	ms
Greece	1	1	2	3						r	ms	r		
Iceland	1	1	3	4						r	ms	r	r	
Ireland	3	3	2	3						ms	ms	r		ms
Italy	3	5	5	6		s			s	ms			ms	ms
Japan	3	5	0	5		s			s		ms		ms	ms
Luxembourg	0	0	1	1									r	
Netherlands	3	4	5	6		s				r	ms	r	ms	ms
New Zealand	3	3	4	5						r	ms	r	ms	ms
Norway	3	4	4	6					s	r	ms	r	ms	ms
Portugal	3	3	2	3						ms	ms		ms	ms
Spain	2	2	3	3						ms			r	ms
Sweden	2	4	5	6		s			s	r	ms	r	ms	ms

continued

Appendix Table (CONTINUED)

A1. Primary Test Scores

Country	No. of obs.				Year									
	M	S	R	Total	1965	1970	1975	1980	1985	1990	1995	2000	2005	2010
Switzerland	0	0	1	1						r				
Turkey	1	1	1	2								r		ms
United Kingdom	4	6	1	6		s			s	ms	ms		ms	ms
United States	4	6	5	7		s			s	ms	ms	r	ms	ms
Asia and the Pacific (9)														
Hong Kong SAR, China	3	4	4	6					s	r	ms	r	ms	ms
India	0	1	1	1		s								
Indonesia	0	0	3	3						r			r	r
Korea, Rep.	3	4	0	4					s	ms	ms		ms	ms
Mongolia	1	1	0	1									ms	
Philippines	1	2	0	2					s				ms	
Singapore	3	4	4	6					s	r	ms	r	ms	ms
Taiwan	3	3	0	3						ms			ms	ms
Thailand	2	3	0	3		s					ms			ms
Eastern Europe (20)														
Armenia	2	2	0	2									ms	ms
Azerbaijan	1	1	1	1										ms
Bulgaria	0	0	3	3								r	r	r
Croatia	1	1	1	1										ms
Czech Republic	3	3	2	4							ms	r	ms	ms

Georgia	2	2	2	2	s				ms		ms
Hungary	4	6	5	7		ms			ms	ms	ms
Kazakhstan	2	2	0	2					ms	ms	ms
Latvia	2	2	2	3			ms	r	ms	ms	ms
Lithuania	2	2	3	3				r	ms		ms
Macedonia, FYR	0	0	2	2				r	r		
Moldova	1	1	2	2				r	ms		ms
Poland	1	2	2	3	s				r		ms
Romania	1	1	3	3				r	r		ms
Russian Federation	3	3	3	4		ms		r	ms	ms	ms
Serbia	1	1	0	1					ms		ms
Slovak Republic	2	2	3	3				r	ms		ms
Slovenia	3	3	3	4			ms	r	ms	ms	ms
Ukraine	1	1	0	1					ms		
Yugoslavia	1	0	1	1		m					
Latin America and the Caribbean (21)											
Argentina	2	1	3	3			m	r	ms		
Belize	0	0	1	1				r			
Bolivia	1	0	1	1			m				
Brazil	2	0	2	2			m		m		
Chile	3	2	3	4	s		m		m	m	ms
Colombia	2	1	4	4			m	r	ms		r
Costa Rica	1	1	1	1					ms		
Cuba	2	1	2	2			m		ms		
Dominican Republic	2	1	2	2			m		ms		
Ecuador	1	0	1	1					m		
El Salvador	1	1	1	1					ms		

243

continued

A1. Primary Test Scores

Appendix Table (CONTINUED)

Country	No. of obs.				Year									
	M	S	R	Total	1965	1970	1975	1980	1985	1990	1995	2000	2005	2010
Guatemala	1	0	1	1									m	
Honduras	2	1	1	2							m			ms
Mexico	2	0	2	2							m		m	
Nicaragua	1	0	1	1									m	
Panama	1	1	1	1									ms	
Paraguay	2	1	2	2							m		ms	
Peru	1	1	1	1									ms	
Trinidad and Tobago	0	0	3	3						r			r	r
Uruguay	1	0	1	1									m	
Venezuela, RB	1	0	2	2						r	m			
Middle East and North Africa (14)														
Algeria	1	1	0	1									ms	
Bahrain	1	1	0	1										ms
Cyprus	2	2	2	4						r	ms	r	ms	
Iran, Islamic Rep.	3	4	4	5		s					ms	r	ms	
Israel	2	2	3	5						ms	ms	r	r	r
Kuwait	3	3	2	4							ms		ms	
Malta	1	1	1	1										ms
Morocco	2	2	3	3								r	ms	ms
Oman	1	1	1	1										ms
Qatar	2	2	2	2									ms	ms
Saudi Arabia	1	1	1	1										ms

Country								
Tunisia	2	2	0	2			ms	ms
United Arab Emirates	1	1	1	1				ms
Yemen, Rep.	2	2	0	2			ms	ms
Sub-Saharan Africa (27)								
Benin	1	0	1	1			m	
Botswana	3	1	2	3		m	m	ms
Burkina Faso	1	0	1	1			m	
Burundi	1	0	1	1				m
Cameroon	1	0	1	1				
Chad	2	0	2	2			m	m
Comoros	1	0	1	1			m	m
Congo, Dem. Rep.	1	0	1	1				m
Congo, Rep.	1	0	1	1				m
Cote d'Ivoire	1	0	1	1				m
Gabon	1	0	1	1		m	m	
Kenya	2	0	3	3	r	m	m	
Lesotho	2	0	2	2			m	
Madagascar	1	0	1	1			m	
Malawi	2	0	4	4	r	m	m	
Mauritius	2	0	3	3	r	m	m	
Mozambique	2	0	2	2		m	m	
Namibia	2	0	3	3	r	m	m	
Senegal	1	0	1	1			m	
Seychelles	2	0	2	2		m	m	
South Africa	2	0	2	2		m	m	
Swaziland	2	0	2	2		m	m	
Tanzania	2	0	2	2		m	m	

continued

Appendix Table (CONTINUED)

A1. Primary Test Scores

Country	No. of obs.				Year									
	M	S	R	Total	1965	1970	1975	1980	1985	1990	1995	2000	2005	2010
Togo	1	0	1	1										m
Uganda	2	0	2	2								m	m	
Zambia	2	0	3	3							r	m		
Zimbabwe	1	0	2	2							r		m	

A2. Secondary Test Scores

Country	No. of obs.				Year									
	M	S	R	Total	1965	1970	1975	1980	1985	1990	1995	2000	2005	2010
Advanced Economies (24)														
Australia	5	6	3	7	m	s			s		ms	ms	ms	ms
Austria	4	4	3	4							ms	ms	ms	ms
Belgium	6	4	4	8	m	s		m		r	m	ms	ms	ms
Canada	6	6	4	7				m	s	ms	ms	ms	ms	ms
Denmark	4	4	4	5						r	ms	ms	ms	ms
Finland	5	5	4	8	m	s			s	r	ms	ms	ms	ms
France	7	5	4	7	m			m		ms	ms	ms	ms	ms
Germany	5	5	4	7	m	s		m		r	ms	ms	ms	ms
Greece	4	4	4	5						r	ms	ms	ms	ms
Iceland	4	4	4	5						r	ms	ms	ms	ms
Ireland	5	5	4	5						ms	ms	ms	ms	ms

Country													
Italy	5	7	4	7		s		s	ms	ms	ms	ms	ms
Japan	6	6	3	8	m	s	m	s		ms	ms	ms	ms
Luxembourg	4	3	3	4	m		m		r		ms	ms	ms
Netherlands	6	6	3	9	m	s	m	s	r	ms	ms	ms	ms
New Zealand	5	5	4	7	m	s	m	s	r	ms	ms	ms	ms
Norway	4	5	4	6				s		ms	ms	ms	ms
Portugal	5	5	4	5					ms	ms	ms	ms	ms
Spain	5	5	4	5		s			ms	ms	ms	ms	ms
Sweden	6	6	4	9	m	s	m	s	r	ms	ms	ms	ms
Switzerland	5	5	4	5					ms	ms	ms	ms	ms
Turkey	3	3	2	3						ms	ms	ms	ms
United Kingdom	7	7	3	9	m	s	m	s	ms	ms	ms	ms	ms
United States	7	7	4	9	m	s	m	s	ms	ms	ms	ms	ms
Asia and the Pacific (13)													
China	1	0	0	1					m				
Hong Kong SAR, China	5	5	4	7	m		m	s	r	ms	ms	ms	ms
India	0	1	0	1		s						ms	ms
Indonesia	3	3	3	3					ms	ms	ms	ms	ms
Korea, Rep.	5	6	3	6		s		s		ms	ms	ms	ms
Macao SAR, China	2	2	2	2						ms	ms	ms	ms
Malaysia	3	3	1	3							ms	ms	ms
Mongolia	1	1	0	1								ms	
Philippines	2	3	1	4				s	r		ms	ms	
Singapore	4	5	2	6		s		s	r	ms	ms	ms	ms
Taiwan	4	3	0	4					ms	m	m	ms	ms
Thailand	5	6	4	8	m	s	m	s	r	ms	ms	ms	ms
Vietnam	1	0	1	1									m

continued

Appendix Table (CONTINUED)

A2. Secondary Test Scores

Country	No. of obs.				Year									
	M	S	R	Total	1965	1970	1975	1980	1985	1990	1995	2000	2005	2010
Eastern Europe (26)														
Albania	2	2	2	2								ms		ms
Armenia	2	2	0	2									ms	ms
Azerbaijan	2	2	2	2									ms	ms
Bosnia and Herzegovina	1	1	0	1									ms	
Bulgaria	4	3	3	4							m	ms	ms	ms
Croatia	2	2	2	2									ms	ms
Czech Republic	4	4	3	4							ms	ms	ms	ms
Estonia	2	2	2	2									ms	ms
Georgia	2	2	0	2									ms	ms
Hungary	6	7	4	8		s		m	s	ms	ms	ms	ms	ms
Kazakhstan	1	1	1	1										ms
Kyrgyz Republic	2	2	2	2									ms	ms
Latvia	4	4	3	4							ms	ms	ms	ms
Liechtenstein	3	3	3	3								ms	ms	ms
Lithuania	4	4	2	4							ms	ms	ms	ms
Macedonia, FYR	3	3	1	3								ms	ms	ms
Moldova	3	3	0	3									ms	ms
Montenegro	2	2	2	2									ms	ms
Poland	3	4	3	4					s			ms	ms	ms
Romania	4	4	2	4							ms	ms	ms	ms
Russian Federation	5	5	3	5						ms	ms	ms	ms	ms

Country									
Serbia	2	2	2					ms	ms
Slovak Republic	4	2	4			ms	ms	ms	ms
Slovenia	4	2	4			ms	ms	ms	ms
Ukraine	2	0	2					ms	ms
Yugoslavia	1	0	1		m				
Latin America and the Caribbean (19)									
Argentina	3	3	3				ms	ms	ms
Brazil	4	3	4		ms		ms	ms	ms
Chile	3	3	4	s			ms	ms	ms
Colombia	3	2	3			ms		ms	ms
Costa Rica	1	2	2					r	ms
Cuba	0	0	1					r	
Dominican Republic	0	1	1					r	
Ecuador	0	1	1					r	
El Salvador	1	1	1					ms	
Guatemala	0	1	1					r	
Honduras	1	0	1						ms
Mexico	3	3	3				ms	ms	ms
Nicaragua	0	1	1					r	
Panama	1	2	2					r	ms
Paraguay	0	1	1					r	
Peru	2	3	3				ms	r	ms
Trinidad and Tobago	1	2	2		r				ms
Uruguay	2	2	2					ms	ms
Middle East and North Africa (19)									
Algeria	1	1	0						ms
Bahrain	2	2	0					ms	ms

continued

Appendix Table (CONTINUED)

A2. Secondary Test Scores

Country	No. of obs.				Year									
	M	S	R	Total	1965	1970	1975	1980	1985	1990	1995	2000	2005	2010
Cyprus	4	4	2	5						r	ms	ms	ms	ms
Egypt, Arab Rep.	1	1	0	1									ms	ms
Iran, Islamic Rep.	4	5	0	5		s					ms	ms	ms	ms
Israel	7	5	3	7	m			m		ms	ms	ms	ms	ms
Jordan	4	4	2	4						ms	ms	ms	ms	ms
Kuwait	2	2	0	2							ms		ms	
Lebanon	2	2	0	2									ms	ms
Malta	2	2	0	2									ms	ms
Morocco	3	3	0	3								ms	ms	ms
Oman	2	2	0	2									ms	ms
Qatar	2	2	2	2									ms	ms
Saudi Arabia	2	2	0	2									ms	ms
Syrian Arab Republic	2	2	0	2									ms	ms
Tunisia	3	3	2	3								ms	ms	ms
United Arab Emirates	1	1	1	1									ms	ms
West Bank and Gaza	2	2	0	2									ms	ms
Yemen, Rep.	0	1	0	1									s	
Sub-Saharan Africa (15)														
Botswana	3	2	1	4						r		m	ms	ms

Ghana	2	2	0	2					ms	ms
Madagascar	1	0	0	1				m		
Malawi	1	0	0	1				m		
Mali	1	0	0	1				m		
Mauritius	2	1	0	2				m		ms
Mozambique	1	0	0	1		m				
Niger	1	0	0	1	m			m		
Nigeria	1	0	1	2		r				
Senegal	1	0	0	1				m		
South Africa	4	2	0	4			m	ms	ms	m
Swaziland	1	0	0	1	m					
Uganda	1	0	0	1				m		
Zambia	1	0	0	1				m		
Zimbabwe	0	0	1	1		r				

NOTES: M indicates math only, S indicates science only, and R indicates reading only.

251

Conclusions

This chapter summarizes the main findings and arguments of the previous chapters and discusses emerging challenges related to education and human development.

This book presented a number of new data sets on educational attainment for a broad number of countries. It introduced estimates of educational attainment for the total, male, and female populations for 146 countries at five-year intervals from 1950 to 2010. This data set improves on our previous work by incorporating newly available census/survey observations and adopting improved estimation methodologies. The other data set presented in this book comprises newly constructed estimates of historical educational attainment for the working-age population from 1870 to 1945 for 89 countries. The estimates are disaggregated by gender and broad age groups of 15–24 and 25–64 years. Another new data set projects educational attainment for the working-age population, disaggregated by gender and by the broad age groups. These data are available for 146 countries from 2015 to 2040 at five-year intervals.

Combining these three data sets, we highlighted the long-term trends of educational attainment for the world and across regions over two centuries from 1870 to 2040.

In 1870, the world's population had very limited access to schooling. According to our estimates, the proportion of the uneducated among the total population aged 15–64 was around 90%. Education occurred mostly in the advanced countries wherein primary education began to expand in the 19th century. Meanwhile, for most developing countries, modern primary education began only in the latter half of the 19th century or the early 20th century. At this time, secondary and tertiary education was still undeveloped in advanced and developing regions of the world.

The 20th century was a century of education. The world has witnessed a dramatic expansion of educational attainment in advanced and developing countries. In most developing countries, the expansion of secondary and tertiary education happened after World War II.

There also has been significant progress toward gender parity, as the gender gaps in educational attainment across education levels have narrowed significantly over the past decades. In 2010, the main remaining departure from near-parity is in some developing regions, including Sub-Saharan Africa, South Asia, and the Middle East/North Africa.

By 2010, the world achieved nearly universal primary education. In advanced countries, almost 90% of the working-age population had attained at least some secondary education, while over a third had attained some level of tertiary education. In developing countries, about two-thirds of the working-age population had attained at least some secondary education, but the percentage of the working-age population that had attained some tertiary level of education remained around 12%, a low number compared to advanced countries.

Over the next 30 years, our projections show a continuous and rapid rise in educational attainment of the working-age population for male and female populations. Parents' desire for their children's education, especially at the secondary and tertiary levels, will continue to remain high. National governments will continue to place education at the top of their policy agendas. The expansion of secondary education will result in a growing demand for tertiary education. In developing countries, over 27% of the working-age population is projected to attain some tertiary education by 2040. The level of educational attainment for the youth population in developing countries is projected to increase at a faster rate than that in advanced countries, continuing to narrow the education gap by 2040. Additionally, the gender gap in educational attainment is expected to disappear in all regions of the world.

More important, it is likely that the world, which has been divided between those who do and those who do not have full access to education over its long history, will see its entire population acquire similar levels of educational attainment by 2040. Of course, this indicator of rough equality applies to number of years of schooling, not necessarily to quality of schooling. This book also provides a newly constructed data set on the quality of education. Our main indicator of quality is an aggregate test score combining results on internationally comparable mathematics and science examinations. These data apply to primary- and secondary-school students in 134 countries at five-year intervals from 1965 to 2010. The data show that students in advanced economies performed considerably better than those in developing countries throughout the period. Thus, there is a large gap in the quality of education between advanced and developing countries and across developing regions.

A good measure of human capital includes measures of the quantity and quality of schooling. Using the aggregate test scores for secondary students as an estimate of the quality of education, we constructed estimates of average educational quality-adjusted human capital stock for adult populations.

An important agenda for many national governments is to establish quantitative targets for education and human development. Our estimates for the distribution of educational attainment by age and gender, and quality of education for individual countries, will assist in designing more-effective education policies.

This book systematically analyzed the role of educational attainment in economic and political development. Educational attainment is one of the key contributing factors behind the world's achievement in economic and political development over the past centuries.

We observed large variations in the growth rates of per-worker GDP across countries and over time. There exist considerable disparities in per-capita income across regions and countries. By adopting the development-accounting approach, we found that differences in average years of schooling explained between 10 and 15 percent of the differences in per-worker output across countries in 2010. The growth-accounting approach showed that about 22% of the world's per-worker GDP growth during 1961–2010 were explained by increases in human capital, while physical capital accumulation and total factor productivity growth accounted for the remainder of output growth.

To investigate the role of educational attainment in economic growth, we utilized two panel data sets—one comprising many variables for a large number of countries from 1960 to 2010, and the other with a more limited number of variables and countries but for a longer period, from 1870 to 2010. The empirical evidence on the causal effect of educational attainment on economic growth is not always strong. But, cross-country growth regressions provided supporting evidence for the positive contribution of overall educational attainment for long-term economic growth. In addition, the regressions showed a positive effect on growth from increasing female school attainment relative to male attainment.

The 20th century was also a century of modernization. Many countries have experienced democratization along with economic development. The cross-country regressions provided strong evidence for modernization with respect to effects of schooling, particularly female schooling, on democracy. These results can be interpreted as an expansion of more educated citizens, leading to higher political participation and greater support for democracy.

In the transition from a low-income, low-education society to a high-income, high-education society, the interaction among income, human capital accumulation, and fertility rates played an important role. There was a sharp reduction of fertility rates and, hence, population growth in many countries in the 20th century. As demonstrated in cross-country regressions, fertility rates were negatively affected, particularly by an increase in female schooling. In other words, the choice of more-educated females to have less children resulted in a lower rate of population growth and, thereby, a higher rate of per-capita income growth.

This book demonstrates the remarkable educational achievements worldwide over the past two centuries. Despite strong educational and human capital growth, however, there remain challenges to current and future educational development.

Removing disparities in opportunities for education still remains a significant challenge. A large portion of the adult population in low-income countries, such as those in Sub-Saharan Africa, still lacks access to basic education. In most emerging economies, including Brazil, China, and India, there exist educational inequalities between genders, and across social groups and economic strata. Disadvantaged children still have limited access to opportunities in education, especially at secondary and tertiary levels.

One of the important challenges in the coming decades will be to ensure the quality, rather than just the quantity, of education for all population groups. Wide disparities in quality of education are highly evident across countries as well as across regions and in social groups within a country. There are deep concerns about the inefficiency of educational systems and poor educational outcomes at all education levels throughout the world, drawing attention to the importance of educational quality.

In the advance from low-income to high-income status, a country has to improve its capacity for technological development by creating more skilled workers through upper-level secondary and tertiary education. In fact, many countries are trying to expand their higher education sector, while at the same time seeking to improve its quality. But developing countries face significant difficulties related to funding, qualified academics, and effective decision making in school administrations. The division between public and private schooling is also an important issue, though not one that we have addressed in this book.

To develop human capital with more diverse competencies and employable skills, it is necessary to strengthen not just general education but also technical and vocational education and training. Some critical areas of skills training include curriculum development, internship program implementation, school-industry partnerships, and retraining and lifelong learning for the workforce.

Education has major consequences not only for economic growth but also for the distribution of income. This book analyzed the contribution of education to cross-national disparities in income levels and growth rates. At the country level, better human capital is positively associated with productivity and economic growth. A faster rate of human capital accumulation in developing countries relative to advanced economies promoted reductions in the worldwide per-capita income gap. In the future, we foresee that human capital, interacting with technologies, continues to play an important role in economic growth and income differences across countries.

Modern economic growth has occurred in tandem with political development. Education has been a key factor to the modernization process. Human capital contributes to the development of representative democracy, which in turn affects human capital accumulation as well as economic development.

The next century will witness how the world and individual countries will advance overall human, economic, and political development. Further movements toward educational equality will moderate income differences across countries and promote further modernization, including a greater prevalence of democracy.

CHAPTER 1

1   Our earlier papers, published in 1993, 1996, 2001, and 2013, on estimates of educational attainment, have been widely cited by more than 10,060 publications as of March 2015, according to *Google Scholar*. Our website (www.barrolee.com) draws an average of 5,900 visitors each month.

2   See Lucas (1988), Barro (1991), and Mankiw, Romer and Weil (1992).

3   See the references and discussions in chapter 4 (4.5, 4.6).

4   See, for instance, Bils and Klenow (2000).

5   See, for instance, Acemoglu, Johnson, Robinson, and Yared (2005).

6   We do not intend to provide a comprehensive comparative history of educational development. There is a vast research literature from various academic disciplines (economics, education, politics, and sociology) that discuss the history of educational expansion and formalization. This literature includes Kandel (1930), UNESCO's *World Survey of Education* (1958, 1961 and 1966), Benavot, Resnick, and Corrales (2006), Benavot and Riddle (1988), and Marlow-Ferguson and Lopez (2002).

CHAPTER 2

1   Tilak (1989) provided a survey of these studies, and Fredriksen (1991) discussed the underlying data.

2   Lee and Barro (2001) show that dropout rates at the primary level for all developing countries were quite high, averaging about 40% in 1970.

3   See Lee and Lee (2014) for details on the original data and estimation methods. The exact sources of original data and estimates for individual countries are available online (http:/www.barrolee.com).

4   A proper accounting of net educational investment also deducts dropouts from gross enrollments. Note that actual enrollment numbers, such as the total number of registered students or average yearly enrollments, reported in censuses and surveys exclude those who have dropped out of school at the time of the survey. However, because students drop out of school during the school year, the actual number of children who finish the school year would be lower than the number measured as enrolled. Dropout rates at the primary level were quite high, averaging about 40% in 1970, for all developing countries (Lee and Barro, 2001). For this reason, when constructing a "stock" measure of educational attainment, we use "completion ratios" to account for all dropouts that happen during the entire cycle of primary and secondary education.

5   See Lee and Lee (2014) for details.

6   We compute the shares of the population aged 5–9, 10–14, 15–19, and 20–24 years old from the sample of all available countries-years observations at ten-year intervals, from 1820 to 1940. If the country does not have actual figures for 1820, we estimate them by using the median value for the subsample that each country belongs to. We then fill in missing observations by using linear interpolation, when this mode of estimation is feasible from the available data. For 26 countries in our sample of 89 countries, no actual observation from the historical demographic statistics is available. We fill in these missing observations by linear interpolation between the estimated median value in 1820 (constructed from available data) and the actual census figure in 1950. See Lee and Lee (2014) for more details.

7   We assume that enrollment ratios ($enroll_j$, j = primary, secondary, and tertiary levels) for the total and female population grow by following a logistic growth time trend, whereas they approach the maximum ratios, $enroll_j^{max}$: $enroll_{j,t} = enroll_j^{max}$ / $(1 + \exp(-\alpha_j - \beta_j time))$. We allow that the intercept and slope parameters vary by level of education and by country. The estimation of the logistic growth trend model is explained in detail in chapter 3.

8   The complete data set, available online, presents the estimates at five-year intervals for each country.

9   Throughout the book, the group of "advanced countries" is defined to consist of 24 countries including Australia, Austria, Belgium, Canada, Denmark, Finland, France, Germany, Greece, Iceland, Ireland, Italy, Japan, Luxembourg, Netherlands, New Zealand, Norway, Portugal, Spain, Sweden, Switzerland, Turkey, United Kingdom, and United States. The data set of enrollment and educational attainment estimates before 1950 does not include Iceland.

10   In 1950, there were approximately 530 million children aged 5 to 14, and 240 million children aged 15 to 19 (UN, 2013). The total number of students enrolled was estimated to be around 200 million in all primary schools and about 40 million in all secondary schools (See UNESCO, 1958, p.15).

11   The computation of the gender ratio requires the male enrollment ratios, which can be computed from the total and female enrollment ratios in Table 2.2 with data on school-age population shares by gender. The data on the population are available from the Barro-Lee website (http://www.barrolee.com).

12   See Lee and Francisco (2012). Subsequent discussions of the related literature and empirical specification in this section are based on this paper.

13   Hanushek and Luque (2003) argued that the methodology of Heyneman and Loxley has serious problems.

14   Feenstra, Inklaar, and Timmer (2013), (http://www.ggdc.net/pwt).

15   See Solt (2013), (http://hdl.handle.net/1902.1/11992).

16   Appendix Notes, available online at http://www.barrolee.com, provide information on the data sources for individual countries. There are additional data, beginning in the 1990s, available from OECD sources for a group of OECD countries. We have decided not to use these additional observations. The OECD sources are often incompatible with the UNESCO sources, because most OECD data come from labor-force surveys based on samples of households or individuals, in contrast to the national censuses in the UNESCO database (see Barro and Lee, 2013).

17   Our most recent update (Barro and Lee, 2013) used 621 observations. The new information comes mostly from the 129 recently available observations from national censuses, which cover recent years around 2000, 2005, and 2010, compiled by UNESCO and the United Nations.

18 The Appendix Table presents the summary of the census/survey information for these countries.

19 ISCED was first developed by UNESCO in 1976 and then revised in 1997 and 2011. See http://www.uis.unesco.org/Education/Pages/international-standard-classification-of-education.aspx for information about ISCED classification and individual ISCED mappings for each country.

20 The discussion in this subsection is based on Barro and Lee (2013).

21 Some census data report the proportion of children who have reached the primary level together with those who have no formal education $(h_u + h_p)$. A number of countries also report the combined proportion of those who have reached secondary schooling or less $(h_u + h_p + h_s)$. In addition, some census data report the combination of children who have reached primary or secondary levels $(h_p + h_s)$. To decompose these overlapping census observations, we use information from illiteracy rates, enrollment ratios, or other censuses. See the Appendix Notes, available online at: http://www.barrolee.com, for more details.

22 See Barro and Lee (2013, Appendix Notes 1) for more details on the estimation of survival rates.

23 See Barro and Lee (2013, Appendix Notes 1) for more details on how to combine forward-flow and backward-flow estimates.

24 The adjustment uses the change in the "adjusted enrollment ratio" for age group a at education level j, after taking account of time lags and the graduates' advance to the next cycle of education.

25 The discussion in the following paragraph is based on Barro and Lee (2013).

26 For countries in which only the completion ratio for total population is available, we break it into age groups based on the typical age profile of completion ratios, constructed using available data for other countries in the same region.

27 See Barro and Lee (2013) for more details.

28 See Barro and Lee (2013, Appendix Notes 1) for more details.

29 See Lee and Lee (2014) for further information.

30 Eurybase is a database on education systems in Europe. (http://www.edac.eu/policies_desc.cfm?V_id=12)

31 Iceland is the only advanced country that is excluded in the sample for the earlier period. The data set for 1950–2010 includes many newly independent states, formed since World War II, including former republics of the USSR.

32 The complete data at five-year intervals, disaggregated by gender and age, is available online (www.barrolee.com).

33 The share of the youth population, aged 15–24, in the overall population decreased steadily in advanced countries, from 26% in 1950 to 19% in 2010, while it decreased from 32% to 26% in developing countries over the same period. See Figure 3.2 in chapter 3.

34 See Barro and Lee (2013) for more detailed discussions.

CHAPTER 3

1 See the explanations in Lutz et al. (2007) and Samir et al. (2010).

2 This methodology and following discussions are based on Lee and Francisco (2012).

3 $\Delta enroll_{j,t}^a$ are constructed by changes in enrollment ratios for age group a in education level j, after appropriately taking account of time lags and graduates' advance into the next education cycle.

4   Samir et al. (2010) also considered a scenario for the educational distribution of net migration for individual countries, which is different from the UN's scenario. With limited data on the exact education profiles of migrants, however, their projections did not take a complete account of migrations by education level. For most countries, the education differentials of migrants have little effect on the educational attainment of the total population.

5   See the discussion in chapter 4.

6   Our projections consider different mortality rates by education level only for the population older than 65 years, while we assume a constant mortality rate, regardless of education level, for the population between 15 and 64 years old in each individual country.

7   In the logistic growth model, the growth rate is time-varying and equals to $\beta_j \, enroll_{j,t}$ $(1 - enroll_{j,t} / enroll_j^{\max})$.

8   We set $enroll_{\text{pri}}^{\max} = enroll_{\text{sec}}^{\max} = enroll_{\text{ter}}^{\max} = 101$.

9   The projected enrollment ratios for each educational level from 2015 to 2040 at five-year intervals can be provided upon request.

10   See Samir et al. (2010) for details.

11   Samir et al. (2010) used the following averages for their four categories: 0 years for E1, 5.2 years for E2, 11.4 years for E3, and 15.5 years for E4. These average durations were then applied to all countries.

CHAPTER 4

1   See http://www.rug.nl/research/ggdc/data/penn-world-table.

2   In this type of model, if the initial human capital is fixed over time, the levels of steady-state physical capital per worker and output per worker increase with the given human capital stock.

3   See Barro and Sala-i-Martin (2004, chapter 5).

4   If the initial ratio H/K is substantially lower than its steady-state value, that is, physical capital is sufficiently abundant compared to human capital, gross investment in physical capital is set to zero, and physical capital stock decreases at a depreciation rate. Barro and Xala-i-Martin (2004, chapter 5) showed that for reasonable parameters, this nonnegative restriction on gross investment is not likely to be binding.

5   If the foremost effects of an epidemic affect children and the elderly rather than working-age adults, the impact of epidemics on per capita output growth is ambiguous. The neoclassical growth theory predicts that a negative shock to population growth can lead to a faster accumulation of capital, and subsequently, to faster output growth. Empirical studies also present conflicting results. Bell and Lewis (2004) found that the Black Death, which killed an estimated quarter of Western Europe's population in the 14th century, had a positive effect on incomes, whereas Hirshleifer (1987) suggested that growth was not rapid in this situation. Bloom and Mahal (1997) showed that the Spanish flu epidemic of 1918–1919, which killed at least 40 million people worldwide, had no significant impact on acreage sown per capita in Indian provinces.

6   However, the effect of initial human capital stock on economic growth is influenced by the level and growth of technology. For example, as discussed in Barro (2012), for a given value of real per-worker output, a higher level of human capital stock can indicate a lower level of initial total factor productivity (TFP) or labor-augmented productivity relative to human capital stock (and physical capital stock). Then, the

effect of initial human capital stock on output growth also hinges on the subsequent change in TFP.

7   If human capital is defined as the skills embodied in a worker, then its use for one activity precludes its use for other activities, and people can claim property rights to it; that is, human capital is a rival and excludable good. In contrast, technology can be nonrival, and, in some circumstances, nonexcludable.

8   A country's human capital is often calculated by the simplified specification, $h = e^{\theta s}$. Klenow and Rodriguez-Clare (1997) and Hall and Jones (1999) used this simple specification to construct a measure of human capital stock.

9   Caselli and Ciccone (2013) showed that the perfect substitutability assumption yields an upper-bound estimate on the increase in output that can be generated by more schooling.

10   We can assume that the rates of return to schooling vary by schooling. Caselli (2005) and Hall and Jones (1999) suggested that rates of return to schooling (θ) change according to the value of schoolings. For instance, $\theta = 0.13$ for $s \leq 4$, $\theta = 0.10$ for $4 < s \leq 8$, and $\theta = 0.07$ for $8 < s$. The results of development accounting based on these values are similar.

11   The estimate of TFP is often called the "index of our ignorance," as Abramovitz (1956) put it. TFP may incorporate many elements other than productivity, such as natural resources and business-cycle factors.

12   $V_k = F_K \times \dfrac{K}{Y} = rK / Y$ and $V_H = F_H \times \dfrac{H}{Y} = wH / Y$, where r is the rental price of capital and w is the wage rate.

13   We can derive (4.13) from a translog-type production function such as $lnY = \alpha_0 + \alpha_k lnK + \alpha_H lnH + \alpha_t t + \dfrac{1}{2}\beta_{KK}(lnK)^2 + \dfrac{1}{2}\beta_{HH}(lnH)^2 + \dfrac{1}{2}\beta_{tt}t^2 + \beta_{HK}(lnH)(lnK) + \beta_{Ht}(lnH)^*t + \beta_{Kt}(lnK)^*t$, where the αs and βs are parameters. To ensure constant returns to scale, the parameters must satisfy the following restrictions: $\alpha_K + \alpha_H = 1$, $\beta_{KK} + \beta_{KH} = \beta_{HH} + \beta_{KH} = \beta_{Kt} + \beta_{Ht} = 0$.

14   A drawback of this approach is that the labor income share of the educated can increase for reasons other than changes in human capital.

15   If different categories of labor inputs cannot be distinguished in the data, the contribution of labor input to growth is measured using the growth rate of aggregate labor weighted by the overall labor share. It can underestimate the true contribution of labor inputs if the composition of labor shifts over time toward types of high-quality labor (see Barro and Sala-i-Martin, 2004, Chapter 10, 10.3.3).

16   The result of growth accounting does not vary much with different assumptions on the rates of return to schooling. We can also consider that schooling quality varies across countries and time, and then, we can calculate the wage share of each labor input assuming the rate of return to schooling quality, which can be measured by test scores (see the relevant discussion in chapter 6). The results of growth accounting do not change much for reasonable ranges of rates of return to schooling quality, which are assumed to be comparable to the rates of return, to the schooling year.

17   Bosworth and Collins (2003) showed that the contribution of education to output growth is small.

18   When we use an alternative measure of the Mincerian-type human capital stock in (4.8), the regression results are qualitatively similar.

19   Changing the time dimension of the sample from a five-year to a ten-year period provides qualitatively similar regression results.

20   *International Country Risk Guide* provides information on ratings of political, eco-
      nomic, and financial risks since the early 1980s (Political Risk Services, Various
      years).

21   Although the use of lagged values as instruments can deal with the endogeneity
      problem to some extent, it would not be fully satisfactory if a strong serial corre-
      lation exists among the explanatory variables. However, it is practically difficult to
      construct an array of fully convincing exogenous instruments in a panel structure
      with too many explanatory variables.

22   If we replace the government consumption measure with that from the PWT 7.0, it
      enters significantly negative.

23   See Barro and Sala-i-Martin (2004, section 9.2).

24   Lipset (1959) asserted "only in a wealthy society in which relatively few citizens
      lived in real poverty could a situation exist in which the mass of the population could
      intelligently participate in politics and could develop the self-restraint necessary to
      avoid succumbing to the appeals of irresponsible demagogues. A society divided be-
      tween a large impoverished mass and a small favored elite would result either in ol-
      igarchy (dictatorial rule of the small upper stratum) or in tyranny (popularly based
      dictatorship)" (p.75).

25   The results are essentially the same if we use the values for 1965, 1970 . . . , 2010
      instead of the averages.

26   We cannot implement the fixed-effects Tobit or probit models that can take care of
      the censoring issue, because there is no sufficient statistic allowing the fixed effects
      to be conditioned out of the likelihood (Wooldridge, 2002).

CHAPTER 5

1   See www.rbarro.com/data-sets.

2   They include Bulgaria, Colombia, Costa Rica, Egypt, El Salvador, Finland, Greece,
     Guatemala, Honduras, Hungary, Ireland, and Nicaragua.

3   Galor (2005) described three distinct regimes that have characterized the process of
     economic development over the long-run period of human history: the Malthusian
     Epoch, the Post-Malthusian Regime, and the Sustained Growth Regime. This char-
     acterization may not apply to all regions, as development paths have often tended to
     be distinctive and divergent.

4   See Galor (2005, Chapter 5) for more details.

5   With inclusion of fertility rate, the sample size substantially shrinks by almost 40%.
     The fertility variable enters statistically significant and negative in the growth regres-
     sions, but makes education and democracy variables less statistically significant. In
     contrast, when we include crude birth rate as a demographic variable, the regression
     results are broadly similar to what we present here. Data for crude birth rate are avail-
     able more frequently than those for fertility rates for the period before 1950. Reher
     (2004) provides comprehensive data on crude birth rate for 145 countries.

6   For a given value of per-worker output, a higher level of human capital stock can
     indicate a lower level of initial TFP relative to human capital stock. Thus, the in-
     significance of initial human capital stock on economic growth may also reflect the
     impacts of the level and growth of technology on subsequent output growth (see the
     discussion in the endnote 6 in chapter 4).

7   This value is roughly similar to the estimate of the breakpoint from the panel regres-
     sion based on the 1960–2010 data (see the regression in column 4 of Table 4.6).

8   The regression results do not change qualitatively when the sample is restricted to 32 countries that have at least four observations on fertility rate (in addition to per capita GDP, democracy, and educational attainment) between 1870 and 1950.

9   See the discussion of the data set by Morrisson and Murtin (2009).

CHAPTER 6

1   Some recent work emphasizes the importance of noncognitive skills (Heckman, Stixrud, and Urzua, 2006). Noncognitive skills include interpersonal skills, communications ability, teamwork skills, persistence, acceptance of social norms, and other "soft" skills. It is difficult to objectively measure such skills.

2   See Altinok, Diebolt, and De Meulemeester (2014) and the World Bank's website on Global Data Set on Education Quality, http://datatopics.worldbank.org/Education/wDataQuery/QAchievement.aspx.

3   The PISA data sets do not allow direct comparability of mathematics and science scores between 2000 and 2003 and between 2000 and 2006, respectively.

4   For the SACMEQ and the LLECE tests conducted for students of grade six, we match the scores to those of grade four for the TIMSS after making adjustments to the SACMEQ and LLECE test scores. This adjustment is made using the estimated relationship between the test scores of grade four and grade eight students from the TIMSS results.

5   For the Sub-Saharan countries, the estimated average growth rate is 0.4% for the secondary test scores and 0.65% for the primary test scores. The estimates are based on the sample of secondary test scores that excludes Ghana and the South Africa Republic from the sample of secondary test scores, because the inclusion of these countries increases the estimates unreasonably high.

6   The full data set can be downloaded at the following link: http://www.barrolee.com.

7   One idea is to use the scores of adult literacy tests administered to the labor force. For example, we can use the differences in the adult literacy test scores for US adults who have completed primary and secondary education in order to convert the primary test scores to secondary test scores. However, this approach cannot distinguish the effects of additional years of secondary schooling from that of differences in school quality between primary and secondary education. Extending this approach to other countries is not easily applicable, either.

8   These countries are Benin, Bolivia, Burkina Faso, Burundi, Cameroon, Chad, Comoros, Congo, Democratic Republic of Congo, Republic of Côte d'Ivoire, Cuba, Dominican Republic, Ecuador, Gabon, Guatemala, Kenya, Lesotho, Namibia, Nicaragua, Paraguay, Seychelles, Tanzania, Togo, Venezuela, and Zimbabwe.

9   This subsection provides a succinct survey on this topic. Please see Lee and Barro (2001), Hanushek (2006), and Hanushek and Woessmann (2011) for more details.

10   See Hanushek (1986) for a related survey.

11   See Hanushek and Woessmann (2011) for a related survey.

12   See the survey by Hanushek and Woessmann (2011).

13   The reverse causation problem would be less severe in cross-country data than in cross-region data, because the mobility of residents in response to school quality is easier within a country than across countries.

14   Fuchs and Woessmann (2007) showed that the relationship between regular standardized testing and student achievement becomes statistically significantly positive in educational systems that allow external exit exams.

15   The participants in Round 1, held from 2008 to 2013, included Australia, Austria, Belgium (Flanders), Canada, the Czech Republic, Denmark, Estonia, Finland, France, Germany, Ireland, Italy, Japan, Korea, Netherlands, Norway, Poland, Russian Federation, the Slovak Republic, Spain, Sweden, the United Kingdom, and the United States. The participants in Round 2, held from 2012 and ongoing until 2016, will include Chile, Greece, Indonesia, Israel, Lithuania, New Zealand, Singapore, Slovenia, and Turkey.

16   We try to construct this test-score measure for the working-age population and find a significant discrepancy between this measure and the PIAAC scores across countries.

17   See Hanushek and Woessmann (2008, 2011) for a survey.

18   Alternatively, we can assume the specification of a quality-adjusted human capital stock measure as follows: $h = \sum_a \sum_j e^{\left(\theta_s + \theta_q q_j^a\right) dur_j^a} l_j^a$ In this specification, the log human capital increases with the level of schooling, but the increase is faster for students at high-quality schools.

19   In the sample, the world average number of years of schooling is 5.7. The value of one standard deviation of test scores in the whole sample is 9.9.

20   Some researchers use international rankings of universities as a measure of school quality at the tertiary level (Aghion et al., 2010). However, these are based on the research outputs of the faculty, which are not necessarily correlated with the quality of school graduates.

21   Hanushek and Woessmann (2012) showed that changes in test performance and growth rates are positively correlated from 1975 to 2000. However, the sample is limited to 15 advanced countries. This result is also subject to the endogeneity problem.

22   The result is similar to the one using an alternative measure of the Mincerian-type quality-adjusted human capital in (6.7).

BIBLIOGRAPHY

Abouharb, M. R., & Kimball, A. L. 2007. A New Dataset on Infant Mortality Rates, 1816–2002. *Journal of Peace Research, 44*(6), 743–754.

Abramovitz, M. 1956. Resource and Output Trends in the United States since 1870. *The American Economic Review, 46*(2), 5–23.

Acemoglu, D. 1997. Training and Innovation in an Imperfect Labour Market. *The Review of Economic Studies, 64*(3), 445–464.

Acemoglu, D. 2002. Technical Change, Inequality and the Labor Market. *Journal of Economic Literature, 40*(1), 7–72.

Acemoglu, D., Johnson, S., Robinson, J. A., & Yared, P. 2005. From Education to Democracy?. *American Economic Review Proceedings, 95*(2), 44–49.

Acemoglu, D., Johnson, S., Robinson, J. A., & Yared, P. 2008. Income and Democracy. *American Economic Review, 98*(3), 808–842.

Acemoglu, D., & Zilibotti, F. 2001. Productivity Differences. *The Quarterly Journal of Economics, 116*(2), 563–606.

Aghion, P., Dewatripont, M., Hoxby, C., Mas-Colell, A., & Sapir, A. 2010. The Governance and Performance of Universities: Evidence from Europe and the US. *Economic Policy, 25*(61), 7–59.

Ahuja, V., & Filmer, D. 1996. Educational Attainment in Developing Countries: New Estimates and Projections Disaggregated by Gender. *Journal of Educational Planning and Administration, 10*(3), 229–254.

Ainsworth, M., Beegle, K., & Nyamete, A. 1996. The Impact of Women's Schooling on Fertility and Contraceptive Use: A Study of Fourteen Sub-Saharan African Countries. *The World Bank Economic Review, 10*(1), 85–122.

Altinok, N., & Diebolt, C., & De Meulemeester, J. L. 2014. A New International Database on Educational Quality: 1965–2010. *Applied Economics, 46*(11), 1212–1247.

Altinok, N., & Murseli, H. 2007. International Database on Human Capital Quality. *Economics Letters, 96*(2): 237–244.

Altonji, J. G., & Dunn, T. A. 1996. Using Siblings to Estimate the Effects of School Quality on Wages. *Review of Economics and Statistics, 78*(4), 665–671.

Anand, S., & Ravallion, M. 1993. Human Development in Poor Countries: On the Role of Private Incomes and Public Services. *Journal of Economic Perspectives, 7*(1), 133–150.

Angrist, J. D & Lavy, V. 1999. Using Maimonides' Rule to Estimate the Effect of Class Size on Children's Academic Achievement. *The Quarterly Journal of Economics, 114*(2), 533–575.

Angrist, N., Patrinos, H. A., & Schlotter, M. 2013. An Expansion of a Global Data Set on Educational Quality (No. WPS6536). The World Bank Policy Research Working Paper.

Baier, S. L., Dwyer, G. P. & Tamura, R. 2006. How Important are Capital and Total Factor Productivity for Economic Growth?, *Economic Inquiry*, 44, 23–49.

Banks, A.S., & Wilson, K.A. 2013. Cross-national time-series data archive. Jerusalem: Databanks International. http://www.databanksinternational.com

Barnard, H. 1854. *National education in Europe: being an account of the organization, administration, instruction and statistics of public schools of different grades in the principal states.* New York: C.B. Norton

Barro, R. J. 1991. Economic Growth in a Cross Section of Countries. *The Quarterly Journal of Economics*, 106(2), 407–443.

Barro, R. J. 1997. *Macroeconomics* (5th ed.). Boston: MIT Press.

Barro, R. J. 1999. Determinants of Democracy. *Journal of Political Economy*, 107(S6), S158–S183.

Barro, R. J. 2012. Convergence and Modernization Revisited (No. w18295). National Bureau of Economic Research.

Barro, R. J., & Lee, J. W. 1993. International Comparisons of Educational Attainment. *Journal of Monetary Economics*, 32(3), 363–394.

Barro, R. J., & Lee, J. W. 1994. Sources of Economic Growth. In *Carnegie Rochester Conference Series on Public Policy*, 40(1), 1–46.

Barro, R. J., & Lee, J. W. 1996. International Measures of Schooling Years and Schooling Quality. *American Economic Review*, 86(2), 218–223.

Barro, R. J., & Lee, J. W. 2001. International Data on Educational Attainment: Updates and Implications. *Oxford Economic Papers*, 53(3), 541–563.

Barro, R. J., & Lee, J. W. 2013. A New Data Set of Educational Attainment in the World, 1950–2010. *Journal of Development Economics*, 104, 184–198.

Barro, R. J., & Sala-i-Martin, X. 2004. *Economic growth* (2nd ed.). Boston: MIT Press.

Becker, G. S. 1960. An economic analysis of fertility. In *Demographic and economic change in developed countries*, 209–231. Princeton, NJ: Princeton University Press.

Becker, G. S., & Barro, R. J. 1988. A Reformulation of the Economic Theory of Fertility. *The Quarterly Journal of Economics*, 103(1), 1–25.

Becker, G. S., & Lewis, H. G. 1973. On the Interaction between the Quantity and Quality of Children. *The Journal of Political Economy*, 81(2), S279–S288.

Becker, G. S., Murphy, K. M., & Tamura, R. 1990. Human Capital, Fertility and Economic Growth. *Journal of Political Economy*, 98(5 Pt. 2), S12–37.

Beer, C. 2009. Democracy and Gender Equality. *Studies in Comparative International Development*, 44(3), 212–227.

Behrman, J. R. and Birdsall N. 1983. The Quality of Schooling: Quantity Alone Is Misleading. *American Economic Review*, 73 (December), 928–946.

Bell, C., & Lewis, M. 2004. The Economic Implications of Epidemics Old and New. *World Economics*, 5(4), 137-174.

Benavot, A., Resnick, J., & Corrales, J. 2006. *Global educational expansion: Historical legacies and political obstacles.* Cambridge, MA: American Academy of Arts and Sciences.

Benavot, A., & Riddle, P. 1988. The Expansion of Primary Education, 1870–1940: Trends and Issues. *Sociology of Education*, 61(3), 191–210.

Benhabib, J., Corvalan, A., & Spiegel, M. M. 2011. Reestablishing the Income-Democracy Nexus (No. w16832). NBER Working Paper.

Benhabib, J. & Spiegel, M. M. 1994. The Role of Human Capital in Economic Development: Evidence from Aggregate Cross-Country Data. *Journal of Monetary Economics*, 34(2), 143–173.

Bils, M., & Klenow, P. J. 2000. Does Schooling Cause Growth?. *American Economic Review*, 90(5), 1160–1183.

Bishop, J. H., & Wößmann, L. 2004. Institutional Effects in a Simple Model of Educational Production. *Education Economics*, 12(1), 17–38.

Bloom, D. E., & Mahal, A. 1997. AIDS, flu, and the black death: Impacts on economic growth and well-being. In D. E. Bloom & P. Godwin (Eds.), *The economics of HIV and AIDS: The case of south and south east Asia* (22–52). Delhi: Oxford University Press.

Blum, A., Goldstein, H., & Guérin-Pace, F. 2001. International Adult Literacy Survey (IALS): An Analysis of International Comparisons of Adult Literacy. *Assessment in Education: Principles, Policy & Practice*, 8(2), 225–246.

Boix, C. 2011. Democracy, Development, and the International System. *American Political Science Review*, 105(4), 809–828.

Bollen, K.A. 1980. Issues in the Comparative Measurement of Political Democracy. *American Sociological Review*, 45(3), 370–390.

Borensztein, E., De Gregorio, J., & Lee, J.W. 1998. How Does Direct Investment Affect Economic Growth?. *Journal of International Economics*, 45(1), 115–135.

Bosworth, B., & Collins, S. M. 2003. The Empirics of Growth: An Update. *Brookings papers on economic activity*, 2003(2), 113–206.

Bratsberg, B., & Terrell, D. 2002. School Quality and Returns to Education of US Immigrants. *Economic Inquiry*, 40(2), 177–198.

Breton, T. R. 2011. The Quality vs. the Quantity of Schooling: What Drives Economic Growth?. *Economics of Education Review*, 30(4), 765–773.

Campbell, J. R., Hombo, C. M., & Mazzeo, J. 2000. *NAEP 1999 trends in academic progress: Three decades of student performance*. ED Pubs.

Card, D., & Krueger, A. B. 1992. Does School Quality Matter? Returns to Education and the Characteristics of Public Schools in the United States. *Journal of Political Economy*, 100(1), 1–40.

Card, D., & Krueger, A. B. 1996. School Resources and Student Outcomes: An Overview of the Literature and New Evidence from North and South California. *The Journal of Economic Perspectives*, 10(4), 31–50.

Caselli, F. 2005. Accounting for cross-country income differences. *Handbook of economic growth*, 1, 679–741.

Caselli, F., & Ciccone, A. 2013. The Contribution of Schooling in Development Accounting: Results from a Nonparametric Upper Bound. *Journal of Development Economics*, 104, 199–211.

Castelló-Climent, A., & Hidalgo-Cabrillana, A. 2012. The Role of Educational Quality and Quantity in the Process Of Economic Development. *Economics of Education Review*, 31(4), 391–409.

Chapman, D. W., & Boothroyd, R. A. 1988. Threats to Data Quality in Developing Country Settings. *Comparative Education Review*, 32(4), 416–429.

Chesnais, Jean-Claude. 1992. *The demographic transition: stages, patterns, and economic implications: A longitudinal study of sixty-seven countries covering the period 1720–1984*. Oxford: Clarendon Press.

Chetty, R., Friedman, J. N., & Rockoff, J. E. 2013. Measuring the Impacts of Teachers I: Evaluating Bias in Teacher Value-Added Estimates (No. w19423). National Bureau of Economic Research.

Chinapah, V., H'ddigui, E. M., Kanjee, A., Falayajo, W., Fomba, C. O., Hamissou, O. & Byomugisha, A. (2000). *With Africa for Africa. Towards education for all*. HSRC, Pretoria.

Cohen, D., & Soto, M. 2007. Growth and Human Capital: Good data, Good results. *Journal of Economic Growth, 12*, 51–76.

Cummings, W. K. 2003. *The institutions of education: A comparative study of educational development in six core nations*. Oxford: Symposium Books.

Deng, Z., & Treiman, D. J. 1997.The Impact of the Cultural Revolution on Trends in Educational Attainment in the People's Republic of China. *American Journal of Sociology, 103*(2), 391–428.

Feenstra, R. C., Inklaar, R., & Timmer, M. 2013. The Next Generation of the Penn World Table. *University of California, Davis and University of Groningen, in process.*

Finn, Jeremy D., & Charles M. Achilles. 1990. Answers and Questions about Class Size: A Statewide Experiment. *American Educational Research Journal, 27* (Fall), 557–577.

Flug, K., Spilimbergo, A., & Wachtenheim, E. 1998. Investment in Education: Do Economic Volatility and Credit Constraints Matter?. *Journal of Development Economics, 55*(2), 465–481.

Fénelon, F. 1681. *Traité De L'education des Filles*. Paris.

Fredriksen, B. 1991. *An introduction to the analysis of student enrollment and flow statistics*. Population and Human Resources Department. Education and Employment Division background paper series: no.91/39. Washington, D.C.: The World Bank.

Fredriksson, P., Öckert, B., & Oosterbeek, H. 2013. Long-term Effects of Class Size. *The Quarterly Journal of Economics, 128*(1), 249–285.

Fuchs, T., & Woessmann, L. 2007. What Accounts for International Differences in Student Performance? A Re-Examination Using PISA Data. *Empirical Economics, 32* (2–3), 433–464.

Fuller, B. 1986. *Raising school quality in developing countries: What investment boosts learning?*. The World Bank.

Galor, O. 2005. The transition from stagnation to growth: Unified growth theory. In A. Philippe, & S.N. Durlauf. (Eds.) *Handbook of economic growth, 1* (171–293). Elsevier.

Galor, O., & Weil, D. N. 1996. The Gender Gap, Fertility, and Growth. *American Economic Review, 86*(3), 374–387.

Galor, O., & Weil, D. N. 2000. Population, Technology, and Growth: From the Malthusian Regime to the Demographic Transition and Beyond. *American Economic Review, 90*(4), 806–828.

Garrouste, C. 2010. *100 Years of Educational Reforms in Europe: A Contextual Database*. JRC Science and Technical Reports, European Commission.

Glaeser, E. L., La Porta, R., Lopez-de-Silanes, F., & Shleifer, A. 2004. Do Institutions Cause Growth?. *Journal of Economic Growth, 9*(3), 271–303.

Glaeser, E. L., Ponzetto, G. A., & Shleifer, A. 2007. Why Does Democracy Need Education?. *Journal of Economic Growth, 12*(2), 77–99.

Glass, Gene V., Cahen, L.S., Smith, M. L., & Filby, N. N. 1982. *School class size: Research and policy*. Beverly Hills, CA: Sage.

Goldhaber, D. D., & Brewer, D. J. 1999. Why Don't Schools and Teachers Seem to Matter?: Assessing the Impact of Unobservables on Education Production. *Journal of Human Resources, 32*(3), 505–523.

Goujon, A. 2002. *Human capital: Population economics in the Middle East*. Cairo: The American University in Cairo Press.

Goujon, A., & Samir, K. C. 2008. Past and Future of Human Capital in Southeast Asia: From 1970 to 2030. *Asian Population Studies*, 4(1), 31–56.

Grossman, G. M., & Helpman, E. 1991. *Innovation and growth in the global economy*. Cambridge, MA: MIT Press.

Hall, R. E., & Jones, C. I. 1999. Why Do Some Countries Produce So Much More Output Per Worker than Others?. *The Quarterly Journal of Economics*, 114(1), 83–116.

Hanushek, E. A. 1986. The Economics of Schooling: Production and Efficiency in Public Schools. *Journal of Economic Literature*, 24(3), 1141–1177.

Hanushek, E. A 1995. Interpreting Recent Research on Schooling in Developing Countries. *World Bank Research Observer*, 10(2), 227–246.

Hanushek, E. A. 2006. School resources. In Hanushek, E. A., Welch, F. (Eds.) *Handbook of the Economics of Education, Volume 2*. Elsevier, 865–908.

Hanushek, E. A., & Kimko, D. D. 2000. Schooling Labor-Force Quality and the Growth of Nations. *American Economic Review*, 90(5), 1184–1208.

Hanushek, E. A. & Luque, J. A. 2003. Efficiency and Equity in Schools around the World. *Economics of Education Review, Special Issue in Honor of George Psacharopoulos*, 22(5), 481–502.

Hanushek, E. A., Schwerdt, G., Wiederhold, S., & Woessmann, L. 2013. Returns to Skills around the World: Evidence from PIAAC (No. w19762). National Bureau of Economic Research.

Hanushek, E. A., & Woessmann, L. 2008. The Role of Cognitive Skill in Economic Development. *Journal of Economic Literature*, 46(3), 607–668.

Hanushek, Eric A., & Woessmann L. 2011. The economics of international differences in educational achievement. In Eric A. Hanushek, S. Machin, and L. Woessmann (Eds.), *Handbook of the economics of education*, Vol. 3. Amsterdam: North Holland, 89–200.

Hanushek, E. A., & Woessmann, L. 2012. Do Better Schools Lead to More Growth? Cognitive Skills, Economic Outcomes, and Causation. *Journal of Economic Growth*, 17(4), 267–321.

Haveman, R., & Wolfe, B. 1995. The Determinants of Children's Attainments: A Review of Methods and Findings. *Journal of Economic Literature*, 33, 1829–1878.

Heckman, J. J., Stixrud, J., & Urzua, S. 2006. The Effects of Cognitive and Noncognitive Abilities on Labor Market Outcomes and Social Behavior. *Journal of Labor Economics*, 24(3), 411–482.

Heckman, J. J., & Walker, J. R. 1990. The Relationship between Wages and Income and the Timing and Spacing of Births: Evidence from Swedish Longitudinal Data. *Econometrica*, 58(6), 1411–1441.

Hedges, L. V., Laine, R. D., & Greenwald, R. 1994. Does Money Matter? A Meta-Analysis of Studies of the Effects of Differential School Inputs on Student Outcomes. *Educational Researcher*, 23(3), 5–14.

Herzer, D., Strulik, H., & Vollmer, S. 2012. The Long-Run Determinants of Fertility: One Century of Demographic Change 1900–1999. *Journal of Economic Growth*, 17(4), 357–385.

Heyneman, S. P., & Loxley, W. A. 1983. The Effect of Primary School Quality on Academic Achievement across Twenty-nine High and Low Income Countries. *The American Journal of Sociology*, 88(6), 1162–1194.

Hirshleifer, J. 1987. *Economic behaviour in adversity*. Chicago: The University of Chicago Press.

Hoxby, C. M. 1998. The Effects of Class Size on Student Achievement: New Evidence From Population Variation (No. w6869). National Bureau of Economic Research.

Hsieh, C. T., & Klenow, P. J. 2010. Development Accounting. *American Economic Journal: Macroeconomics*, 2(1), 207–223.

Huber, E., Rueschemeyer, D., & Stephens, J. D. 1993. The Impact of Economic Development on Democracy. *The Journal of Economic Perspectives*, 7(3) 71–86.

Human Fertility Database. Max Planck Institute for Demographic Research (Germany) and Vienna Institute of Demography (Austria). Available at www.humanfertility.org (data downloaded on September 24 2013).

Institut National d'Etudes Démographiques. Database. Available at http://www.ined.fr/en/pop_figures/developed_countries/developed_countries_database

International Monetary Fund. Various years. *International financial statistics*. Washington, D.C.: IMF.

Islam, R., Ang, J. B., & Madsen, J. B. 2014. Quality-Adjusted Human Capital and Productivity Growth. *Economic Inquiry*, 52(2), 757–777.

Jones, B. F. 2011. The Human Capital Stock: A Generalized Approach (No. w17487). National Bureau of Economic Research.

Jorgenson, D. W., Stiroh, K. J., Gordon, R. J., & Sichel, D. E. 2000. Raising the Speed Limit: US Economic Growth in the Information Age. *Brookings papers on economic activity*, 1, 125–235.

Kalemli-Ozcan, S. 2002. Does the Mortality Decline Promote Economic Growth?. *Journal of Economic Growth*, 7(4), 411–439.

Kalemli-Ozcan, S. 2003. A Stochastic Model of Mortality, Fertility, and Human Capital Investment. *Journal of Development Economics*, 70(1), 103–118.

Kandel, I. L. 1930. *History of secondary education: A study in the development of liberal education*. Boston: Houghton Mifflin Company.

Kane, T. J., & Staiger, D. O. 2008. Estimating Teacher Impacts on Student Achievement: An Experimental Evaluation (No. w14607). National Bureau of Economic Research.

Kaneko, M. 1986. *The Educational Composition of the World Population: A Database*. Education and Training Department Report no. EDT 29. The World Bank.

Klenow, P., & Rodriguez-Claire, A. 1997. The Neoclassical Revival in Growth Economics: Has It Gone Too Far?. In B. S. Bernake & J. Rotemberg (Eds.), In *National Bureau of Economic Research Macroeconomics Annual 1997*, 12 (73–103). Cambridge, MA: MIT Press.

Knack, S., & Keefer, P. 1997. Does Social Capital have an Economic Payoff? A Cross Country Investigation. *Quarterly Journal of Economics*, 112, 1251–1288.

Kremer, M. R. 1995. Research on Schooling: What We Know and What We Don't, A Comment on Hanushek. *The World Bank Research Observer*, 10(2), 247–254.

Krueger, A. B. 1999. Experimental Estimates of Education Production Functions. *Quarterly Journal of Economics*, 114(2), 497–532.

Lavy, V. 2010. Do Differences in Schools' Instruction Time Explain International Achievement Gaps? Evidence from Developed and Developing Countries (No. w16227). National Bureau of Economic Research.

Lazear, Edward P. 2003. Teacher Incentives. *Swedish Economic Policy Review*, 10(3), 179–214.

League of Nations. Various years. *Statistical yearbook of the League of Nations*. Geneva.

Lee, J. W. 1993. International Trade, Distortions, and Long-Run Economic Growth, *IMF Staff Papers*, 40, June, 299–328.

Lee, J. W., & Barro, R. J. 2001. Schooling Quality in a Cross–Section of Countries. *Economica*, 68(272), 465–488.

Lee, J. W., & Francisco, R. 2012. Human Capital Accumulation in Emerging Asia, 1970–2030. *Japan and the World Economy*, 24(2), 76–86.

Lee, J. W., & Lee, H. 2014. Human Capital in the Long Run. Working paper, Korea University.

Lee, W. Y. 1995. Women's Education in Traditional and Modern China. *Women's History Review*, 4(3), 345–367.

Leung, K.S.F. 2006. Mathematics education in east Asia and the west: Does Culture Matter? In: *Mathematics education in different cultural traditions-a comparative study of east Asia and the west*. New York: Springer.

Lindert, P. 2004. *Growing public*. Cambridge, UK: Cambridge University Press.

Lindo, J. M. 2010. Are Children Really Inferior Goods?. *Journal of Human Resources*, 45(2), 301–327.

Lipset, S. M. 1959. Some Social Requisites of Democracy: Economic Development and Political Legitimacy. *American Political Science Review*, 53(1), 69–105.

Lockheed Marlaine E., Adriaan M. Verspoor & associates. 1991. *Improving primary education in developing countries*, Oxford University Press for the World Bank.

Lucas, R. E. 1988. On the Mechanics of Economic Development. *Journal of Monetary Economics*, 22(1), 3–42.

Lutz, W., & Goujon, A. 2001. The World's Changing Human Capital Stock: Multi-state Population Projections by Educational Attainment. *Population and Development Review*, 27(2), 323–339.

Lutz, W., Goujon, A., Samir, K. C, & Sanderson, W. 2007. Reconstruction of Populations by Age, Sex and Level of Educational Attainment for 120 Countries for 1970–2000. *Vienna Yearbook of Population Research*, 193–235. Vienna: International Institute for Applied Systems Analysis (IIASA).

Maddison, A. 2003. *The world economy: Historical statistics*. Paris: OECD.

Maddison, A. 2007. *Contours of the world economy, 1–2030 AD*. New York: Oxford University Press.

Mankiw, N. G., Romer, D., & Weil, D. N. 1992. A Contribution to the Empirics of Economic Growth. *The Quarterly Journal of Economics*, 107(2), 407–437.

Manuelli, R. E., & Seshadri, A. 2010. Human Capital and the Wealth of Nations. Working paper. University of Wisconsin-Madison.

Marlow-Ferguson, R., & Lopez, C. (Eds.). 2002. *World education encyclopedia*: IR (Vol. 2). Farmington Hills, MI: Gale Cengage.

Meyer, J. W., Ramirez, F. O., & Soysal, Y. N. 1992. World Expansion of Mass Education, 1870–1980. *Sociology of Education*, 65(2), 128–149.

Mingat, A., & Tan, J. 1998. The Mechanics of Progress in Education: Evidence from Cross-country Data. World Bank Policy Research Working Paper No. 2015. Washington, DC: The World Bank.

Mitchell, B. R. 2003a. *International historical statistics: Africa, Asia & Oceania, 1750–2000* (4th ed.). London: Palgrave Macmillan.

Mitchell, B. R. 2003b. *International historical statistics: The Americas, 1750–2000* (5th ed.). London: Palgrave Macmillan.

Mitchell, B. R. 2003c. *International historical statistics: Europe, 1750–2000* (5th ed.). London: Palgrave Macmillan.

Monroe, P. 1911. *A cyclopedia of education.* New York: The Macmillan Company.

Montanino, A., Przywara, B., & Young, D. 2004. Investment in Education: The Implications for Economic Growth and Public Finances. Brussels: Directorate-General for Economic and Financial Affairs. The European Commission. (Economic Papers No. 217).

Morrisson, C., & Murtin, F. 2009. The Century of Education. *Journal of Human Capital,* 3(1), 1–42.

Mulligan, Casey B. 1999. Galton Versus the Human Capital Approach to Inheritance. *Journal of Political Economy,* 107(6), 184–224.

Murnane, R. J., Willett, J. B., Duhaldeborde, Y., & Tyler, J. H. 2000. How Important Are the Cognitive Skills of Teenagers in Predicting Subsequent Earnings?. *Journal of Policy Analysis and Management, 19*(4), 547–568.

Murtin, F. 2013. Long-term Determinants of the Demographic Transition, 1870–2000. *Review of Economics and Statistics,* 95(2), 617–631.

Murtin, F., & Wacziarg, R. 2011. The Democratic Transition (No. w17432). NBER Working Paper.

National Center for Health Statistics (US). Division of Vital Statistics, United States. National Vital Statistics Division, United States. National Office of Vital Statistics, & United States. Bureau of the Census. Vital Statistics Division. 1969. *Vital Statistics of the United States.* United States Bureau of the Census.

Nelson, R. R., & Phelps, E. S. 1966. Investment in Humans, Technological Diffusion, and Economic Growth. *The American Economic Review,* 56(1/2), 69–75.

OECD & Human Resources Development Canada. 1998. *Literacy skills for the knowledge society: Further results from the international adult literacy survey,* Paris and Ottawa.

OECD & Statistics Canada. 1995. *Literacy, economy and society—results of the first international adult literacy survey.* Paris and Ottawa.

Organisation for Economic Co-operation and Development (OECD). 2000. *Literacy in the information age: Final report of the international adult literacy survey.* OECD, Paris, and the Ministry of Industry, Canada.

Osili, U. O., & Long, B. T. 2008. Does Female Schooling Reduce Fertility? Evidence from Nigeria. *Journal of Development Economics,* 87(1), 57–75.

Political Risk Services. Various years. *International Country Risk Guide.* Syracuse, NY.

Pritchett, L. 2001. Where Has All the Education Gone?. *The World Bank Economic Review,* 15(3), 367–391.

Przeworski, A. (Ed.). 2000. *Democracy and development: Political institutions and well-being in the world, 1950–1990* (Vol. 3). New York: Cambridge University Press.

Psacharopoulos, G. 1994. Returns to Investment in Education: A Global Update. *World Development,* 22(9), 1325–1343.

Psacharopoulos, G., & Arriagada, A. M. 1986. The Educational Composition of the Labor Force: An International Comparison. *International Labor Review, 125*(5), 561–574.

Psacharopoulos, G., & Arriagada, A. M. 1992. The Educational Composition of the Labor Force: An International Update. Population and Human Resources Department. Education and Employment Division background series paper: no. 92/49. Washington, D.C.: The World Bank.

Psacharopoulos, G., & Patrinos, H. A. 2004. Returns to Investment in Education: A Further Update. *Education Economics, 12*(2), 111–134.

Psacharopoulos, G., & Woodhall, M. 1985. *Education for development: An analysis of invest-ment choices*. Oxford University Press for the World Bank.

Redding, S. 1996. The Low-skill, Low-quality Trap: Strategic Complementarities between Human Capital and R&D. *The Economic Journal, 106*(435), 458–470.

Reher, D. S. 2004. The Demographic Transition Revisited as a Global Process. *Population, Space and Place, 10*(1), 19–41.

Romer, P. M. 1986. Increasing Returns and Long-Run Growth. *Journal of Political Economy, 94*(5), 1002–1037.

Romer, P. M. 1987. Growth Based on Increasing Returns Due to Specialization. *The American Economic Review, 77*(2), 56–62.

Romer, P. M. 1990. Endogenous Technological Change. *Journal of Political Economy, 95*(5), S71–S102.

Rousseau, J. J. 1762. Émile ou de l'Éducation. *Profession de foi du Vicaire savoyard*. Paris: Garnier.

Samir, K. C., Barakat, B., Goujon, A., Skirbekk, V., Sanderson, W., & Lutz, W. 2010. Projection of Populations by Level of Educational Attainment, Age, and Sex for 120 Countries for 2005–2050. *Demographic Research, 22*(15), 383–472.

Schoellman, T. 2012. Education Quality and Development Accounting. *The Review of Economic Studies, 79*(1), 388–417.

Schofer, E., & Meyer, J. W. 2005. The World-Wide Expansion of Higher Education. CCDRL Working Papers No.32.

Schultz, T. P. 1985. Changing World Prices, Women's Wages, and the Fertility Transition: Sweden, 1860–1910. *The Journal of Political Economy, 93*(6), 1126–1154.

Schultz, T. P. 1997. Demand for children in low income countries. M.R. Rosenzweig and O. Stark (eds.) *Handbook of Population and Family Economics, 1*(1), 349–430.

Shang, Q., & Weinberg, B. A. 2013. Opting for Families: Recent Trends in the Fertility of Highly Educated Women. *Journal of Population Economics, 26*(1), 5–32.

Solow, R. M. 1956. A Contribution to the Theory of Economic Growth. *The Quarterly Journal of Economics, 70*(1), 65–94.

Solow, R. M. 1957. Technical Change and the Aggregate Production Function. *Review of Economics and Statistics, 39*(3), 312–320.

Solt, F. 2013. The Standardized World Income Inequality Database Version 4.0, Iowa City: University of Iowa. http://myweb.uiowa.edu/fsolt/swiid/swiid.html

Soysal, Y., & Strang, D. 1989. Construction of the First Mass Education Systems in 19th Century Europe. *Sociology of Education, 62*(4), 277–288.

Stevenson, H. W., Lee, S., Chen, C., & Lummis, M. 2008. Mathematics Achievement of Children in China and the United States. *Child Development, 61*(4), 1053–1066.

Tilak, B. G. 1989. Education and its Relation to Economic Growth, Poverty, and Income Distribution: Past Evidence and Further Analysis. Discussion paper no. 46. The World Bank.

Tocqueville, A. D. 1835. *Democracy in America*. London: Long-mans, Green.

Unger, J. 1982. *Education under Mao: Class and competition in canton schools, 1960–1980*. New York: Columbia University Press.

United Nations. 1955. *Demographic yearbook 1955*. New York.

United Nations. 1991. *Global estimates and projections of population by sex and age, the 1990 assessment*.

United Nations. 2013. *World population prospects: The 2012 revision*. New York: Department for Economic and Social Affairs.

United Nations, Department of Economic and Social Affairs, Population Division, 2013. *World population prospects: The 2012 Revision, Key Findings and Advance Tables.* ESA/P/WP.227

United Nations Development Programme. 1990. *Human development report 1990.* Oxford University Press.

United Nations Educational, Scientific, and Cultural Organization (UNESCO). 1958. *World survey of education II: Primary education.* Paris: UNESCO.

United Nations Educational, Scientific, and Cultural Organization (UNESCO). 1961. *World survey of education III: Secondary education.* Paris: UNESCO.

United Nations Educational, Scientific, and Cultural Organization (UNESCO). 1966. *World survey of education IV: Tertiary education.* Paris: UNESCO.

United Nations Educational, Scientific, and Cultural Organization (UNESCO). 1983. *Statistics of educational attainment and illiteracy, 1970–1980.* Paris: Division of Statistics on Education, UNESCO.

United Nations Educational, Scientific, and Cultural Organization (UNESCO). 1987. *Toward a methodology for projecting rates of literacy and educational attainment.* Paris: Division of Statistics on Education, UNESCO.

United Nations Educational, Scientific, and Cultural Organization (UNESCO). 1993. *World education report.* Paris: UNESCO.

United Nations Educational, Scientific, and Cultural Organization (UNESCO). Various years. *Statistical yearbook.* Paris: UNESCO.

Ursúa, J. F. 2011. Macroeconomic Archaeology: Unearthing risk, Disasters, and Trends. Unpublished, Harvard University, April.

U.S. Bureau of Education. Various years. *Report of the commissioner of education.* Washington, D.C.: U.S. Government Printing Office.

Uzawa, H. 1965. Optimum Technical Change in an Aggregative Model of Economic Growth. *International Economic Review,* 6(1), 18–31.

Weil, D. N. 2004. *Economic growth.* Boston: Addison-Wesley.

Wils, A. 2007. *Window on the future: 2025—Projections of education attainment and its impact.* Washington, DC: Academy for Educational Development.

Woessmann, L. 2003. Schooling Resources, Educational Institutions, and Student Performance: The International Evidence. *Oxford Bulletin of Economics and Statistics,* 65(2), 117–170.

Wooldridge, J. M. 2002. *Econometric Analysis of Cross Section and Panel Data.* Boston: MIT Press.

World Bank. 2013. *World Development Indicators 2013.* Washington, D.C.: The World Bank.

Yousif, H. M., Goujon, A., & Lutz, W. 1996. *Future population and education trends in the countries of North Africa.* Laxenburg, Austria: International Institute for Applied Systems Analysis. (Research Report RR–96–11).

Note: The letter 't' following locators refers to tables; the letter 'f' refers to figures.